PRENTICE-
HALL
POCKET
ENCYCLOPEDIA

HOME
DECORATING

PRENTICE-HALL
POCKET
ENCYCLOPEDIA

HOME
DECORATING

Contributing authors
John McGowan · Roger DuBern

PRENTICE-HALL CANADA, INC.
SCARBOROUGH, ONTARIO

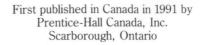

First published in Canada in 1991 by
Prentice-Hall Canada, Inc.
Scarborough, Ontario

First published in Great Britain in 1991
by Dorling Kindersley Limited,
9 Henrietta Street, London WC2E 8PS

Designed and edited by Swallow Books,
260 Pentonville Road, London N1 9JY

Canadian Cataloguing Publication Data

McGowan, John
Prentice-Hall pocket encyclopedia of
home decorating

ISBN 0-13-718438-7
1. Interior decoration – Amateurs' manuals.
I. Dubern, Roger. II. Brumstead, Elaine, 1929–
III. Title. IV. Title: Pocket encyclopedia of
home decorating.

NK2115.M23 1991 747 C91-093165-8

Typeset by Bournetype, Bournemouth
Reproduced by Colourscan, Singapore
Printed in Singapore by Kyodo Printing (Co) Pte Ltd.

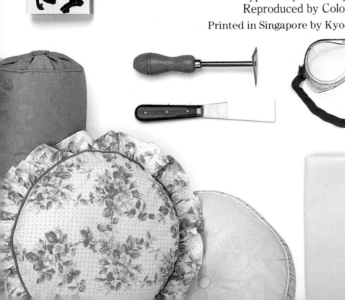

CONTENTS

Introduction Page 6

INTRODUCTION

Obtaining a professional finish when decorating is easy if you take the trouble to find out how to do each job properly, and arm yourself with the correct equipment and materials. The cardinal rules are to take your time, and to work carefully; do not cut corners and never skimp on any part of the job. Decorating is no longer cheap; all materials are expensive. However, by doing a thorough job you will save money in the long run. The room will stay looking good for far longer than if you skimp. If you rush at it, ignoring the rules and then settle back into an armchair before the paint has dried, you will probably have created an eyesore which will be hard to live with. In no time at all, you will find yourself having to start again from scratch, spending more money – but this time doing it the right way!

This book is an invaluable addition to your decorating library; it will enable you to produce top-quality results with any task, from painting a door to laying a carpet. It does not matter whether you have had any previous experience; you will find that the easy-to-follow, concise, step-by-step instructions will give you the confidence to complete any job successfully. Even those unavoidable technical terms that confuse and baffle the inexperienced decorator are explained fully in a simple glossary. In addition, there are a host of handy hints and tips to help you to avoid all the traps and pitfalls which would otherwise spoil a job and cause delays.

The book has been planned carefully to take you through each aspect of the main decorating jobs: painting, wallpapering, tiling and laying floor coverings. Finally, it offers invaluable guidance on shelving, dressing a window and sewing projects – providing a total guide to redecorating a room.

One of the most frustrating aspects of do-it-yourself projects is finding that you have not got the correct

Drilling equipment
A hand drill (top) can be used if you do not have an electric one. The awl (above) is used to make starting holes in flat surfaces for screws.

piece of equipment for the job. This means having to stop work to mount a lengthy search for the vital tool. It is even more annoying then to discover that you have not got a particular item and that the shops are all closed. To help you to avoid this major inconvenience, there is a complete list of the items that you will need for each job at the beginning of each chapter. You will find that, where necessary, precise details are given for each tool.

One of the best ways to learn about decorating is to study your previous mistakes. A fault-finding guide is given, where relevant, which explains what may have gone wrong with your previous efforts.

The chapter on painting begins by explaining the differences between the various paints, from primer

Making shades
The steps show the various stages of making curtains and shades, and the different methods of hanging.

Curtains
A wide range of both unlined and lined curtains is dealt with. The most suitable types of fabric for each style of curtain are listed, and their compatibility with types of lining material. Accessories such as curtain tracks and rods are also illustrated and discussed.

to latex and alkyd, and how to estimate the quantity needed for a particular job. Both the protective and decorative aspects of paint are discussed, and the effects that colors can have on a room. The key to perfect painting is found in a correctly prepared surface: stripping old paint, filling cracks and holes in walls, woodwork and metalwork are all outlined before we move on to techniques for applying paint correctly. Finally, the tricks of applying decorative textures and finishes are fully explained.

The chapter on wallpapering stresses the importance of choosing the right type of paper and pattern for a particular job – and also helps you to solve that common dilemma of how many rolls to buy. Hanging wallpaper and ceiling paper can only be

Equipment
The equipment illustrated is accompanied by brief descriptions of the variations where necessary, and their suitability for the different types of job.

Fittings and accessories
Fittings and accessories for all types of home furnishings are also included. Clear directions show how to sew them.

Sewing equipment
A wide selection of equipment suitable for both the amateur and the professional is illustrated, and the uses of the various items are described. The step-by-steps are illustrated with contrasting color thread for clarity.

Wallpapering
The concise and easy-to-follow step-by-step instructions enable you to tackle the job with confidence.

Sewing projects
The wide variety of bedcoverings is supplemented by features on related items, such as hems, ruffles, seams and edgings. The profusion of different types of patterned fabric is also illustrated and discussed.

Hacksaw (above, top)
This implement is useful for cutting either metal or wood, especially when creating shelves.

Paintbrushes (above, bottom)
The well-prepared do-it-yourself enthusiast will have a variety of brushes for all types of jobs.

accomplished if you are able to reach every part of the room safely and easily: so this chapter also shows you how to set up a secure working platform, both on flat surfaces and on stairs. The question of how to prepare a room is covered in detail, including how to strip off old paper and make the necessary repairs to create a smooth background surface. Finally, the techniques for measuring, cutting, pasting and hanging the paper are illustrated, with special emphasis given to tricky areas such as windows, light fixtures and radiators.

To round off the chapter, textured wall coverings – silk, burlap, grasscloth, and so on – are described and illustrated, together with the special techniques required for hanging them correctly.

The third chapter explains the secrets of successfully tiling floors, walls and ceilings. Every

Techniques
The various techniques for achieving a professional finish are not only illustrated, but also explained in the text.

Table linens
Styles of tablecloths, napkins and table mats are included, together with decorative techniques such as quilting and appliqué, which not only provide a professional touch, but can also change an otherwise ordinary item into an heirloom.

type of tile is dealt with – ceramic, cork, mirror, brick, plastic, quarry, vinyl and marble – together with individual details such as tile sizes, and how to estimate the quantities that you will need. Again, the correct preparation of walls, floors and ceilings is discussed, and there is a section on how to plan the tiling for a well-balanced effect. This is followed by the necessary techniques for hanging or laying each type of tile.

The fourth chapter deals with other types of floor covering, emphasizing the all-important business of preparing floorboards and concrete floors perfectly, to ensure that your new floor covering gives long-lasting wear. All the stages in laying carpets (including stair carpets) and suitable padding, wood and sheet vinyl are covered, and are backed up with essential advice

Cutting equipment
Guidance is given about how to store your cutting equipment safely, and how to take care of it so that it will have many years of useful life.

Tools and equipment
*Each chapter contains
clear illustrations of all
the necessary tools and
materials for the job.*

on choosing the best and most effective floor covering for any situation.

Storage and shelving is the basis of a room's furniture, and Chapter Five concentrates on this. The various methods of building all types of shelves are shown with, of course, precise instructions for putting them up soundly. The chapter ends with a brief look at other storage units.

Curtains, shades and sewing projects provide the finishing touches to a room, and these are covered in the last two chapters. Whether you are hanging curtain rods, need to know about fabrics, making lined or unlined curtains, choosing and hanging shades, or making cornices, you will find all the information you need. The book concludes with a section on sewing

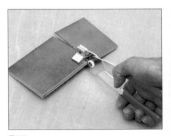

Tiling
*The steps clearly show what
equipment you need for tiling, and
how to use it.*

Thimbles, pins and threaders
*Thimbles are a must when you are
working with heavyweight fabrics,
or with dense materials, such as
leather. Ball-headed pins in
different colors help you to see
where the pins are as you sew. A
needle threader is an extremely
useful gadget.*

sheets, pillowcases, valances, quilts, bed covers, tablecloths and pillows.

Nowadays it is vital that we, as householders and consumers of an enormous range of products, do all that we can to help protect our environment and to conserve world resources. We can play our part by using environment-friendly products in our home decorating jobs and, wherever possible, making use of recycled materials – old timber being a prime example. When buying products, check that any aerosols you choose to use are ozone-friendly and that wood preservatives are water-base. Also familiarize yourself with the latest water regulations for your area, since they are there to protect the quality of our water supply.

Jig saw
If you need to cut intricate or awkward shapes, a jig saw is ideal for the purpose.

Using the materials
Even if you have never used the materials before, the step-by-step illustrations make it clear what to do.

Trimmings
There is a wealth of trimmings available for all types of sewing projects – tassles, braids, piping, ruffles and fringes. This variety is reflected in the optional techniques illustrated throughout the text.

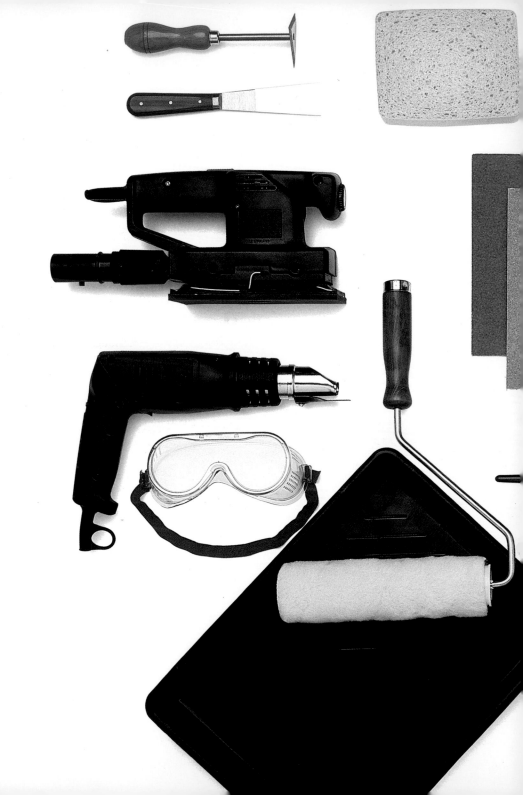

CHAPTER ONE

PAINTING

Good paintwork is to a house what a good complexion is to a human face. It reflects the general condition and attitudes of the owner, it provides a background for more striking features and highlights, and lends an individual quality to the whole appearance.

Modern materials give better and faster results than ever before and a quality paint job will last for many years with new, hard-wearing paints. Although paints are now sold under various descriptions, such as high gloss, satin or eggshell finish, water-base (latex) paint is still used for walls and ceilings and alkyds and oil-base paints for woodwork and metalwork. It is still usually cheaper to paint than to paper.

Careful preparation of surfaces before painting is all-important if you want results that measure up to your expectations. Flaws and cracks that are left untreated will rapidly reappear and may even be exaggerated against a new finish, leaving you with no choice but to strip off the new paint and start all over again.

Tools and equipment

Cheap tools produce poor results. However tempting it is to save money, this is always a false economy, because good-quality equipment lasts longer, even improving with age; is more satisfying to use; and, most importantly, produces a finer finish. Before using any equipment, check that it is thoroughly dry and rust-free, as rust creates indelible stains. Clean tools thoroughly and store them in a cool, dry, well-ventilated place.

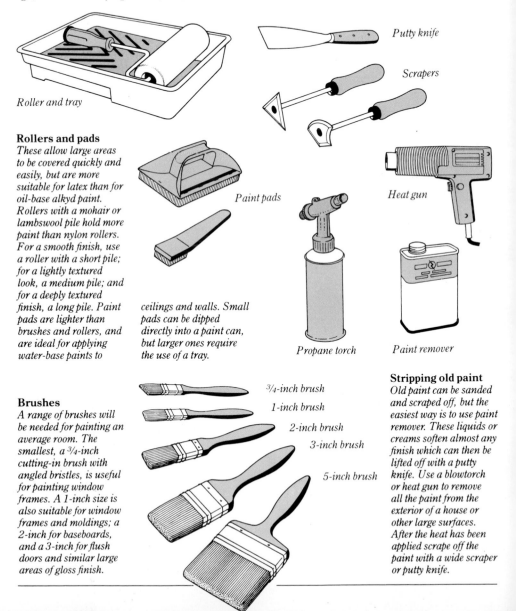

Roller and tray

Putty knife

Scrapers

Paint pads

Heat gun

Propane torch

Paint remover

Rollers and pads
These allow large areas to be covered quickly and easily, but are more suitable for latex than for oil-base alkyd paint. Rollers with a mohair or lambswool pile hold more paint than nylon rollers. For a smooth finish, use a roller with a short pile; for a lightly textured look, a medium pile; and for a deeply textured finish, a long pile. Paint pads are lighter than brushes and rollers, and are ideal for applying water-base paints to ceilings and walls. Small pads can be dipped directly into a paint can, but larger ones require the use of a tray.

Brushes
A range of brushes will be needed for painting an average room. The smallest, a ³/₄-inch cutting-in brush with angled bristles, is useful for painting window frames. A 1-inch size is also suitable for window frames and moldings; a 2-inch for baseboards, and a 3-inch for flush doors and similar large areas of gloss finish.

³/₄-inch brush
1-inch brush
2-inch brush
3-inch brush
5-inch brush

Stripping old paint
Old paint can be sanded and scraped off, but the easiest way is to use paint remover. These liquids or creams soften almost any finish which can then be lifted off with a putty knife. Use a blowtorch or heat gun to remove all the paint from the exterior of a house or other large surfaces. After the heat has been applied scrape off the paint with a wide scraper or putty knife.

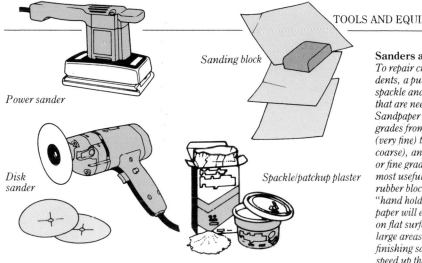

Power sander

Sanding block

Disk sander

Spackle/patchup plaster

Sanders and fillers

To repair cracks and dents, a putty knife, spackle and tray are all that are needed. Sandpaper comes in grades from No. 000 (very fine) to No. 12 (very coarse), and the medium or fine grades are the most useful. A wooden or rubber block used as a "hand hold" for abrasive paper will ease the work on flat surfaces. For large areas, electric finishing sanders help to speed up the work.

Painting problems

Painting faults can always be traced back to an error in preparation, poor working conditions or incorrect application. Inadequate cleaning and sanding of surfaces, overbrushing or overthinning of the paint, and overloading the brush are some of the most common mistakes made by amateurs.

If a coat of enamel fails to retain its sheen, you may have left insufficient drying time between coats. Overbrushing and overthinning of the paint may also give this result. Where a previous coat of paint is still visible through a new finish, either the wrong undercoat was used, or there are insufficient undercoats.

Again, overbrushing, overthinning or overstirring may also dilute the paint and allow previous colors to show through.

On woodwork, paint will peel if the surface is not correctly prepared; with latex, dirt and dust or mildew may be the problem.

All these problems can be cured by allowing the paint to harden for a week, then rubbing it down with sandpaper and cleaning the surface before applying fresh alkyd or latex.

For blisters on woodwork, cut out the bubble and fill it with wood putty. Sand down and dust off before applying fresh alkyd. If the blistering is excessive, strip the paint off and start again.

Some red pigments will bleed into a new coat, so apply a barrier coat in between.

Specks and pimples
Specks and pimples are caused by dust in the paint. A badly sanded surface may also leave a speckled finish.

Runs and wrinkles
Runs, sags and wrinkles form if the paint is applied too thickly, or if it has not been adequately brushed out.

Blisters
Blisters are caused by painting on a damp surface or on to old, soft, or lifting paint. Heat may also be a cause.

Brushmarks
Brushmarks may be caused by a poor-quality brush, painting too thickly, or not sanding a worn surface.

Paints and varnishes

Paint serves a dual purpose – to decorate and to protect a surface. Paints are available for both interior and exterior use, but it is outside where protection is of paramount importance. Paints can be divided into three categories: preparatory paints, such as primers and undercoats; top coats, including alkyd and latex; and special purpose paints, such as masonry and floor paints. Most paints are made up of three ingredients: pigment, which provides color; a binder, usually a resin, which causes the pigment to stick to the surface; and a liquid, either oil or water, which combines the two. Top coats are divided into alkyd (resin-base) and oil-base paints, which are available in glossy enamel and flat finishes, for use on wood and metal; and water-base paints or latex, which come in flat or semi-gloss finishes, and are used on plaster, paper and brick.

Varnishes also decorate and protect a surface, but provide a transparent covering. They are used solely on bare wood, allowing the pattern of the wood grain to show through.

Choice of paint is the first major decorating decision, and it is worth taking time to choose the most suitable color. It is also important to select the right type of paint for each job to avoid repeating the work before you are ready for a change.

For exterior paint jobs the type of paint you choose depends on the surface to be painted. Different surfaces require different treatment, so take time to determine the best protective covering in order to ensure a good-looking and long-lasting finish.

Masonry paint on brick

Latex enamel on wallpaper

Primer, undercoat and enamel on wood

Paints

There are several types of preparatory paints which are applied to the surface before the top coat. Primers create a uniform surface on wood and metal. Aluminum primer-sealer (not to be confused with aluminum paint) seals off stains, such as water damage marks. Undercoat is designed to obliterate all other colors and to provide a good surface prior to using an enamel top coat.

Of the top coats latex paints spread easily and are thinned with water while alkyd paints have more covering power and are thinned with paint thinner or turpentine. For interior work there are three different finishes: flat for walls and ceilings; semi- or high-gloss enamels for windows, doors and other wordwork; and deck enamel for floors and steps. Flat finishes are quick-drying and free of odor. Enamels take more scrubbing and abuse than flat finishes and are available, in addition to the high glosses, in duller lusters such as satin and eggshell.

A range of special-purpose paints tackle specific painting problems, such as those formulated to be self-cleaning or resistant to discoloration, condensation, or mildew.

Varnishes

Varnishes are widely used to give protection and also to enhance the decorative properties of wood. Polyurethane varnish is used for wood and comes in gloss, semi-gloss, and satin (dull) finishes. You can also buy seal and stain combined, in a variety of colors. There is a range of tough varnishes, sold as marine varnish, which are suitable for exterior decorative wood.

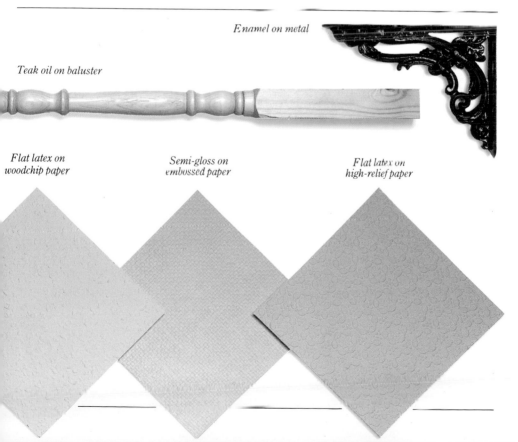

Enamel on metal

Teak oil on baluster

Flat latex on woodchip paper

Semi-gloss on embossed paper

Flat latex on high-relief paper

Choosing the right paint

Buy a well-known brand, or a store brand product from a reputable home center. Unknown, cheap paints, particularly latex, sometimes produce an inferior result with little durability.

It is best to estimate the quantities you will need and to buy the full amount in one batch to be sure of consistent color. This is particularly important if you are having the paint custom-mixed by the supplier. Paints of the same type can be mixed, provided they come from the same manufacturer. If you are mixing your own paint, make a note of the quantities and names of pigments used.

The small area of color on a manufacturer's color chart rarely gives a clear idea of how the paint will look in a room. The combined effect of the color on the walls and the ceiling may intensify the shade as much as 50 percent above the paint color chart. Always consider the color of the paint in relation to the rest of your decorating scheme.

Whichever type of paint you use, always use the correct type of preparatory paint. This is as important as choosing the right top coat. Use primers to seal porous surfaces such as unsized plaster, and to act as a key on metal surfaces. There are different types of primers for wood, wallboard, plaster, brick, concrete and metals. Use undercoat on primed surfaces, this will reduce the number of top coats you have to apply.

Never use latex paint on metal surfaces because they are water-base paints and will cause rusting.

When to use latex paint
Of all the top coats, latex is the easiest to apply. On new surfaces it is usual to use a thinned paint-and-water coating as a primer. On previously painted or papered surfaces, latex should be built up coat by coat, allowing each layer to dry in between. Latex is not ideal on bare wood, since the water content raises the grain, producing a rough finish. Use it on internal walls and ceilings (opposite).

When to use solvent-thinned paint
These need to be more thoroughly brushed out than latex and should be applied in thin coats to avoid runs. Dripless (thixotropic) alkyds, however, are laid on in a thick layer, without much brushing. This is simply a protective finishing coat, so previous colors must be obliterated by layers of undercoat. Use alkyds on exterior and interior wood and/or metal (opposite). Generally, these paints do not need to be thinned, unless being used in a spray gun.

Enamel needs to be brushed on extremely carefully, since the high gloss finish will show up irregularities. Like latex, it needs to be built up coat by coat, allowing each layer to dry.

Choosing the right varnish

As with paints, it is best to choose a well-known brand to be sure of a quality finish. If you are treating exterior wood, it is particularly important to choose a protective, exterior-quality product. Varnish will last longer on mahogany-type woods than on coarser woods, such as oak and Western red cedar. If you plan to add a coat of varnish over a stain, check that they have compatible chemical bases.

DEALING WITH LEADED PAINTS

Lead is no longer used in paint. However, some old paintwork may still contain lead. If you think this may be the case, take the following precautions:

• Don't use a blowtorch or heat gun, as it creates toxic fumes.

• Don't use dry sandpaper, as it creates dust.
• Put debris in the garbage can, don't burn it.
• Use gloves, and wash your hands afterwards.

If you use spray paint, try to find CFC-free aerosols as far as possible.

SUITING THE PAINT TO THE SURFACE

Different areas of a house require very different treatment. Never cut corners on the preparatory work. Some areas, such as children's furniture, need virtually no preparation and only one or two coats of paint. Others, such as exterior woodwork, may need much preparation – knot sealer, primer and undercoat – before applying several top coats, so plan carefully before you start.

Internal walls and ceilings
Sealer or undercoat on new surfaces; top coat with latex – flat or semi-gloss, alkyd – flat, semi-gloss or gloss enamel.

Children's furniture
Prime and seal new or bare wood; apply semi- or high gloss enamel.

Doors, windows, stairs, baseboards
Prime new or bare wood, apply semi- or high-gloss enamel for all woodwork; floor varnish, all-in-one-type stain or deck enamel for stairs and baseboards.

Wood siding
Scrape off; rub down with sandpaper; apply suitable wood preservative, then paint with exterior latex or alkyd. Apply two coats of primer and top coat on new wood.
Other woodwork: Sand; apply knot sealer and prime bare patches; then apply undercoat and top coat.

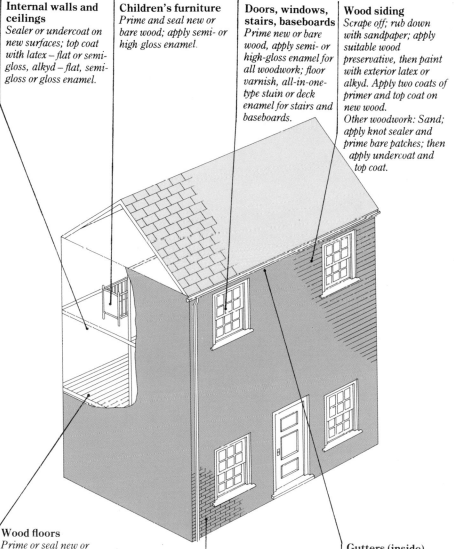

Wood floors
Prime or seal new or bare wood with wood sealer; choose shellac, floor varnish, polyurethane floor paint or deck enamel.

Brickwork
Brush down; point defective joints; apply latex exterior masonry paint.

Gutters (inside)
Repair defective joints; apply asphalt roof paint. (outside) Wire-brush, prime bare metal; apply undercoat and top coat.

The effects of color on a room

Color has the power to transform a room. It can raise and lower ceilings, it can expand and reduce walls, it can disguise and highlight individual features and it can soothe or excite. A dark room can be brightened with a light reflecting sheen, and warm, dark colors can make a large, cold room feel more cozy. Your decision may be influenced by existing furnishings, and in many rooms the paintwork may need to act as a neutral backdrop to more vibrant accessories. Remember that when applied, the accumulated color will intensify the shade of the color chart, as many home decorators have discovered too late!

Diminishing a large room
Color can influence the apparent size and shape of a room. Light shades will bring space to a small room and dark tones foreshorten a large one. A low ceiling will appear higher if it is painted a paler shade than the walls. To disguise the room shape even more, apply a single dark color over the ceiling and walls then break it up with spotlights (above). Complementary textures and the judicious addition of strong color, as illustrated here, will also ensure that, for the most part, the eye focuses on the lower half of the overall decorating scheme.

Enlarging and lightening a small room

As a dark color can help to make a large room look more cozy, so a lighter color can enlarge a smaller space. A pale, receding background shade will lighten and open up a dark room (left) and will help to conceal pipes, radiators and irregular window shapes. The effect is enhanced by a coordinating color effect. The use of paintings or prints can also give additional weight to the overall effect. Cool shades, such as the frosty blue, monochromatic color scheme (below), lend a cool feeling of light and space to a sunny room. Sparkling white woodwork and silver chrome accessories add to the effect, helping to give a clean, modern air to what is otherwise a traditional room.

Establishing moods

Those who demand a stimulating home environment probably enjoy strong primary colors, broken up with neutrals. Others who need a restful, relaxing atmosphere may prefer natural and more muted tones. The aspect of the room should also be considered when selecting paint color. A burnt orange shade (above) gives warmth to a large room with harsh light coming through the windows.

FURNISHINGS

When planning the color scheme for a room, it is important to take the furnishings into account. All the examples on this page make the furnishings a complementary or focal point of the overall interior design.

Furnishings include carpets, curtains and chair coverings. If you can't invest in a whole new suite of furniture, slip covers or throw-overs can do the job just as well and much more cheaply. They are also versatile, easy to clean and can be changed with the seasons.

Planning

New decoration will only be as good as the planning and preparation of the work. The first step in any redecoration job is to decide on the extent of the initial structural and repair work required, before estimating time, costs and quantities of materials needed. This work will depend on the age and condition of the house.

In a post-1950s house the lumber is unlikely to be well seasoned. The woodwork may split, shrink and warp away from the walls, causing cracks that need filling. Many modern homes, however, do have the advantage of low-maintenance accessories, such as plastic gutters and downspouts, and anodized aluminum windows that do not need paint.

Different problems arise in older houses. The walls, usually solid, encourage dampness which must be cured before decorating can begin. The lath and plasterwork in ceilings and walls deteriorate over time, so cracked plasterwork will need to be repaired or replaced before painting or wallpapering. A thick layer of paint is likely to have built up on the woodwork over the years. If the paintwork tends to chip badly, you should strip it back to the bare wood. Preparation may take more time than decoration.

Estimating quantities

To estimate the amount of paint you need for any interior paint job, you need to know the square feet of wall surface to be painted and the number of square feet a gallon of the paint you are planning to use will cover. The label on the paint can usually specifies how many square feet a gallon will cover.

Remember, an imperial gallon covers 25 percent more than an American gallon.

To calculate the square footage of walls, measure the perimeter of the room and multiply this figure by its height. The result is the square footage of wall space to be covered. Divide the number of square feet to be painted by the number of square feet a gallon will cover. The result is the number of gallons you will need to complete the job. Exactly the same formula applies to the task of determining how much paint you will need in order to completely cover the ceiling. Always risk buying too much rather than too little.

Ceilings
Multiply the length by the width and remember to allow for alcoves.

Walls
Measure the perimeter of the room without deducting window and door areas. Multiply this figure by its height.

Doors, windows and baseboards
An average window measures 43 square feet. Doors measure 43 square feet (21 square feet per side), including frame and trim. For baseboards, multiply the length by the height.

Covering rates of paints

The covering power of paints varies with the type of paint, the porosity of the surface and the thickness of the coat applied. Dripless enamel and jelly-like paints, for example, will not cover as large an area as alkyd or latex, but since the coating is thicker, fewer coats may be required. Most stains and varnishes will go further than paint, while primers will not stretch as far. Bare plaster and textured surfaces absorb more liquid, so it is often more economical to add water to a first coat than to apply an extra top coat.

The type of paint, the color and the surface determine the number of coats to be applied. You will need an extra coat, for example, when covering a dark color with a lighter one, but not when using a dark final color. When decorating previously unpainted wood, use primer and an undercoat before one or two coats of gloss. If painting over old enamel, you may need to apply one or two coats of undercoat to create a good base. A third coat of latex is sometimes needed to obliterate a dark background. High-gloss latex may also need an extra coat. The table (right) gives specific coverage areas.

Paint type	Covering area (in yd^2 per ½ gal)
Latex primer (wood)	7–8
(metal)	9–11
(plaster)	5–9
Aluminum primer-sealer	11 13
Alkyd primer/undercoat	15–16
Alkali-resistant primer	9–11
Primer-sealer	10
Stain-blocking primer	6–12
Metal primer	9–11
Undercoat	15
Alkyd	17
Alkyd (dripless)	12
Alkyd gloss (oil-base)	12
Eggshell latex	15
Latex, flat (dripless solid)	14
Latex, semi-gloss	15
Aluminum paint	12–14

POINTS TO REMEMBER

• Make sure that you have enough paint before you begin.
• Apply paint in clear dry weather with temperatures above 40 degrees.
• All surfaces should be clean and dry (with latex paint, there can be some moisture on the wood).
• Repair defective downspouts and gutters.
• Check all caulking and flashing.
• Reputty crumbling window sash.
• Nail loose boards in place.
• Fill cracks and nail holes with wood putty.
• Sand off flaking, blistered paint.
• Protect metal with rust-inhibitive primer.

ESTIMATING PAINT FOR EXTERIORS

House paint normally covers about 500 square feet of surface per American gallon, 625 square feet per imperial gallon. With these estimates and the dimensions of the house, it is easy to determine the approximate number of gallons of paint that will be required by the following procedures:
1. Average height of house = distance from foundation to eaves for flat-roof types; add 2 feet to this for pitched roofs.
2. Average height × distance around foundation = surface area in square feet.
3. Surface area ÷ 500 = number of gallons of paint (or primer) required for each coat.
There is no need to calculate trim paint. The average house – six to eight rooms – requires a gallon.

A three-coat job is the best for new work – one coat of primer and two top coats. Do not make the error of assuming that if three coats are desirable, more coats are bound to be even better. One coat is often sufficient when repainting a surface in good condition. When the old paint is worn or a long time has elapsed since the last painting, two coats are recommended.

Stripping old paint

It is not always necessary to strip off old paint, for if the gloss on woodwork is sound and smooth, it will form an ideal base for fresh paint. Plaster surfaces must be clean and smooth before paint is applied. Paint that is peeling, badly cracked or chipped should be completely removed. Test the surface with masking tape, if it pulls paint away, strip away all of the old finish. Most of the methods described here also apply to varnishes.

Choosing the method

Dry scraping is hard work and can leave gouge marks, so unless the paint peels off readily, it is best to use heat or paint-stripper to soften the finish. Heat stripping is the easiest way to treat a large area, but the heat must be carefully applied so as not to burn the wood. If an open flametorch seems too risky, an alternative is an electric paint softener which uses no flame and scrapes as it softens.

Propane torch

1 *Hold the torch about 6–8 inches from the surface, starting at the top. Play it across the paint until the paint begins to melt.*

2 *Scrape off paint immediately after application of heat. Sweep the flame over the remaining paint until it slides off. Use a scraper to scrape paint off moldings.*

Paint stripper

1 *Brush the liquid on thickly with short strokes and working in one direction only.*

2 *After about 20 minutes strip off the softened layers of paint with a putty knife.*

3 *Remove any remnants and sludge using a coarse cloth or steel wool.*

Peel-off stripper

1 *Apply a thick layer of paste and let it eat through the layers of paint.*

2 *After several hours the layer can be peeled off, leaving a clean sub-surface.*

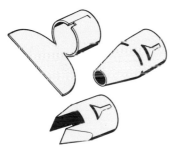

Heat gun
Operating like an immensely powerful electric hairdryer, a heat gun blasts out a stream of hot air which will melt the paint in its path. Direct the gun at an area of paint, and when it softens, after a few seconds, peel off the coat with a scraper. For stripping paint around windows and tricky areas, special nozzle attachments are available (above). Although effective, some heat guns are noisy and heavy to use.

SAFETY TIPS

With paint stripper:
• Always wear gloves and long-sleeved clothing to avoid skin burns, and don't smoke.

• Cover nearby furnishings.
With heat stripper:
• Keep buckets of water handy in case of fire.

• Never place your fingers in the air stream.
• Catch burning peelings in a metal tray, never in newspaper

How to fill cracks and holes

Time spent filling cracks and holes will be well rewarded in the final result. Standard interior-grade cellulose fillers are suitable for most inside plaster or wooden surfaces to be repainted. Use spackling compound to repair cracks, nail holes and small gouges in plaster. Build up thin layers of spackle and when the surface is slightly raised let it dry, then sand down. To patch wide cracks and holes in walls and ceilings, apply two layers of patching plaster plus a layer of fine-textured finishing plaster. Let each layer dry completely before adding the next. Finish all patches by sanding with fine paper and, as with all new plaster, always prime before painting.

For filling gouges and dents in wood, you can buy putty sticks that come in a variety of colors to match finished wood paneling.

How to apply spackling compound

1 *Score the crack with the side of a putty knife to widen the cavity for the spackle.*

2 *Brush away any debris, then dampen the crack with a wet paintbrush or sponge.*

3 *Pack the spackle tightly into the crack and smooth it down with a knife. Let it dry.*

4 *Rub dry spackle with a block wrapped in fine-grade sandpaper until smooth and flat.*

Preparing ceilings

First remove any light fixtures that may impede the work, turning off the power first and sealing any exposed wires afterwards. Then assess the condition of the existing paint and plasterwork.

If the paint is discolored by nicotine stains, apply a coat of aluminum sealer paint. Dried water stains, caused by a leaking roof or pipes, will show through latex, so these need to be coated with an oil-base primer-sealer. Kitchen ceilings are often coated with accumulated grease, which will prevent the paint from sticking if it is not removed. Likewise, soot or dust deposited on the ceilings above a fireplace must be thoroughly cleaned off to prevent it from showing through and discoloring subsequent layers of paint.

Fill any superficial cracks with spackle. In an old house, if paint is peeling, scrape off the flakes and either wash off the rest or coat the ceiling with primer-sealer before repainting. If paint dust has accumulated, seal with a coat of stabilizing primer. Loose ceiling paper should be stripped off, but any which is firmly attached can be left and painted. It is not always advisable to paint over wallpaper, but it can be done if the paper does not have a texture that will show through or colors that might bleed through the paint; use latex paint. Remember that a ceiling may have been papered because it is badly cracked though structurally sound, therefore, ceiling paper in good condition is best left alone.

Preparing walls

More preparation is needed if a wall is to be painted than if it is to be papered. Fresh plaster walls can be painted with latex paint as soon as the trim is nailed: use two coats. With oil-base paint use three coats and let the plaster cure for at least 90 days before painting. If you cannot wait that long, plaster can be prepared for alkyd by treating the surface with a solution of 2 pounds of zinc sulfate dissolved in 1 gallon of water.

Walls of plywood and most composition wallboards are painted in the same way as plaster walls. Some wallboards are extremely porous and will require a sealer coat. How many coats you apply depends on the condition of the surface, change in color, and the type of paint.

CLEARING THE ROOM

- Remove all lightweight furniture and move heavy pieces to the center of the room. Do not forget to empty the drawers of anything that you may need.
- Take down any pictures and store them.
- Roll up the carpet and take any rugs or mats to another room.
- Cover the floor and any remaining furniture with secured drop cloths.
- Remove all of the hardware from the doors and the windows, propping them open wherever it is necessary.
- Remove all of the switch plates and outlet plates in the room and cover any openings with masking tape.
- If it is necessary, vacuum the floor and wipe any dust from the surfaces which are to be painted.

FINAL PREPARATIONS

Make sure you have all the necessary tools and materials before you start.

All surfaces to be painted must be prepared thoroughly. Use a coarse sandpaper to remove damaged paintwork, then finish off with paper of a finer grain. Wash any remaining painted surfaces with either an ammonia solution or household cleaner. If you plan to paint over old wallpaper then you should test to see whether its colors will bleed. Clean the ceiling if necessary. Holes in the walls or ceiling must be filled, as must any holes in the woodwork or trim.

Plan to paint from the ceiling downwards.

Preparing bare wood

Whether it is brand new or stripped of old paint, all bare wood to be painted needs a coating of primer, undercoat and gloss finish. To ensure a smooth finish, the surface should first be rubbed down with sandpaper or a power sander. Rough surfaces may call for coarse paper, but a final smoothing with a fine grade will ensure a good finish.

After any cracks are filled with spackle or patching plaster, knots in the wood will need a coating of shellac to prevent the resin from staining the paintwork. To seal the pores in the wood and to provide a sound, stable base for undercoat, a coat of primer is applied. Most woods will take white or pink wood primer, but particularly resinous woods need aluminum primer. Universal primer may be used, although specific products give a better result.

Since undercoat is heavily pigmented for hiding power, always select the color recommended by the manufacturer for use under the chosen finish. You may find that it is necessary to apply more than one coat of undercoat in order to leave a smooth base for the gloss finish.

Preparing wood for enamel

1 *Sand and wipe the surface, then brush a layer of sealer on to any wood knots.*

2 *Let it dry for a couple of days. Then brush on the primer to provide a stable base.*

3 *Allow to dry, then apply at least one coat of well-stirred undercoat (more if necessary).*

Wood filler

Where wood is to be given a clear varnish or lacquer finish instead of a coat of paint, waterproof wood filler, which comes in a variety of wood colors, can be used. One type comes as a putty-like material; another, which also dries to a natural wood color and can later be stained to any shade, is sold as paste and separate hardener to be mixed together. Both types should be worked well into the surface with a putty knife and allowed to set before sanding down and applying an oil- or spirit-base stain. Take care not to spread the filler into the grain beyond the immediate split or nail hole. Small gaps that tend to form in window frames and at joints can be packed and pushed down with a finger before smoothing off with a damp cloth. Always use an oil-base wood

Applying wood filler
Work the filler down into the surface.

filler on particleboard, since it is very porous.

Dents can also be treated by using wood filler to build up the surface. Make sure that it is of the appropriate color.

Preparing metal

Rust is the enemy of ferrous metals (those that contain iron and steel) and must be kept at bay with a rust-inhibiting primer and a coat of polyurethane paint. Even small chips in the surface paint can allow moisture to seep below the paint film and encourage corrosion, especially in window frames in rooms where condensation is a problem.

First locate the areas of rust and remove all traces with a wire brush or with a brush attachment on an electric drill, but always protect your eyes with safety goggles. Finish with fine sandpaper or steel wool, then clean with paint thinner. Rust reforms rapidly, even overnight, so apply a rust-resistant zinc chromate primer immediately before painting. On small tools or surfaces that are hard to sand, brush off as much rust as you can, then apply a gel-like rust remover as directed. You can lessen your work on a large surface by applying a rust convertor – a special primer that turns solid well-bonded rust into a protective coating.

Treating rust

1 *Scrape off any rust and peeling paint with a wire brush. Inspect the area carefully to ensure that no trace of rust remains.*

2 *Before the rust has time to reform, seal the metalwork with zinc chromate primer, giving vulnerable points an extra coat.*

PREPARING PAINTWORK

● Before applying a fresh coat to existing paintwork, the surface must be free from stains, dirt and dust, or the new finish will look uneven and will soon start to flake.
● Remove surface dirt by brushing, washing or vacuuming and use a pointed handle or knife to clear dust particles from hard-to-get-at corners.
● When washing down the area, use ammonia solution or household cleaner, and prevent water from dripping down behind electric outlets.
● Before painting window frames from inside, always ensure that outside frames are thoroughly clean so that dirt is not picked up on the brush. Wipe down sills and other wooden surfaces with a lint-free rag moistened with paint thinner.
● Allow all surfaces to dry thoroughly before applying paint.

How to apply paint

Latex and other water-base paints will usually brush straight from the can, but half-full cans of oil-base paints develop a skin. Lift off the layer of solidified paint, then stir thoroughly. Dripless paints, however, should never be stirred. Alkyd and latex paints demand slightly different techniques, as shown below. (The jelly-like thixotropic paints, designed to go on in one coat, should be brushed sparingly.) There is no need to scrape off surplus paint, but try not to load too much paint on to the brush initially. Before applying a second coat of paint, dust the surface with a lint-free rag to ensure that no specks spoil the finish. Complete each surface in one session to prevent dried paint lines from forming.

Brushing on gloss finish

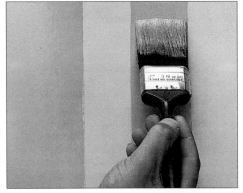

1 *Dip the end of the brush into the paint and wipe off the excess. Avoid dipping it too deep, or the paint will trickle down on to your hand.*

2 *Begin with two or three short downward strokes in the direction of the grain. Change direction to spread the paint, then work with the grain again.*

3 *Reload the brush and paint another strip, leaving a gap the size of the brush width. Then paint across to fill the area between the strips.*

4 *Brush vigorously over the whole area, finishing off with vertical strokes. When dry, sand each coat with fine sandpaper before applying the next coat.*

Brushing on latex

1 *Select a wide brush for quick application. Coat it generously with paint and apply it in horizontal bands about 2 feet wide.*

2 *With flat latex, finish off with zigzag strokes. With semi-gloss, which dries faster, finish off with light, upward strokes.*

Using a roller or pad

Before applying paint with a roller, first cut in the edges with a brush or an edging roller. Make your first stroke upward and increase the pressure on the roller until all the paint is deposited. Follow with a down stroke over the same area and then roll crosswise to assure even coverage. Always start in a dry area and roll toward one that was just painted, blending in the edges. Check for skips as you progress. For hard-to-get-at corners you can buy a special doughnut-shape edging roller that coats both side of a corner at once. Try not to roll too fast or spin the roller at the end of the stroke as this causes spattering. Always stop the roller before you lift it from the wall. Use lighter pressure to feather out the final strokes.

When using a paint pad, dip the pad lightly into the paint can and wipe away the excess on the side. You can also use a special applicator to load the paint evenly on to the pad. Smooth on the paint in random directions (right). Reload the pad with paint as soon as you notice the layer begin to become too thin.

Using a roller
Start with random, zigzag strokes, then smooth out with horizontal strokes in both directions.

Using a paint pad
Smooth on the paint in a random fashion.

Painting flat surfaces

The first consideration when preparing to paint a large area is the light. Try to avoid starting in natural light and finishing in artificial, or you may find yourself covering the same area twice. You should also complete ceilings and individual walls in one session, since if you stop mid-wall for a meal-break or for the night, the dried paint line will show conspicuously through the final finish.

Before applying latex, close the windows to stop the paint from drying too quickly so that you have time to join up the wet edges of each section. When the room is finished, open the windows to accelerate drying time. For ease of working, try to get as close as possible to the ceiling. Bare walls need a diluted coat of latex to prime the surface before applying a first coat, but already painted surfaces need no primer. If the paint does not cover well, do not try to thicken the coat, but let it dry and apply an extra coat. For a perfectly smooth finish, you may need two or three coats.

While painting, keep a rag dampened with water for latex paints, or with turpentine for alkyd paints, to clean up paint spatters. As a general rule, paint a room from top to bottom, so that disturbed dust does not fall on to wet paint and so that drips and runs can be painted over later.

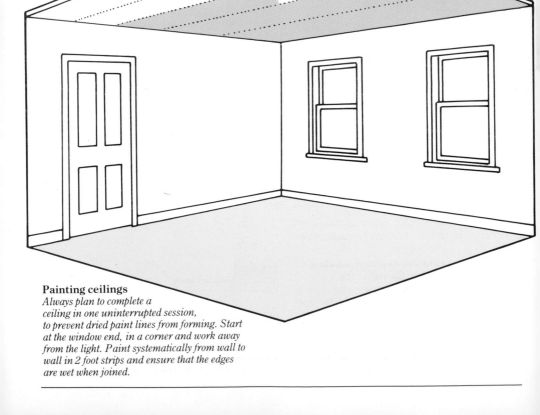

Painting ceilings
*Always plan to complete a
ceiling in one uninterrupted session,
to prevent dried paint lines from forming. Start
at the window end, in a corner and work away
from the light. Paint systematically from wall to
wall in 2 foot strips and ensure that the edges
are wet when joined.*

Painting walls
*Start at the top corner of a wall nearest the window.
Cover the wall in broad, horizontal bands and work down
to the baseboard. Cut in with a narrower
brush around windows and door frames.
If using a roller, first coat the edges
with a narrow brush.*

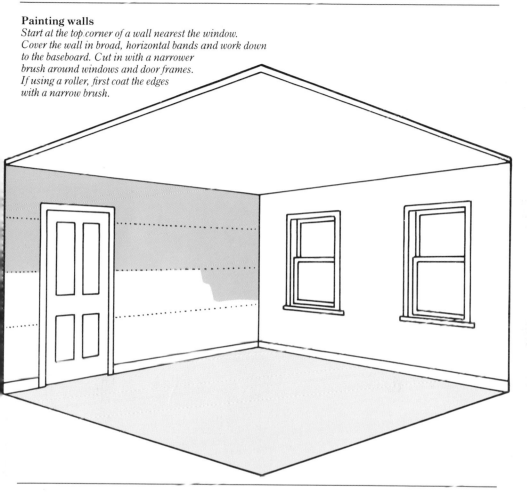

Painting baseboards

Painting baseboards can be a tedious and time-consuming job. However, it can be made easier if you tackle it in the following way.

Use a 2-inch brush and a piece of old card (right). Rest the card on the top of the baseboard, or tuck it down between the baseboard and the wall. This prevents the paint from smudging on to the walls.

At the corners, dab a lightly loaded cutting-in brush into the crevice and draw away the excess paint. To protect the floor, slide a piece of cardboard below the baseboard.

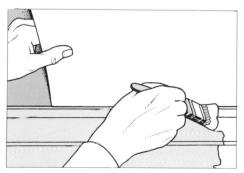

Using card to protect the walls
Insert card between the baseboard and the wall.

Using ladders

A variety of convertible step ladders is now
available, which will either slide or swing out
into a straight ladder, for using against the wall.
Make sure your ladders are sturdy. Ensure
that the connections will not allow the ladder to
slip when extended and remember that a
stepladder is firmly footed only when the
spreader is fully opened and locked. Always
ensure that the ladder reaches at least 3 feet
above the highest level at which you wish to
stand, and never stand above the second step
from the top. Face the ladder as you climb and
do not lean over too far to either side while
painting. For larger areas, such as stairwells
and ceilings, use a secure, stable working
platform (pages 48–9).

A clip-on shelf
*This serves as a handy
platform for equipment.*

Non-slip ladders
*Ladders which stand on
two levels are useful on
stairs, provided there are
suction pads on the feet.*

Convertible ladders
*The sections can be
moved around to form
a straight ladder, or a
self-supporting type at
a variety of angles.*

Painting radiators

Radiators should always be painted when cold
and allowed to dry thoroughly before the heat
is turned on again, or the finish will be
impaired. If your radiators have never been
painted be sure that they are thoroughly
cleaned of grease and rust. Rust must be
removed if the paint is to stick. The best prime
coat for radiators is red-lead paint. After
priming, any ordinary interior paint can be
used, but avoid paints with a metal pigment,
since this will reduce radiating power. Paint
only the visible portions, leaving the rest bare
metal for greater heating efficiency. Shiny
aluminum placed behind the radiator will
reduce heat loss through the wall. If the
radiators were previously painted, and the
paint is cracked or peeling, it may be necessary
to remove all of it with paint remover or a wire
brush before repainting.

Painting stairs and stairwells

The stair area should be painted last, since halls and landings are likely to be scuffed when moving furniture from room to room; also, as the nucleus of the house, it forms the main color link between individual rooms and upper and lower floors. First set up a secure working platform for reaching even the least accessible parts of the stairwell (right). Remove carpet and fittings, clean the entire staircase and repair any faults such as creaking and uneven stairs, cracks, dents or splits. Follow the usual order of work, beginning with the landing ceiling, then the walls of the stairwell, working from the top down, and finally the stairs, balusters and the banisters. Throughout the work, keep the movement of doors and people to a minimum until the paint has dried, to reduce dust. If the wood is to be varnished and its color changed, first fill any holes or splits and coat it with a woodstain.

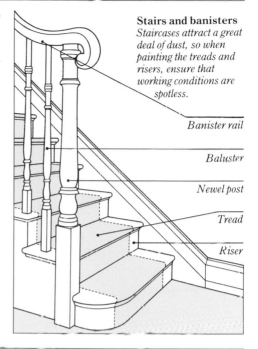

Stairs and banisters
Staircases attract a great deal of dust, so when painting the treads and risers, ensure that working conditions are spotless.

Banister rail

Baluster

Newel post

Tread

Riser

Painting kitchens and bathrooms

Steam and condensation are the main problems to be solved when redecorating these rooms. Good ventilation in the form of efficient exhaust fans will help to minimize the effect of moisture, and a layer of latex on walls and ceilings will provide an easily washable surface, especially if it has a slight sheen. Anti-condensation latex paints containing insulating material are now available to help offset some of these problems. These paints now come in a wide range of colors. Avoid gloss finish on walls and ceilings, since it exaggerates condensation and irregularities. Copper pipes can be given a layer of undercoat then gloss, and will not need primer. Normal gloss will withstand temperatures of up to 194°F (90°C), although white and pale colors may yellow at over 158°F (70°C). Alternatively, a metallic paint can be used. These are corrosion and heat resistant and give luster to both hot and cold pipes.

Avoid water-base paints, since they tend to soften and crack when heated. Never paint connections of fitting nuts on pipes; they could prove difficult to remove if they are sealed with a layer of paint. If you are repainting sound paint, simply wash down the surface and sand it to make a base for the new paint.

PAINTING EXTERIOR WALLS

- Start at the top of the house and work down.
- Divide the house into sections, using natural breaks as demarcation lines. Begin with fascia boards, gutters and soffits, then tackle the walls and downspouts and finish with the windows and doors.
- Work in horizontal strips one block at a time.
- Do not apply masonry paint in cold weather, as it may damage the paint.
- Porous surfaces, such as masonry and stucco, absorb about 50 percent more paint than wooden surfaces.
- Try to work in the shade and move around the house in the same direction as the sun.

Painting doors

Always remove doorknobs, keyhole plates, hooks and other hardware before painting, to avoid smudges and runs and to speed up the work. Store them carefully with their screws and loosely refit between coats to allow doors to be opened and closed. Clean keyholes and the top edges of doors thoroughly so that dust specks are not picked up on bristles and spread over the surface. Complete any necessary repairs, such as fixing hinges and sanding down a sticking door, before painting.

Aim to paint doors after walls and windows but before baseboards and in one continuous session to prevent dried paint lines from forming. Doors need semi- or high-gloss enamel finish for protection against normal wear and tear; they represent the largest area of gloss finish in most homes. An undercoat is necessary – even if the existing paint surface is sound and the new color is darker than the old. Use two undercoats, however, when covering a dark or strong color with a paler shade, and sand between coats. There is no need to paint the top edge of a door, unless it is visible from stairs above. However, a painted edge will collect less dust than bare wood. If the door is to be painted in different colors on each side, paint the hinge edge the same color as the outer face and the lock edge the same color as the inner face if the door opens into the room.

Following the sequence shown below, paint first with vertical strokes, then cross-brush to fill in the gaps. Finish off with upward strokes.

Paneled doors
1 *Use a 1-inch brush to paint the moldings.* 2 *Paint the panels with a 2- or 3-inch brush.* 3 *Paint the vertical center sections.* 4 *Cover the top, middle and bottom horizontal bands.* 5 *Complete the vertical outside sections and edges, and finally the frame.*

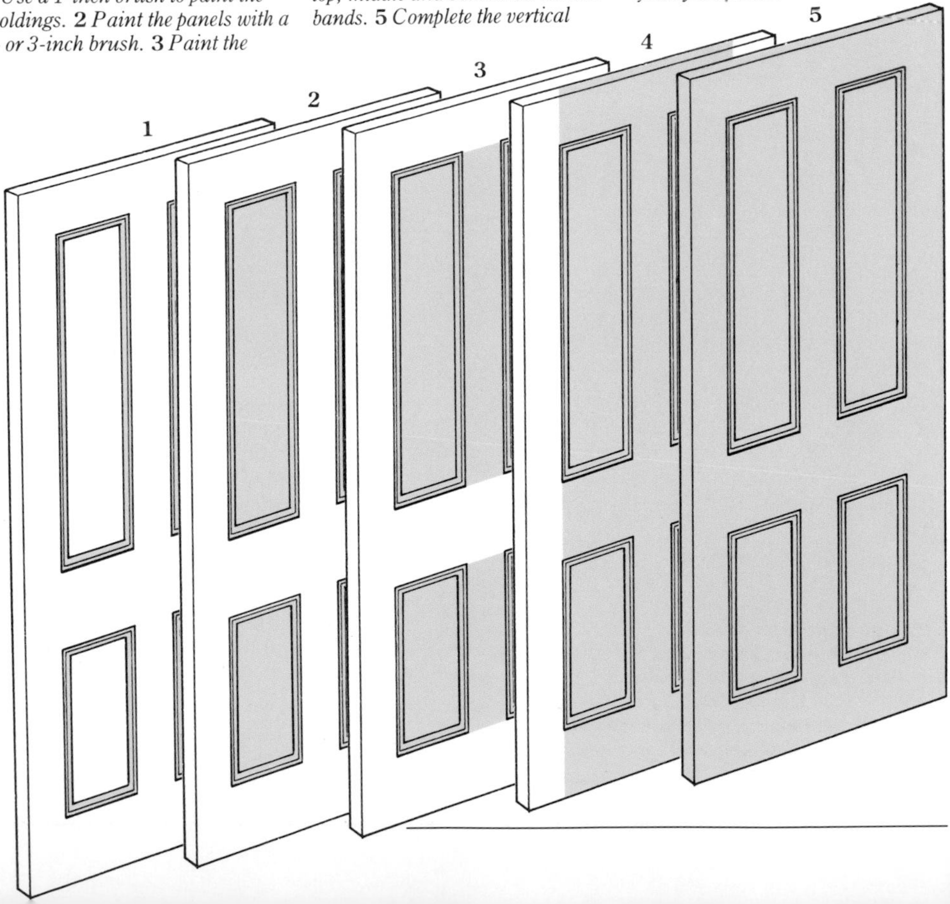

Painting panels and edges

Always paint the panels (left) from each end, toward the middle, and do not overload the brush, or the paint may run. When painting edges (above), use a small brush: this will prevent paint ridges from forming. The top edges of doors do not need to be painted unless they can be seen from above. For when to paint the panels, see the working sequence on the opposite page. Sand each coat with fine-grade sandpaper to make a base for the next.

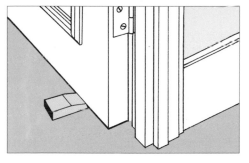

Propping the door open

Prop a flush or paneled door open by tapping a wedge under it. This exposes both the hinge and handle edges for painting, and avoids the risk of your being trapped in the room when you have removed the door handles. Allow each coat to dry thoroughly before closing the door.

FLUSH DOORS

When painting flush doors, start at the top and work down in sections. To cover the area quickly, use a 3-inch brush. Start at the top corner of the hinge side and work in 9 inch^2 sections until you reach the bottom corner on the handle side. Begin with vertical strokes, then cross-brush to spread the paint and finish off with light, upward strokes before moving on to the next section. When painting the edges, take care not to allow the paint to build up into ridges and, where possible, take the paint over the corners. You will find a small 2 inch brush easiest for the edges. Try to avoid the common mistake of applying too much paint to the top of the door and too little to the sides. Work quickly so that the edge of each 9 inch^2 painted section can be covered before it dries.

Painting windows

Window frames, which suffer both condensation and changes of temperature, are subjected to the worst conditions of all interior woodwork. Repair any damage and prepare the surface before painting. Paint any openable windows as early in the day as possible to allow time for them to dry. You will need a 1-inch brush and, if you choose, a paint shield.

The order of working for individual parts of a window is determined by its construction. For the best results, follow the order given below for double-hung and casement windows and always finish painting in the direction of the wood grain.

Cutting in

It is worth practicing the cutting-in technique to get a fine line on glazing bars, frames and edges. Place a loaded brush about $\frac{1}{8}$ inch from the edge and carefully push it toward the join. Press lightly down and draw the brush swiftly along to make a long, clean line. If you do not feel confident about using this method, use a paint shield or masking tape instead (see opposite page). The effect will be the same.

Double-hung windows
Follow the order of painting shown (right and below). 1 First open both windows so that there is an 8 inch overlap. Paint the bottom meeting rail of the top one and the accessible upright sections. 2 Almost close both top and bottom ones and paint the rest of the top one. 3 Then cover the bottom one, leaving it to dry thoroughly. 4 Almost close the windows (use matchsticks to prevent them from sticking) and paint the soffit. 5 Finally, paint the exposed parts of the inner and outer channels, and then paint the sill.

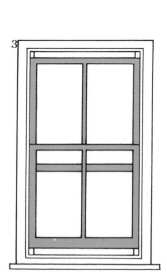
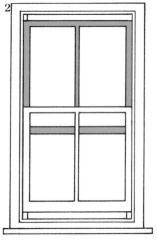
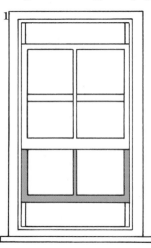
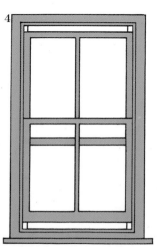
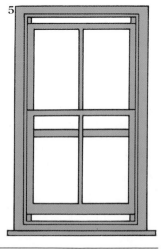

Casement windows
1 *First remove catches and handles and store in a safe place. If one window is stationary, begin with the one that opens, painting the muntins (where the glass joins the wood).* 2 *Then do the crossbars, starting from the top ones if necessary.* 3 *Then move on to the crossrails, again starting from the top.* 4 *Go on to the sides and the edges.* 5 *Finally, paint the frame and meeting sill. Always paint the sill last, otherwise paint will get on to your clothing. Leave the stay until last also, to allow the window to be adjusted during painting.*

Tips on keeping paint off glass

To guarantee a neat edge around window panes, try protecting the glass with a paint shield as you work, or apply masking tape (right) before you begin. Press the tape firmly down to prevent paint from creeping under the edges, and remove it before the final coat is dry to avoid peeling a layer of paint off the frame. Always allow the paint to overlap slightly on to the glass, to prevent moisture from seeping between the putty and the glass and causing the wood to rot. Splashes can be scraped off when dry with a razor blade or paint thinner.

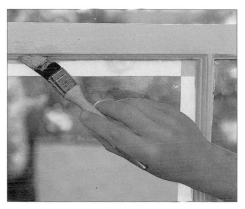

Neat edges for window panes
Masking tape protects the glass as you work.

Textures and finishes

A wide range of attractive paint finishes can be achieved by brushing, sponging, rolling, or dabbing a design into a colored glaze, or by stenciling on a shape, while textured paints can be rollered or combed into a raised pattern. These effects need no special skill and in many cases can be completed more rapidly than a standard painting job.

Decorative finishes

No specialized tools are needed beyond normal painting equipment, but you must use the correct paint for the basecoat and the right glaze. For the background, an oil-base paint with an eggshell dull luster finish produces the best results. Ordinary latex can be used, but it is more absorbent and so produces a less crisp finish. Glazes can be shiny, flat or transparent. Transparent oil glazes can be bought ready-made, to be tinted with universal stainer or artists' oil-colors. Alternatively, a glaze can be made up from one part linseed oil, one part turpentine, one part drying agent, a little whiting and some color. Extra whiting will reduce the sheen. A third type of glaze is made from oil-base paint, diluted with paint thinner.

Textured paints

Textured paints create a subtle decorative finish and can be used to cover a badly cracked surface. Some are also flexible, so that if a ceiling or wall "moves," the cracks remain covered. They are available in both a ready-to-use and powdered form for mixing to the right consistency. Some automatically leave a raised pattern when applied, while others are textured by hand after application, with combs, brushes or rollers.

Dragging

A fine, striped pattern is achieved by "dragging" a brush through a superficial coating of transparent oil glaze. First brush on the background coat and allow it to dry. Then brush on an even coating of colored oil glaze in a broad band. While it is still wet, run the dragging brush down through the glaze to score straight lines. Then glaze and drag the next band of wall. You may find it easier to work with another person, one applying the glaze while the other uses the dragging brush.

This is one of the most elementary of woodgraining techniques, giving the surface the appearance of raw silk, although it will also bring out any irregularities and faults in woodwork. Always drag the brush in the same direction as the woodgrain, and drag away from corners on panels so that pools of glaze cannot form there. Treat moldings first and let them dry. Curving lines and cross-hatching can also give an unusual and attractive effect. You can buy traditional "dragging" brushes, but an ordinary decorating brush will produce the same effects.

Dragging
To achieve a straight line down a high wall, bring the first stroke down as far as you can, then drag the brush up from the bottom to overlap the first one. Vary the position of the edges to hide them.

Sponging

A mottled or stipple pattern can be created with a large natural sponge and a little patience. Unlike dragging and ragging, sponging usually involves adding color to a neutral background, instead of removing patches of color. First apply a coat of paint to the wall and leave it to dry for 24 hours. Then pour some thinned colored glaze into a shallow bowl. Dampen a sponge, dip it lightly into the glaze and dab on to a sheet of newspaper to absorb the excess. When the pattern becomes a delicate speckle on the paper, begin work on the wall. As the design begins to fade, refill the sponge with glaze. Allow the coat to dry, then fill in any gaps. For a softer effect, apply a second glaze color to the wall.

Sponging
Lightly sponge the second glaze color over the first, changing direction and position frequently to avoid repetition of patterns.

Ragging

The tucks and creases of a bundled-up rag, the woven design of burlap, or pieces of old lace curtain can create interesting textured patterns. When the base coat is dry, apply an even layer of glaze to a small area of the wall, brushing thoroughly to even out the coverage. While the glaze is still wet, lightly roll a clean, lint-free, bundled-up rag in random directions on the color until a pattern forms. Use a dabbing and pushing action with a slight twist for a clear design. Apply the glaze to the next patch and continue, allowing a small overlap of pattern each time. Replace the rag when it starts to lose its effect. This job can be done by two people, one painting the glaze, the other using the rag. If the color dries too quickly, moisten it with a damp sponge. Ragging looks best on walls and ceilings, where the distinctive patterns can be fully appreciated.

Ragging
The glaze should be stippled or sponged before applying the rag, to hide brushmarks.

APPLYING TEXTURED PAINTS

Ensure that the surface is clean, dry, sound, and free from flaking paint. If you are applying self-texturing paint, it will automatically create its own texture as you roller or brush it on. With ordinary textured paint, apply a coat first, then work the textured pattern into the smooth layer of paint. A variety of effects can be created with different implements, such as a plasterer's comb, a swirl brush, a stipple brush and patterned rollers. Experiment on a piece of board before committing the pattern to the wall, to avoid time-consuming errors.

Stenciling

Stencils allow for more individual variations than other decorative finishes. Stenciling kits are available, but it is not difficult to design and cut out your own stencil. To make a stencil, draw a design on stencil paper or cardboard and make the cutouts with a craft knife. When designing a stencil, be sure to include ties, or strips that separate the shapes and link the cutout areas to the edges of the stencil. Ties should be at least one-eighth inch wide. You can transfer any drawing to a stencil, but you must add ties if the original has none. To make the cutouts, hold the stencil firmly in place and keep the craft knife upright. As you cut, rotate the stencil so that you always stroke the knife in the same direction.

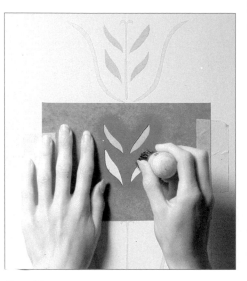

Stenciling
Use a stencil brush to apply the color.

Painting a mural

As with *trompe l'oeil* (opposite page), the only limit in mural painting is your imagination. Murals are normally thought of as being applied to walls, but floors, ceilings and furniture can also be decorated in this way. The preparation is simple, and the materials can be purchased in any art supply store.

You can achieve very bold designs with stark outlines (below), or more muted and subtle effects. Landscapes, abstract designs and human compositions are some varieties you may want to consider. If you do not feel confident about making your own design, work from photographs or paintings.

First sketch your image on graph paper, then divide the wall into the same number of squares, but enlarged in proportion to fill the allocated space. Copy the outline on the wall, floor, ceiling or furniture in pencil, one square at a time, then fill in the colors, using masking tape and a thin brush for the edges.

Using masking tape
Attach masking tape to the outlines, then apply the color (right). Start with the paler shades and let each section dry before moving on to the next. Brush on the paint thickly to reduce the number of coats required. Finally, remove the masking tape, fill in any gaps in the color, and apply a thin, black line to the edges (far right).

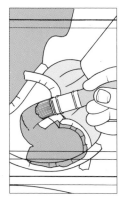

Painting furniture

When preparing surfaces, be meticulous in removing all dirt and loose paint. It is particularly important to do this for painting furniture, since it is in everyday use and defects can easily be seen. To remove peeling, chipped paint from intricate chair and table legs, cream remover is the best choice. It forms a jelly-like cover that clings long enough to lift the old finish. Use a stiff brush and coarse steel wool to scrub away the residue.

The decorative paint effects described on this page and previous pages can easily be used to decorate furniture as well as walls. Any item, from a picture frame to a wardrobe, can be given a sponged, stippled, dragged or rag-rolled finish, or a more complicated effect can be produced, like the bird's-eye maple pattern shown (right). Decorated furniture can provide an interesting and inexpensive contrast to plain walls and furnishings.

One of the simplest paint effects is called spattering, for which you will need a fairly thin glaze and a thick brush. You will also need a second brush or strip of wood. Tap your glaze-laden brush hard against the other brush, while holding both brushes over the surface to be painted. This action will cause droplets of color to spatter across it. You will find that a finer spatter can be achieved if you dip a round artist's brush in some thinned glaze, holding it over the surface to be painted with one hand while you "tickle" the bristles with the forefinger of the other.

Bird's-eye maple

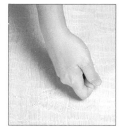 

1 *Tint the base coat with yellow ochre, and the graining color with raw sienna and burnt umber. To make "creased ribbons," drag a dry brush across the glaze. To create "eyes" dab your knuckles into the wet glaze.*

2 *Leave for 15 minutes if using an oil glaze. The graining is created by using a burnt-sienna-colored crayon or a fine artist's brush. Draw the graining lines while the glaze is wet. Make the lines wander around the dots.*

Stippling

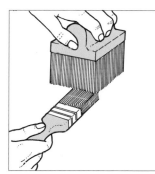 

1 *Stippling produces a subtle finished effect. Apply a base coat which is several tones lighter than, or a different color to, the glaze. Prime the stippling brush well with a small amount of glaze before use.*

2 *Wipe off any excess glaze with an old rag to prevent the color from building up. Work quickly in sections, stippling over the edges. Don't allow the glazes to become tacky, or you won't be able to blend them easily.*

TROMPE L'OEIL

The decorative effects you can produce by the use of *trompe l'oeil* are limited only by your imagination. You can create the illusion of another dimension on a flat surface, or improve badly proportioned features. Paneling, beading, fabrics, landscapes and animals are just some possibilities.

Try a *trompe l'oeil* paneled effect on a flat door. Paint it first with white enamel. For the recessed panels, use a white semi-gloss latex tinted with raw umber to produce a greenish-gray color. Use masking tape to keep the lines straight. To give the illusion of shadows, add darker lines to two sides of the panels.

Chapter Two

Wallpapering

Modern wallpaper is no longer simply paper – but includes a wide choice of synthetic and fabric materials, designed to wash, wear, strip and hang more easily than old-fashioned papers. Vinyls and washable papers are as easy to clean as paintwork, and strippable papers, that can be removed without water, make preparation quick, clean and simple when redecorating. Improved designs, colors and finishes have introduced a wide range of choice.

Once you have decided on the type of wallcovering, measure the areas carefully, double check the figures and calculate quantities. Choice of pattern and color will, to some extent, be determined by local availability, existing furnishings and price. Prices vary widely for the same paper, particularly as it is often cheaper to buy paper in stock than to order, so it is usually worth calling around to the different suppliers.

Unlike painting, wallpapering can be done gradually and will conceal minor cracks. Thorough preparation, however, is important to ensure a smooth finish.

Tools and equipment

A full set of wallpapering tools is not a large investment, particularly as some general household items form part of the collection. The only expensive piece of equipment you might need would be a steam stripper for removing difficult papers, and this can be rented. Choose overalls with pockets large enough to hold brushes, scissors and a sponge. A kit of decorating tools should last a lifetime. Just ensure that, at the end of a job, everything is cleaned of paste in warm, soapy water and thoroughly dried.

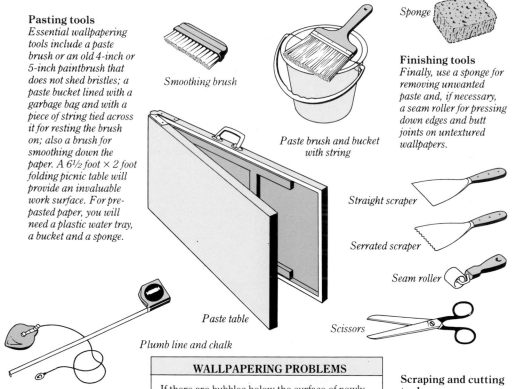

Pasting tools
Essential wallpapering tools include a paste brush or an old 4-inch or 5-inch paintbrush that does not shed bristles; a paste bucket lined with a garbage bag and with a piece of string tied across it for resting the brush on; also a brush for smoothing down the paper. A 6½ foot × 2 foot folding picnic table will provide an invaluable work surface. For pre-pasted paper, you will need a plastic water tray, a bucket and a sponge.

Smoothing brush

Sponge

Finishing tools
Finally, use a sponge for removing unwanted paste and, if necessary, a seam roller for pressing down edges and butt joints on untextured wallpapers.

Paste brush and bucket with string

Straight scraper

Serrated scraper

Seam roller

Paste table

Scissors

Plumb line and chalk

Measuring tools
For marking an accurate guide line before hanging, you will need a plumb line and a pencil for walls, and a chalkline for ceilings (or walls). When measuring out the paper, use a flexible steel tape measure, or a metal straight edge.

WALLPAPERING PROBLEMS

If there are bubbles below the surface of newly pasted paper, this is because the paste has not been adequately brushed out. If the paste is still wet, peel back the paper and rebrush. If dry, cut a cross through the bubble with a sharp knife and paste down the flaps.

If the paper won't stick to the wall, this may be due to a damp or unsized porous wall, the wrong paste, insufficient paste, or not leaving the glued paper to soak for long enough.

Scraping and cutting tools
You will need a straight and, possibly, a serrated scraper for removing wallpaper, and a pair of scissors about 10 inches long for making straight, accurate cuts. A trimming knife and a smaller pair of household scissors are also handy when making intricate cuts around complicated shapes.

Setting up workstations

Always set up a safe working platform before attempting to decorate ceilings and stairwells. In most houses this can be improvised using a combination of ladders and boards. The exact arrangement will depend on your staircase, but the system shown below can be adapted for most stair shapes. If the stairwell is particularly high, however, renting a narrow scaffold tower may be the best solution. When using step ladders, always ensure that they are fully open and that the shelf is pushed well down. When climbing ladders, remember to empty pockets of scissors and knives.

Stairs and stairwells
Put a step ladder on the top landing and lean a straight ladder against the head wall with its foot firmly lodged against a stair riser. Then link them with boards. For the lower levels, put a step ladder in the hall and form a platform with planks resting on a ladder step and a stair.

Wrap cloth around the tops of the ladder to protect the wall and to prevent it from slipping.

For spanning gaps of over 5 feet, use two planks doubled up and secured together with nails or strong tape.

Always lean a long ladder into a stair so that it lodges firmly against the riser.

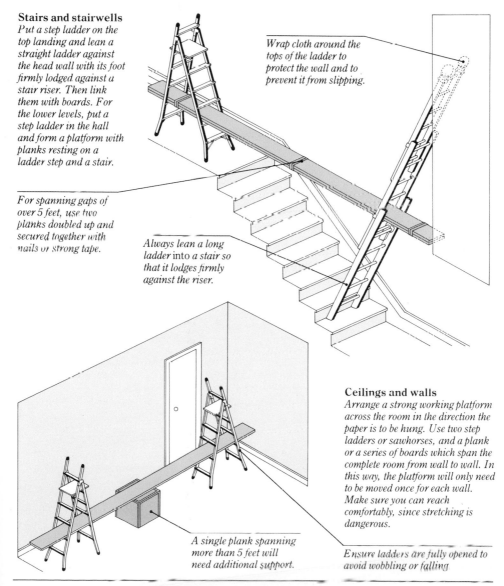

Ceilings and walls
Arrange a strong working platform across the room in the direction the paper is to be hung. Use two step ladders or sawhorses, and a plank or a series of boards which span the complete room from wall to wall. In this way, the platform will only need to be moved once for each wall. Make sure you can reach comfortably, since stretching is dangerous.

A single plank spanning more than 5 feet will need additional support.

Ensure ladders are fully opened to avoid wobbling or falling

Wallcoverings

The range of modern wallcoverings, their decorative styles and practical properties can be overwhelming, so to limit choice, consider practical details first. You can choose wallpapers that are washable, prepasted, scuff-resistant, pretrimmed, and strippable. Some of these also have insulating and water-resistant properties. Many of these new "wallpapers" are not made of paper at all, but of vinyl, metallic foil, burlap, fabric, cork, and even wood. Vinyl-faced wallcoverings with a backing of either cloth or paper are the most widely-used. Standard wallpapers are often purely decorative and less hard-wearing; however, they can help to disguise an imperfect surface.

When selecting wallcoverings remember that the color, pattern, and design of a wallpaper can be used to influence the appearance of a room, altering its style and proportions immeasurably.

Price may also influence your decision. The range is wide, from the cheapest printed paper to expensive silks, and it is worth shopping around for the best prices. It may not be possible to cover an entire room in an expensive fabric, so consider using one or two rolls as a panel against a less expensive but harmonizing backdrop. Remember that rolls on display are generally cheaper than papers ordered from a pattern book.

Most wallcoverings are supplied in rolls that are 27 inches wide, but wider rolls at 54 inches are sometimes available. You will usually find details of the sizes specified in the manufacturer's pattern book.

Types of paper

When selecting wallpaper, it is important to match the color, pattern and texture to the size, shape and general style of individual rooms. It is, however, equally important to choose a suitably practical material for the job. Some areas, for example, will need resilient papers, others demand easily sponged surfaces. Ease of hanging may also influence your choice, particularly if you lack experience.

The hardest papers to hang are the thin, cheap types which tear easily when wet with paste, particularly when pulled around corners. Medium, heavyweight, washable and vinyl papers are stronger and tolerate rougher handling. Paste smudged on the decorative side of the paper can leave a stain, so the easily wiped vinyl-coated papers and paper-backed vinyls can be an advantage in this respect.

Since they are nonporous, these papers are ideal for steamy rooms, such as kitchens and bathrooms, while heavy vinyls, which resist stains and scuffs, are suitable for hallways, stairs and landings.

For bathroom or powder rooms you can get wallcoverings that will withstand moist conditions.

Prepasted wallcoverings save the time and trouble of mixing and applying paste. Most of these also come pretrimmed so you don't have to cut the selvages as each strip is hung. If the paper is not pretrimmed, it must be cut and matched the same as unpasted paper. Prepasted papers are hung directly from a tray of water in which they are first soaked for the time specified by the manufacturer, then pulled straight up and onto the wall. Water trays are usually sold with the paper and are folded to shape from heavily waxed cardboard. A bathtub or long kitchen sink will also work.

TIPS ON BUYING WALLCOVERINGS

- Check that you receive the exact design you ordered from the supplier.
- Check that all rolls have the same lot number.
- Check shades before hanging because there may be some color discrepancy within the same batch. If there is variation, hang darker colors nearer the window and avoid using differing shades on the same wall.
- Avoid thin, cheap papers, as they tear easily after pasting.

PAPER AND FABRIC WALLCOVERINGS

The chart below illustrates the extremely varied range of textures and types of wallcoverings. From the gleam of metallic foil to the glow of woven fibers, from the luxury of silk to the light heartedness of simple prints. There is something to suit every taste and pocketbook.

From the outer strip inward:
Metallic foil
High-relief paper
Hand-printed paper

From the outer strip inward:
Off-white lining paper
Expanded vinyl
Prepasted paper
Textured vinyl
Relief vinyl

From the outer strip inward:
Standard wallpaper
Plain embossed paper
Flocked paper

From the outer strip inward:
Grasscloth
Woven fabric
Silk
Burlap

When to use lining paper

Lining paper is basically blank wallcovering stock which is commonly used in older homes to smooth out rough or cracked surfaces before application of wallpaper; it is often used to cover up the textured plasterwork so common to homes built in the 60s. Lining papers come in different weights and types, depending on what surface they are to be used for. The super heavyweight lining papers can be used directly over grooved woodpaneling, tile, cement block, and peg board. It bridges the cracks and grooves making them undetectable after your wallcovering is hung over the lining paper. Lining paper is also recommended by some manufacturers before hanging foils, light-reflective wallcoverings, unbacked fabrics and grasscloths that would silhouette any irregularities in the walls. It minimizes the possibility of mildew and staining, maximizes adhesion and provides a smoother wall surface.

Wallpapers

The range of standard wallpapers is vast, with patterns and colors to suit all tastes. These smooth, untextured papers are usually not expensive, but are the least resilient of wallcoverings.

Embossed papers come in a variety of textures, from basketweave to imitation plaster. Some are composed of two layers of paper; these heavy papers are supplied plain and are designed to be painted.

Woodchip is another plain, heavy paper which is designed for painting. It is useful for disguising small imperfections on a surface. It consists of a heavy paper base covered in wood chips, creating a pleasing texture suitable for any size and shape of room.

There is a range of wallcoverings that have pronounced relief patterns, which can be random patterns, or can imitate stone, pebbles, tiles or stucco. Designed to be painted, these high relief papers are good for concealing lumpy surfaces.

Hand-printed papers are printed by block or screen methods rather than by machine. Available mainly through interior designers, roll widths and lengths in these papers are not always standard.

Flocked papers may have either a paper or vinyl base, with a pattern of fine pile on the surface. They need to be handled with care so that the surface does not become stained with paste. Vinyl-base types are more durable, easier to clean, and some are prepasted.

Borders and friezes can add a touch of color and variety to an otherwise plain decor and, if skillfully placed, can make a ceiling look higher or lower. They are often designed to coordinate with wallpaper lines. Borders can be used just below the ceiling, around windows or doors, as a chair rail or to emphasize architectural features.

CHOOSING THE RIGHT ADHESIVE

It is vitally important to choose an adhesive compatible with your wallcovering, or it may ruin your decoration. So it makes sense to choose your wall-covering before buying your adhesive. Don't be tempted to buy only one kind of adhesive for a variety of wallcoverings: it will probably be a false economy. As a general rule, the heavier the paper, the thicker the paste should be.

For vinyl and heavyweight papers, there are, in addition to powders, a number of premixed pastes used straight from the tub. For vinyls and other impervious materials, it is essential to use a paste which contains fungicide, on both the top covering and the lining, to prevent mold from growing under the surface. Fungicides are poisonous, so always wash your hands after using these pastes. Some materials, such as burlap and grasscloth, demand a special heavyweight paste. With fine materials, such as silks, it is better to paste the wall not the fabric.

Plastic wallcoverings

These include papers with a plastic coating, and vinyl, light-reflective and foil varieties.

Washable paper has a thin, transparent vinyl coating which makes it easy to clean and resistant to stains, so it is ideal for kitchens, bathrooms and children's rooms. However, it is difficult to remove once hung. Some types are available prepasted.

Vinyl paper is not to be confused with washable paper, although it can easily be cleaned by scrubbing with a soft brush. It must be hung using an adhesive containing fungicide. It consists of a thick layer of vinyl bonded onto a paper backing.

Prepasted paper has a backing precoated with water-active adhesive. It is dipped in water before hanging. This ensures an even layer of adhesive and avoids the time-consuming job of pasting the paper.

Expanded vinyl is used for sealing a wall that is prone to condensation. It also helps to seal a poor surface before adding the wallcovering, and can provide a certain amount of insulation against cold and noise.

Textured vinyl is designed to be painted. It is tougher than embossed paper and cannot be spoiled by pressing out. The pattern is raised or embossed by a heat process after printing. This provides a relief effect while retaining a smooth backing.

The new breed of metallic foils are finely embossed with light-reflective inks that cast a pearlescent luster rather than the harsh glare generally found in the earlier foils and mylars. A smooth wall is essential so lining paper may be necessary, since the shine highlights any defects in the surface beneath.

Comparing types of wallcovering

The durability of wallcoverings varies. Vinyls and some of the thicker fabrics stand up well to wear and tear, while thin papers and delicate fabrics are more vulnerable. Embossed paper is more resilient than a standard single paper, since the embossed texture added in the factory gives extra weight.

Wallcovering, properly hung, will last for years. Most of today's wallcoverings, even the most elegant are washable, though some are easier to clean than others. Papers divide into three sorts: spongeable types (which can be gently sponged clean); washable types (which can be washed with a wet, soapy cloth); and scrubbable types (which withstand washing with a mild abrasive). Fabrics are more prone to staining than papers, and vinyl less so.

To increase washability, stain resistance and color retention, some wallcoverings such as textile fabrics and burlaps can be treated with a clear plastic coating.

Synthetics are the strippable wallcoverings that have very smooth, durable surfaces. They do not generally change their physical shape after pasting.

The most luxurious finishes are usually the most expensive and often demand a slightly different hanging technique (pages 58–9). Greater care is needed to keep paste off the surface and avoid expensive cutting mistakes. Once hung they usually have a long life.

PASTING

Coverings with a paper backing are usually easier to hang than those without and can be pasted like normal wallpaper. Most paper-backed wallcoverings expand when pasted. It is therefore important to allow the paper to "soak" for a few minutes until expansion is completed before applying it to the wall.

Some wallcoverings are available prepasted, and the adhesive has to be activated by immersing the wallcovering in a water tray. A compromise has to be made by the manufacturers as to how much paste is applied, and on some impervious surfaces there may be a surplus of paste which will have to be wiped away with a damp cloth.

Textured wallcoverings

Texture in wallcovering influences the atmosphere of a room. Shiny surfaces, such as foils, reflect light and are cool to the touch and to the eye. Lustrous finishes, such as silks and satins, are elegant and cool but soft. Heavier, matt textures, such as burlaps, tweeds and linens, absorb the light and give a warmer, more muted and relaxed effect. Many materials also act as heat or sound insulators and most wear better than paper.

For smoothing textured wallcoverings into place, seam rollers are generally taboo because they can easily flatten or burnish the seams; a soft roller, pad smoother or clean hands are best. Your fingers or the gentle tapping of a smoothing brush will keep seams down.

Burlap

This resilient fabric is available with or without a paper backing and in a wide range of colors and patterns. It can also be painted with alkyd paint or latex. It is useful for hiding imperfections in walls and for use in areas prone to condensation. However, it should not be used where it is likely to get dirty, as it is difficult to clean.

Paper-backed burlap is pasted and hung like traditional wallpaper with a layer of adhesive on the back. With unbacked burlap, apply paste to the wall before hanging the strips. Flatten each strip into place with a roller and take care not to pull the material or it will stretch and leave an uneven surface. Overlap successive strips and complete all the walls before trimming, in case the material shrinks. Trim top and bottom with a craft knife against a wide-bladed scraper. Make neat seams by cutting through each overlap with a very sharp craft knife against a steel straightedge. Remove the left-over piece and press down the join.

Trimming burlap
Use a very sharp knife to trim seams neatly.

TEXTURED COVERINGS AT A GLANCE

- Sheets, fabrics and burlaps should be preshrunk if they do not have a backing and applied with a non-staining paste.
- Grasscloth is a fragile fabric consisting of natural grasses woven into a fine cotton warp and bonded onto a paper backing. It must be hung carefully and with a special adhesive.
- Silk is available plain or patterned, stuck to a paper backing. It is important not to get paste on the face of the material as it stains easily.
- Woven fabrics are sold also with a paper backing. Alternatively, furnishing fabric and sheets can be cut into lengths and applied to a prepasted wall.
- Cork is available mounted onto a painted paper backing. It must be hung carefully with a special premixed adhesive.

Silk

Luxurious and long-lasting, silk suits a sophisticated decor. It is very delicate, so take great care when handling not to stretch or crease it. To prevent adhesive or water marks from staining the silk, apply the paste to the wall, making sure that there are no bumps in the adhesive, or these will show through.

Measure the lengths required, allowing 2 inches for trimming. Cut carefully, using a sharp knife against a straightedge. Always double-check your measurements to avoid costly mistakes. If you need to divide a strip around a corner, you may find it easier to make a rough cut with scissors, then score through with a craft knife for a neat and perfectly straight edge. Smooth onto the wall with a soft roller and make neat seams as for burlaps.

Foil

Made from metallized plastic film on paper backing, foil provides a light-reflective surface. This makes an ideal covering for bathrooms, but only on walls that are perfectly smooth, as foil exaggerates irregularities. Two types are available: ordinary and prepasted. With the ordinary type, each length is pasted with a foam roller. The prepasted type is immersed in water to activate the paste. Hang the foil from the top down and smooth it onto the wall with a clean sponge. Take care to match the pattern accurately and to get the design straight, since mismatching will be obvious. Trim the top and bottom edges, then butt the joins and, finally, flatten them gently with a seam roller, or better still, with a soft roller.

Finishing the join
Use a seam or soft roller to ensure butt joins are neat.

Grasscloth

Oriental in origin, this woven fabric is made from natural grasses woven with cotton and glued to a paper backing. To hang grasscloth, paste it as normal, but cover the face of the pasting table first with a strip of lining paper, to protect the fabric. Do not fold the cloth or it will leave a hard crease line. Apply strips to the wall and smooth them down with a clean roller. Using a piece of cardboard, crease a trimming line at the ceiling and the baseboard. Only when the adhesive is dry should you trim each length with a craft knife, using a steel straightedge. Like burlap, grasscloth is often difficult to clean, so it should not be used where it might easily get dirty.

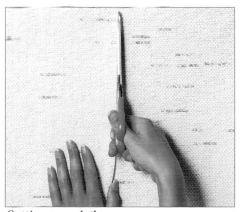

Cutting grasscloth
Cut slowly and use sharp scissors or a craft knife for a neat line.

SUITING THE WALLCOVERING TO THE ROOM

When choosing wallcoverings, it is important to consider the suitability of the paper or fabric for the room. Each room has its own problems and needs; it may be prone to condensation, for example, or it may need to be insulated against cold or noise.

Certain rooms, such as kitchens and children's rooms, need paper that is washable and hard-wearing. The range of wallcoverings now available means that you can choose for both practicality and decorative effect.

Hall/landing
Vinyl
Washable paper
Woodchip paper
Embossed paper
High-relief paper
Relief vinyl

Bedroom
Standard paper
Flocked paper
Embossed paper
High-relief paper
Fabrics

Children's room
Washable vinyl
Woodchip paper
Standard paper
Cork

Bathroom
Metallic foil vinyl
Relief vinyl
Moisture-proof vinyl
Washable paper

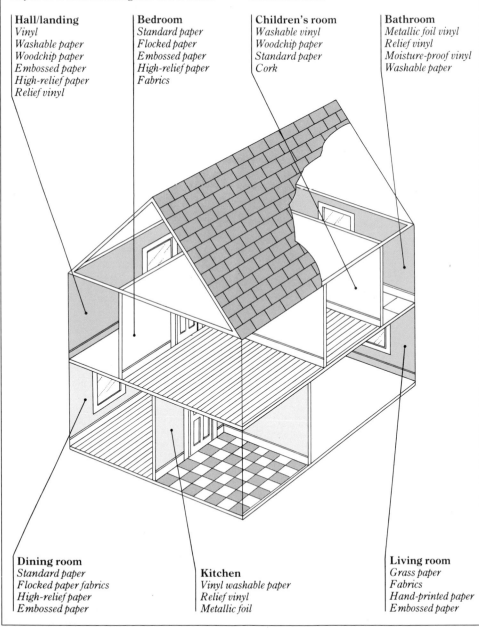

Dining room
Standard paper
Flocked paper fabrics
High-relief paper
Embossed paper

Kitchen
Vinyl washable paper
Relief vinyl
Metallic foil

Living room
Grass paper
Fabrics
Hand-printed paper
Embossed paper

Estimating quantities

Wallcoverings are packaged in bolts of two or three single rolls containing 36 square feet each, regardless of width. Allowing 10 percent for waste, a single roll will cover about 30 square feet of surface. With the average 8 foot ceiling you usually get 3 or 4 ceiling-to-floor strips from a 2-roll bolt. To determine the number of rolls needed for a given room, use a yardstick or steel tape and take measurements in feet. Multiply the height by the distance around the room. Then divide by 30. From this result substract one-half roll for each normal size window and door. You now have the number of rolls you'll need. Use the chart to double check your estimates.

ROOM ESTIMATING CHART					
Distance Around Room in Feet	Single Rolls for Wall Areas Height of Ceiling			Number Yards for Borders	Single Rolls for Ceilings
	8 Feet	9 Feet	10 Feet		
28	8	8	10	11	2
30	8	8	10	11	2
32	8	10	10	12	2
34	10	10	12	13	4
36	10	10	12	13	4
38	10	12	12	14	4
40	11	12	12	15	4
42	12	12	14	15	4
44	12	13	14	16	4
46	13	14	15	17	6
48	14	14	16	17	6
50	14	15	16	18	6

BORDERS AND CEILINGS

Borders are sold by the linear yard, not by the roll. They come in various widths for application between ceiling and wall. To estimate how much you need, add the distance around the room in feet and divide the total by three to get the number of yards required.
Ceilings To estimate the amount of paper needed to cover a ceiling, multiply its width by length (in feet) and divide by 30 to get the total number of single rolls required.

Choosing patterns

Complicated patterns are usually best avoided by the beginner, especially in a room with lots of alcoves and corners. Simple, repeat patterns are equally problematic, since the eye will quickly pick up any mismatching. These usually fall into two types: straight "cross match" patterns which have horizontal repeats, and patterns with diagonal repeats. "Free match" designs, however, match automatically.

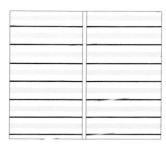

Free match pattern
Pattern matching is easiest when the pattern is small and random.

Straight across match pattern
Horizontal patterns are unsuitable for sloping ceilings.

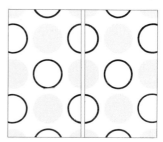

Drop match pattern
A vertical pattern will emphasize uneven corners.

Color and pattern for effect

Pattern, like color, influences the mood and shape of a room. Florals, for example, tend to be restful, while geometrics may create a more stimulating atmosphere. Designs can be used to play visual tricks: vertical lines help to "raise" a ceiling, while horizontal lines "widen" a room; three-dimensional geometrics give the impression of depth, whereas small designs give a feeling of space; and large motifs diminish the size of a surface. Motifs have the power to focus interest on a feature or disguise irregularities when they are taken over an entire room. For the best effect, avoid having too many patterns in one room, do not combine florals with geometrics and always set off a pattern with a plain background, floor or furnishings.

Floral patterns
Fresh spring colors lend warmth and character to a bleak, angular room (left). Large sprigs have the effect of opening out a room and raising a ceiling, particularly when arranged in vertical strips. If the pattern is carried on to the blinds or furnishings, the warming and softening effect increases. In a small room with irregular shapes – an attic, for example – a miniature floral in random sequences would be more suitable, since a regular line will highlight crooked walls or ceilings.

A printed collage
Menus, wine labels, newspapers and magazines will form an unusual wallcovering. A collage is best pasted on to a small area to form a feature in a bathroom (below), or a child's bedroom.

Geometric patterns
These instantly give a room a clean and modern feel – particularly suitable for a bathroom (right). Ideally, the lines should complement any other verticals and horizontals. The angles of the room must be straight or the lines will exaggerate any irregularities. A tiny motif within the geometric pattern will help to soften lines, and one or two colors should also be repeated in other parts of the room. Plain, bright-colored accessories are shown to best advantage.

Motifs and color schemes
The pattern used in the conservatory above has been chosen to reflect the purpose of the room. The coordinated effect has been achieved by picking up the main color of the pattern throughout the room and matching accessories to the white background.

Preparation and pasting

The finished look of any decorating job depends to a very large extent on good preparation. This includes not only removing all traces of the existing paint and paper and ensuring a clean, firm surface, but also cutting materials correctly to size and covering the pasting surface in an even and methodical manner. It is important to set up a workstation that will enable you to reach all parts of the room safely and easily (page 49).

Stripping off old wallpaper

Any existing wallcovering should be stripped off to leave bare walls, since seams, peeling, blistering or a strong pattern in the old paper may show through the new. The fresh adhesive may also pull the old covering away from the wall, together with the new paper you have just hung. The key to stripping wallpaper is to take time and care over the job. The paper should not be scraped off too vigorously or lumps will be gouged from the plaster, leaving more holes to fill in later. Be patient with stubborn areas and continue soaking and scraping until the paper loosens. Standard wallpapers are removed by sponging with warm water until the paper is soft enough to scrape off. Strippable papers are simply peeled off their backing paper. Stubborn papers which hold fast may be removed more easily with a steam stripper.

Stripping normal wallpaper

1 *Remove wallpaper by soaking with warm water and removal concentrate, using a large brush or sponge. Thicker papers may need an extra soaking.*

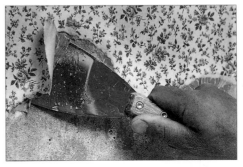

2 *Once the paper is soaked, you can begin scraping. Keep the scraper as flat as possible to avoid gouging the plaster.*

PREPARING SURFACES

You can paper over old wallpaper, provided it still adheres tightly. If it is loose, peeling or blistering it will show through new paper, so it should all be removed. You can not hang a vinyl wallcovering over old paper; it will pull the paper off when it dries. The easiest way to remove old wallpaper is with steaming equipment that you can rent by the day. Soaking with a sponged-on solution of water and removal concentrate also works but it takes longer. Remove loosened covering with a scraper. To prepare new plaster or new wallboard for papering, first seal the surface with shellac or an oil-base paint, then brush on a coat of wall sizing. Make sure the new plaster has cured before sealing it. Strippable papers are simply peeled off their backing paper.

Stripping vinyl wallpapers

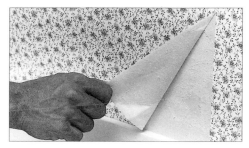

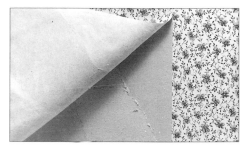

1 *Strippable wallcoverings are removed by releasing the edge of the paper with your fingernail or a utility knife and pulling carefully upward, not outward, to avoid ripping the backing.*

2 *Underneath vinyls you will find a layer of backing paper. This can act as a base paper for the new wallcovering. If, however, the backing paper comes away in places, it must be removed completely.*

Stripping difficult papers

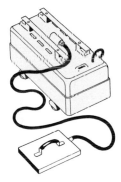

1 *Washable and overpainted papers are made to withstand water, so first score the surface using a wire brush or serrated scraper to break down the surface before soaking.*

2 *A steam stripper is simple to use and creates less mess than soaking and scraping. Steam generated by the machine passes through a plate held close to the wall. This loosens the paper which is then scraped off.*

A steam stripper
This enables you to strip wallpaper from a large area more quickly than soaking and scraping and with relatively little effort. It is worth renting one if you have a lot to do.

WHEN TO SIZE A WALL

Size serves as a base for preparing old or new surfaces for wallcovering and can usually be brushed, rolled or sponged on the wall. Size acts as a sealer to tie together any paint pigment or other troublemaking materials on the surface and separate them from the wallcovering. It also helps slide the wallcovering into position and is added assurance that the wallcovering will stick and that your seams will not open later. The size you use is determined by the wall surface and the type of wallcovering you plan to hang. Read both the wallcovering and paste manufacturer's instructions and consult your dealer.

Measuring and cutting

Measure the height of each wall at both ends and in the middle to give you a maximum length for your strips of paper and allow an additional 4 inches before cutting. This gives an extra 2 inches at both ceiling (or picture rail) and baseboards for neat trimming. Measure ceilings in the same way and allow an excess of 2 inches on ceilings for trimming onto the side and window walls. Unroll a few feet to check which way up the pattern should be. Trim off the end of the roll and either cut off lengths as you go, or, to speed up the job, cut several lengths, so that one length can be soaking while you are hanging another (but mark consecutive numbers on the back and make a note of which end is the "top"). When cutting to match use a metal tape measure to mark out lengths, then use wallpaper shears to cut your paper. When using a plain or a random-patterned paper, work from one roll of paper and cut equal lengths. With a diagonally matching "drop match pattern" paper, work from two or three rolls at a time to minimize waste in pattern matching. Drape lengths over a table and align them carefully before cutting.

Measuring out lengths
When measuring out lengths of wallpaper, use a metal tape measure, and allow at least 4 inches of paper for trimming.

Straight across match patterns
Cut equal lengths from the same roll of wallpaper, and allow a small margin where necessary.

Drop match patterns
Always match up drop match patterns carefully before you begin measuring and cutting the lengths of paper for pasting.

Pasting and folding

Paste should be mixed until all lumps are dissolved and allowed to stand for a couple of minutes. To ensure a good covering of paste, coat the brush generously, then paste systematically and in good light. Be sure to cover the entire area because unpasted areas will show up as blisters on the wall. After applying paste to about two thirds of the strip, fold the top down, allowing paste to rest against paste, pull the unpasted strip onto the table, paste, then fold the bottom edge up.

Soaking
Allow 3–5 minutes after pasting to let the wallcovering soak before hanging. This will give it time to expand or shrink on the work surface rather than on the wall causing mismatching or parting of the seams when dry. Simply leave it on a clean, dry surface after you have applied the paste and continue pasting more strips. Keep the soaking time constant for each strip to avoid variations in stretching.

BATCHES

Never skimp when ordering paper, since running out can cause considerable problems. Although you may be able to buy another roll with the same design, the colors in the pattern might be a remarkably different shade, which will show in bright light. Check that each roll you buy bears the same number. To avoid running out, ask whether you can buy a spare roll, on the condition that you will be able to return it if you do not need it.

Pasting and folding

1 *Paste the central portion of paper, then the long edge nearest to you.*

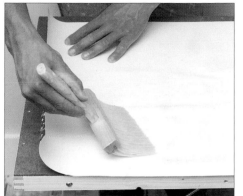

2 *Brush the paste over to the opposite long edge, spreading the paste evenly.*

3 *Fold the pasted half over onto itself, not on to the unpasted paper.*

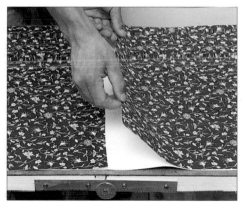

4 *Paste the second half, then fold it over and let the whole strip soak.*

Folding long lengths

When pasting a long length of paper, arrange the pasted sections into folds, pasted-side to pasted side. Do not allow paste to smudge on to the decorative side. Be careful not to crease the folds, since this will leave unsightly marks when the paper is hung.

Accordian folds
These folds make handling easier when working on ceilings or stairwells or when hanging lining paper.

Marking guide lines on ceilings and walls

Walls and ceilings are often not exactly square; to be sure paper hangs straight, you must establish a true vertical with a plumb line. To do this, hang a weight or "plumb bob" at the end of a string; tack the string at the top of the wall so it is closer to the starting door or window than the width of the wallcovering roll and the weight hangs just above the floor. Chalk the string, hold it taut near the weight, and snap it against the wall to get the true vertical. Do this as each new wall is begun and recheck as you go.

Straight guide lines on ceilings are made by measuring equal distances from the wall at each end of the ceiling and snapping the chalkline between the two points.

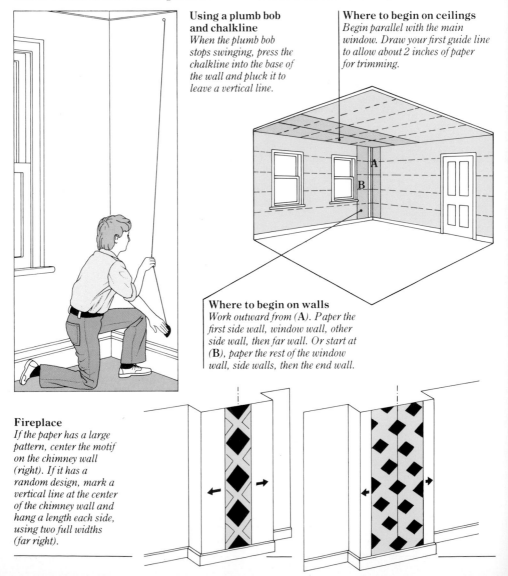

Using a plumb bob and chalkline
When the plumb bob stops swinging, press the chalkline into the base of the wall and pluck it to leave a vertical line.

Where to begin on ceilings
Begin parallel with the main window. Draw your first guide line to allow about 2 inches of paper for trimming.

Where to begin on walls
Work outward from (A). Paper the first side wall, window wall, other side wall, then far wall. Or start at (B), paper the rest of the window wall, side walls, then the end wall.

Fireplace
If the paper has a large pattern, center the motif on the chimney wall (right). If it has a random design, mark a vertical line at the center of the chimney wall and hang a length each side, using two full widths (far right).

Hanging lining paper on walls

Lining paper is hung horizontally, so each strip must be as long as the wall's width. Joining short strips is not advisable, since it is difficult to get a perfect seam.

Mark a guide line for the first length (see opposite), start at the top of the wall and work downward to the baseboards. The first strip should overlap onto the ceiling by about 1 inch before being trimmed off. Each strip should overlap around the corner onto the next wall by about ½ inch. As you work butt each subsequent horizontal strip closely to the previous strip. Always use the same adhesive as for the top wallcovering and be sure it is thoroughly dry before hanging the wallcoverings over it (usually 36 hours).

Hanging horizontal lining
Unfold the paper and smooth it onto the wall.

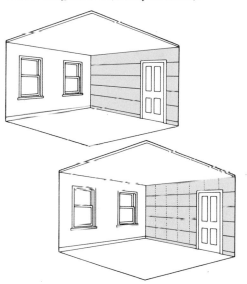

Where to begin lining on walls
Lining paper should be hung in horizontal layers on walls (top). If the surface is bad apply a double layer of paper, known as cross-lining (above). Hang the first layer vertically and the second horizontally.

Patch lining

Where only a small part of the wall needs to be lined, try patch lining. Hang enough lining paper to cover the poor area with an overlap of a few inches, but do not stick down the edges. Allow the paste to dry, then tear off a rim of paper to leave a softened feathered edge to the patch. However, do not add small, straight-edged pieces to a damaged strip, as the seams will show.

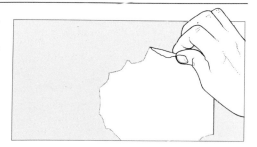

Patching damaged lining
Tear around the patch for a soft line.

How to hang wallpaper

The secret of successful wallpapering is to be thorough, methodical and careful when matching patterns. Before you begin hanging the wallcovering, it is a good idea to inspect each roll for any flaws or color deviations. This will not only prevent a disappointment but will also help uncurl the wallcovering and make it easier to work with when you actually start hanging. Having lined any poor or rough surfaces, cut and pasted strips, established a starting point and marked straight guide lines, the paper is ready to hang. The first strip is lined up against the guide line, smoothed into place, then trimmed. Subsequent strips are carefully brushed into place to form good pattern matches and neat butt seams.

Applying the paper

1 *Standing square to the wall, unfold the top half of the paper. Position the edge against the vertical guide line. Leave a 2-inch trimming edge at the top.*

2 *Run the wallpaper brush firmly down the center of the aligned length. Brush outward to expel any air bubbles and smooth the paper neatly onto the wall.*

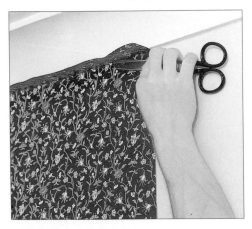

3 *Align the lower half of the paper, then run the back of the scissors along the paper at the ceiling angle.*

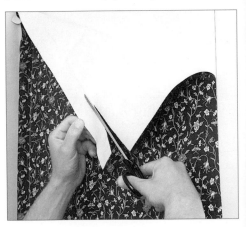

4 *Carefully peel back the paper again and trim along the crease with the wallpaper scissors.*

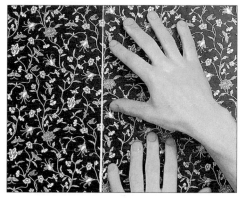

5 *Smooth the trimmed paper back onto the wall with the wallpaper brush. Hang the second strip of paper.*

6 *Align the strip from the top of the wall, matching the pattern. Smooth the seams with a seam roller.*

Mismatching

It is almost impossible to complete a wallpapering job using patterned paper without some mismatching. The usual points are corners, around doors, windows and fireplaces. When deciding where to end the papering, choose a point which will not be too obvious. At the edge of a door or window, for example, use a part of the pattern which blends with the other strips ending there, but does not match them exactly. Accurate matching above doors and above and below windows requires using parts of full-width strips, which wastes paper. Corners are hardly ever perfectly straight and will often be mismatched, although it will be a great deal less noticeable than a mismatched flat wall.

Carrying pasted paper

To carry pasted paper easily and safely to the wall, loop the folded sections over your arm, pasted sides together. This will prevent you from smearing paste onto your clothes, will enable you to mount the ladder easily with the paper, and will ensure that the strip is not crushed. Long strips of folded paper can be supported on a roll. Make sure that the ladder is adjusted properly before you ascend.

BUTT AND OVERLAP SEAMS

There are two ways of joining the seams when hanging wallpaper, butt and overlap. The most widely used is the butt method, in which the edges fit tightly up against each other with no overlap, ensuring that the strips stay together as they dry. To do butt seams hang the first strip, and then slide the second strip by hand toward the first until they meet. Continue sliding until a tiny ridge forms; this ridge will disappear as the paste on the paper dries.

Overlapping seams are made by overlapping the strips and then cutting through both of them with a very sharp craft knife.

If the paper you buy is not pretrimmed, the selvage – the undecorated border – must be cut off both edges of the roll.

How to carry a strip of pasted paper
When carried in this way with the folded section looped over your arm, the top of the fold should be in position to be installed next to the ceiling line.

Hanging lining paper on ceilings

It is advisable to use lining paper on ceilings with old paint or a rough, cracked or textured surface. Without a lining, wallpaper may crease and stretch on uneven surfaces, paste may take a long time to dry on glossy surfaces, and gaps may form through shrinkage.

Lining paper is normally hung at right angles to the top covering on both ceilings and walls, so that the seams in the two layers do not coincide. Use the same paste as for the top wallcovering, but hang the lining immediately, since there is no need to let it soak. Let it dry for 36 to 48 hours before pasting on the top covering. When learning the art of paper hanging, it is worth practicing with lining paper to perfect the technique.

Applying the lining paper

1 *Set up a safe working platform and mark a chalkline on the ceiling. If you have an assistant, have him or her stand by with a clean brush to support the paper.*

2 *Align the first portion of the pasted paper with the chalkline. If you are working alone, use a spare roll of paper to support the rest of the paper while you work.*

3 *Keep the remainder of the strip close to the ceiling and smooth down the paper to eliminate air bubbles. Mark a crease line with a scraper at the edges.*

Lining a ceiling
Prepare the ceiling (page 60) and mark a chalkline for the first strip of paper (page 64). The first strip of lining paper is usually hung at right angles to the main window. In this way, the lining will lie at right angles to the top layer of wallpaper, which is usually hung parallel with the window (page 64). Begin lining in a corner and allow about 2 inches of paper to be turned onto the window wall for trimming. Also allow an extra 2 inches for trimming onto the side walls.

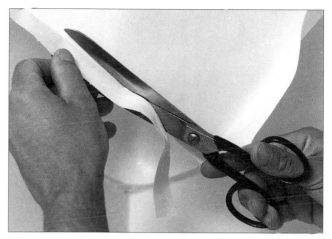

Cleaning scissors
For neat trimming, stand paste-clogged scissors and shears in a jar of hot water from time to time. This will dislodge the adhesive and so guarantee that you get clean cuts. If the paste hardens, it may need to be washed off in clean, soapy water.

Trimming lining paper
Trim along the crease line with a pair of sharp, clean scissors or a craft knife. If the walls are to be prepared, leave a ¼-inch margin of paper on each wall. Successive strips are hung in the same way, ensuring that the edges of all the strips are neatly butt-seamed (page 67).

Hanging vinyl

Scrubbable and damage- and stain-resistant all-vinyl papers are simply the most durable wallcoverings made. They should be used wherever dirt and wear are prime considerations, such as in kitchens, bathrooms, hallways, and children's rooms. All-vinyl coverings are available in cloth- or paper-backed versions or as cloth impregnated with vinyl on a paper backing. They are smoother than vinyl-coated papers, on which the vinyl is thinner; when stressed, all-vinyl coverings tend to stretch rather than tear. They are usually moderately priced. Many professional hangers rank cloth-backed vinyls as the coverings easiest to work with. Because vinyl coverings lack porosity, mildew can develop in the underlying paste, so fungus-resistant vinyl adhesives must be used.

Trimming expanded vinyl
At baseboards, gently press the material into the angle, mark a cutting line, and trim with scissors or a knife.

Hanging prepasted paper

Prepasted paper has a coated backing of dried paste which is activated by immersion in water. Water trays often come with the wallpaper or you can use any container that is long and deep enough. Fill a water tray about two thirds full with clear cold water. It is necessary to re-roll each cut strip so that the face of the paper is on the inside. Loosely re-roll the first strip to be hung from bottom to top with pattern side in, pasted side out and soak as directed (usually less than a minute). Then take the top of the strip, gradually unroll it, moving up the ladder to hang it at the ceiling line. Smooth down, working from the center to the edges with a clean, damp sponge or smoothing brush, wiping away any paste that oozes out at the edges. Once the strip is hung, move the water tray under the location of the next strip.

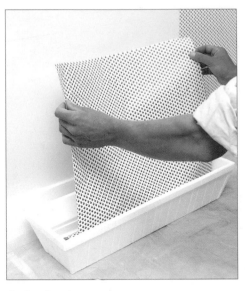

Activating the paste
Carefully pull up the top edge of the roll, allowing the water to drain back into the water tray.

Borders and friezes

Borders and friezes add an inexpensive finishing touch to a newly decorated room. Although traditionally fitted at ceiling or picture rail level, they can be used to good effect to accent a wall, or to trim a sloping ceiling, for example. A decorative strip can reduce the apparent height of a tall ceiling, elongate a short room, coordinate disparate colors, or enliven a quiet room. Borders and friezes look best against a neutral background, but can be used with patterned coordinates. They should not be applied until at least 48 hours after hanging wallpaper.

A softening effect
In a simple, neutral room (left) a soft frieze adds a warm and friendly touch, particularly if it picks up a color in the furnishings. In a room without pattern, a frieze can become a feature.

A coordinated effect
On a vibrant wall, the border needs to link with either the pattern or the color of the wallpaper for a properly unified effect (right).

Papering arches

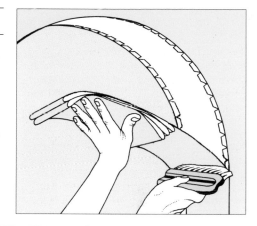

Paper the outer wall first and wrap a 2-inch margin of paper into the arch. Make small, triangular cuts in the edge. This will allow the paper to follow the curve of the arch without tearing. Fold the flaps around the corner and smooth them down. Paper the inside of the arch in two pieces, the exact width of the arch, working from the bottom to the apex of the arch and making a neat butt seam at the top.

Papering arches
Carefully align the edges of the paper with the arch.

Papering corners

Seams are less noticeable if they fall in a corner, so unless a width of paper conveniently ends in a corner, you will need to cut it into two strips. Internal and external corners are treated in much the same way. When less than a full width is needed to reach a corner, you should measure from the edge of the last strip into the corner. Turn the paper face down to mark off the width needed and double-check that the strip is being cut from the correct edge, or the pattern will not match. Pencil guide marks to indicate which edges are to fall in the corner. When the first strip is in place, the leftover piece is hung on the new wall. Make sure that its edge is covering the seam.

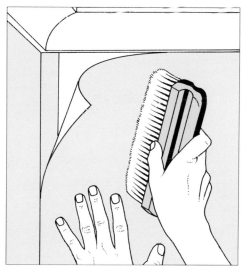

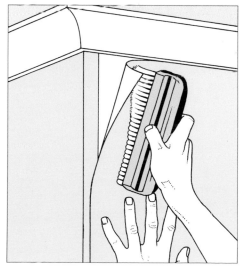

Internal and external corners
Vertically divide a strip of paper between the two walls, allowing a small overlap. Paste the first strip. Mark vertical lines on the next wall before pasting the leftover piece. If the paper is patterned, check that the patterns match before smoothing down the paper.

Papering stairwells

The height of most stairwells poses the problem of how to reach the tops of the walls and how to handle very long strips of paper. The first essential is therefore to set up a safe workstation (page 49).

Although it runs against the normal procedure of working away from the light, it is easiest to hang the longest strip first and work away from it in both directions.

When measuring strips, mark the paper to allow for the slope of the stairs (right). Allow each strip to hang below the longest drop. Carefully crease the paper along the baseboard, then trim to fit. After pasting, fold each strip accordian-style for ease of handling (page 63) and, if possible, enlist a helper to support the strip of paper as it is hung.

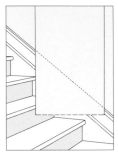

Measuring for the stair angle
Allow for the slope of the stairs when measuring strips, so that the paper falls below the longest drop. Crease the paper along the baseboard and trim.

If you use a prepasted paper, always roll each strip twice in the water tray to ensure that water reaches all parts of the dried paste on the back of these long strips of paper. First immerse the piece, pattern outward, in the water tray, so that the bottom end extrudes, then re-roll it until the end which will lie at the top of the wall emerges.

Papering around fireplaces

The way to tackle a fireplace depends on the mantelpiece. If it reaches right across the chimney wall or to within 1 inch of the corners, treat the wall above and below the mantel as two separate areas. Hang the paper down to the mantelpiece and make a horizontal cut. Then hang the lower half of the strip and make a butt seam where the pieces meet (page 67).

If the mantelpiece spans only a part of the wall, hang the strip as one piece. Brush on the top half of the paper and cut along the rear edge of the mantelpiece. Then cut carefully around the contours of the fireplace, using a utility knife or sharp household scissors for intricate shapes (below left). Smooth the paper into place with a brush. When papering chimney walls, try to make any necessary joins and overlaps on the side, recessing walls (below right).

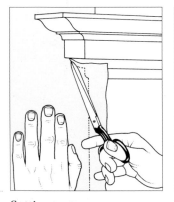

Cutting contours
Use sharp household scissors for intricate cuts.

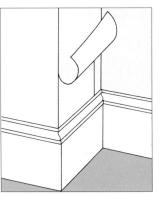

Seams and overlaps
On chimney walls make seams on the side walls.

PAPERING AROUND RADIATORS

Some radiators can now be tilted forward for decorating, but most are fixed. Either remove the radiator or tuck enough paper behind it to leave a "fully papered" look. Cut a slit if necessary for wall brackets supporting the radiator and push the strips down behind. If the paper is visible below the radiator, butt seam the strips at the base of the wall and trim carefully along the top of the baseboard.

Papering around outlets and switchplates

First switch off the power. Modern, flush-fitting sockets and switches are simple to trim around neatly. First loosen the cover plate, then hang the paper up to the electrical fitting. Cut a hole in the paper, about ¼ inch smaller than the size of the plate. Then smooth the paper on to the wall and replace the plate.

Some older-style electrical outlets and switches are fixed in a block. Press the paper against the switch and make small cuts from the center of the fitting to about ½ inch beyond its edges. Brush the paper around the block and trim the flaps (right top). With ceiling rosettes, make radial cuts instead.

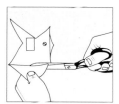

Light switches
Make a cut to each corner, outward from the center, then trim along each edge with a sharp pair of scissors.

Ceiling lights
Make a series of radial cuts from the center to the edge, and trim off the tongues of paper with a trimming knife.

Papering around windows and doors

The shape of the window frame will determine the papering technique. In a window recess, paper the inside walls first, cutting the paper to align exactly with the edge of the outer wall (below left). Then hang a strip on the outer wall, with a small margin overlapping into the papered recess, and match the pattern carefully. The trickiest rooms to wallpaper are attics and lofts where there are unusual angles. Where dormer windows have triangular-shaped wall recesses, turn a 1 inch margin of paper from the outer wall into the recess. Cut pieces to cover the recess walls precisely and overlap the margin (below right). When papering around wide picture windows, first cut, match and hang the middle strips above and below the window, then hang the side strips as with other types of window. Adjust the middle strips slightly to minimize any mismatching. Then smooth and trim.

Papering doorways
Hang complete strips until less than a full width of paper is needed to reach the door frame. Cut out an L-shaped piece of paper, leaving about 2 inches excess all around for trimming. Hang the paper from the ceiling down to the top of the frame and trim along the line. Make a diagonal cut about 1 inch long, working away from the top corner of the frame to allow the rest of the strip to be smoothed into place. Crease the paper along the top of the frame, then cut. Crease the paper along the vertical, then trim.

Papering around windows
Paper the inside walls first (right) as described above, cutting the paper to fit. Alternatively, paper the outer walls first, cutting away excess paper. Leave a small overlap on the vertical side, brushing the flaps into the recess of the window, top and bottom. Trim at the window edge. Finally, paper the sides of the recess. Set it back ¼ inch to prevent the paper from fraying.

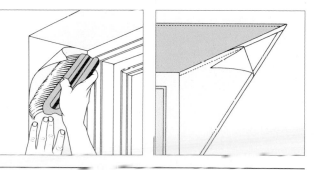

CHAPTER THREE

TILING

Tiles are a decorative and practical way to cover large surface areas throughout your home with a range of materials that offer great scope for individual style and design. Tiles are resistant to water, heat and most household chemicals. They are hard-wearing, easy to clean and demand little maintenance. Although time-consuming, the laying of tiles requires no special skill, particularly with modern adhesives and lightweight tiles.

Beyond the wide range of ceramics, tiles are now produced in a variety of materials. Cork, brick, mirrored glass, vinyl, acoustic (fiberboard) and metal tiles offer new textures and can be installed in much the same way as ceramic. Mural and mosaic tiles have opened up new individual design possibilities, and heat-, frost-resistant and other special-purpose tiles have broadened their practical value.

Tools and equipment

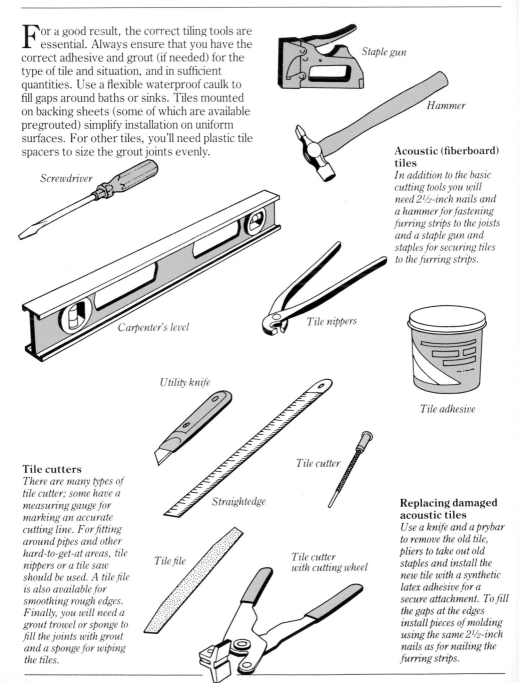

For a good result, the correct tiling tools are essential. Always ensure that you have the correct adhesive and grout (if needed) for the type of tile and situation, and in sufficient quantities. Use a flexible waterproof caulk to fill gaps around baths or sinks. Tiles mounted on backing sheets (some of which are available pregrouted) simplify installation on uniform surfaces. For other tiles, you'll need plastic tile spacers to size the grout joints evenly.

Staple gun

Hammer

Screwdriver

Carpenter's level

Tile nippers

Utility knife

Tile cutter

Straightedge

Tile file

Tile cutter with cutting wheel

Tile adhesive

Acoustic (fiberboard) tiles
In addition to the basic cutting tools you will need 2½-inch nails and a hammer for fastening furring strips to the joists and a staple gun and staples for securing tiles to the furring strips.

Tile cutters
There are many types of tile cutter; some have a measuring gauge for marking an accurate cutting line. For fitting around pipes and other hard-to-get-at areas, tile nippers or a tile saw should be used. A tile file is also available for smoothing rough edges. Finally, you will need a grout trowel or sponge to fill the joints with grout and a sponge for wiping the tiles.

Replacing damaged acoustic tiles
Use a knife and a prybar to remove the old tile, pliers to take out old staples and install the new tile with a synthetic latex adhesive for a secure attachment. To fill the gaps at the edges install pieces of molding using the same 2½-inch nails as for nailing the furring strips.

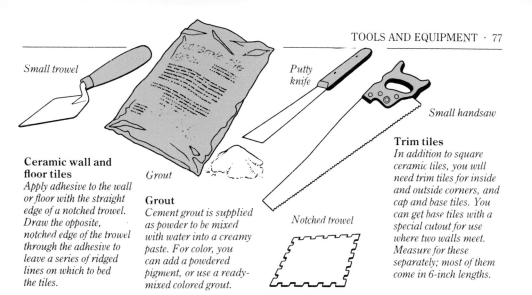

Small trowel

Putty knife

Small handsaw

Ceramic wall and floor tiles
Apply adhesive to the wall or floor with the straight edge of a notched trowel. Draw the opposite, notched edge of the trowel through the adhesive to leave a series of ridged lines on which to bed the tiles.

Grout

Grout
Cement grout is supplied as powder to be mixed with water into a creamy paste. For color, you can add a powdered pigment, or use a ready-mixed colored grout.

Notched trowel

Trim tiles
In addition to square ceramic tiles, you will need trim tiles for inside and outside corners, and cap and base tiles. You can get base tiles with a special cutout for use where two walls meet. Measure for these separately; most of them come in 6-inch lengths.

Choosing the right adhesive

As with wallpapers, it is crucial to choose the correct adhesive for the type of tile, the conditions and the area in which it is to be used. Ceramic tiles should be installed with ceramic-tile adhesive, which is sold premixed or in powder form.

Waterproof types are available for shower stalls and sink backsplashes, frost-proof types for use on patios or balconies; and heat-resistant ones for kitchens and fireplaces. There is also a flexible epoxy adhesive for tiling over a surface which is prone to movement, such as hardboard and particleboard: it often comes in three parts to be mixed before use. A thick-bed adhesive should be used on uneven surfaces. For even surfaces, thinset adhesive is preferable, as it is easier to use.

Cork tiles should be installed with either non-flammable cork wall- or floor-tile adhesive, or a water-based contact adhesive, depending on the instructions supplied. A specific adhesive is also available for brick tiles. Many mirror, vinyl and metallic tiles are self-adhesive. For each 10½ square feet of tile, you will need about 1¾ pints of adhesive.

OTHER USEFUL EQUIPMENT

Mirror tiles are supplied with adhesive tabs. No equipment is needed beyond the basic measuring and cutting tools. For cork wall and floor tiles, marking and cutting tools are required and a cork wall- or floor-tile adhesive. Brick tiles are difficult to cut, so use an electric grinder, a circular power saw with a masonry disk, or a tungsten-carbide rod saw fitted in a hacksaw frame. Use brick-tile adhesive; for pointing, a dry mortar mix or a pointing compound and a brick jointer. Vinyl tiles require chalklines for marking out the floor, a utility knife or scissors, and a straightedge for cutting. Use vinyl flooring adhesive unless tiles are self-adhesive. As with cork, these kinds of tile do not need grouting.

TIPS ON BUYING TILES

- It is cheaper to buy tiles in boxes than singly.
- Count part tiles as whole tiles for estimating purposes, but remember that a large cork or vinyl tile can be cut into several border pieces.
- Always check tiles for chips and color differences when you get them home.
- Allow a few extra tiles (about 5 percent) for breakages and for future repairs.
- When cutting tiles, always exert even pressure and keep the tile supported, to make sure that the break is clean.

Types of tile

Ceramic tiles come in a wide range of colors, patterns, textures and shapes. Use glazed tiles on walls; either unglazed or glazed tiles are suitable for floors. Plain tiles are often colored to match standard bathroom fixtures, and can be combined with complementary patterned tiles. You can also buy matching ceramic trim and tile accessories. Some patterned tiles can be used as random cameos within plain tiling, while others are designed to be used in groups to complete a motif. Both smooth and textured finishes are available – also hand-painted tiles, which are very expensive but can be used sparingly in strategic places. Heat-resistant and frost-proof tiles are also available. Other materials, such as cork, metal, glass and vinyl, offer an additional range of design effects.

Ceramic tiles come in a variety of sizes but the most commonly used are 1, 4¼, 6, 8 and 12 inches square. These are normally sold by the square foot but some dealers will break up a box to give you the exact number you require. Make sure to measure and estimate accurately (pages 84–5), and allow a few extra tiles for breakages and for future repairs.

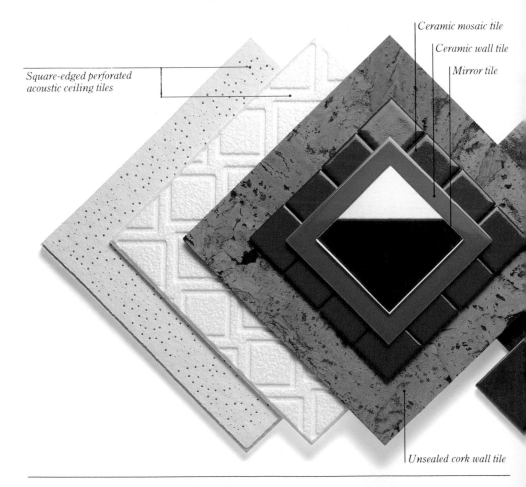

Ceramic mosaic tile

Ceramic wall tile

Mirror tile

Square-edged perforated acoustic ceiling tiles

Unsealed cork wall tile

Ceiling tiles

Tiling is a fast, easy and attractive way to transform an unsightly ceiling. Standard tile sizes are 12×12, 12×24, 24×24 and 24×48 inches. The larger sizes are called panels rather than tiles. Acoustic tiles, made of compressed wood or mineral fibers, are the most widely used for ceilings. They are effective at deadening noise and are fire resistant; some are made of completely fireproof materials. Ceiling tiles may be installed either by fastening them directly to furring strips on an existing ceiling with staples or ceiling tile cement, or by fitting them into place within a metal grid suspended from the ceiling. Tongue and groove acoustic panels are slipped into place without special fastening, and can be lifted out for cleaning or access to pipes and wiring.

POINTS TO REMEMBER

- Always take time to plan the job carefully before installing tiles. The position of the first tile determines the end result.
- Remember to allow for grout joints when mapping out the tiling area.
- Choose adhesives and grout to suit both the tiles and the room conditions.

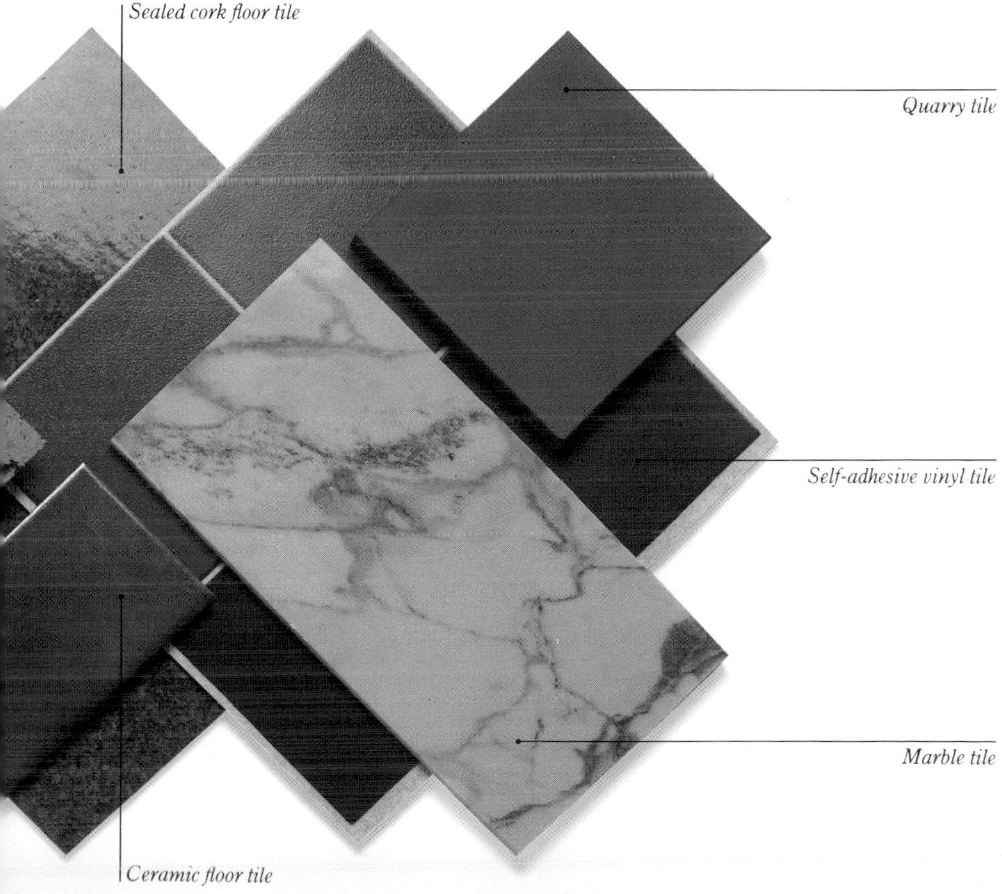

Sealed cork floor tile

Quarry tile

Self-adhesive vinyl tile

Marble tile

Ceramic floor tile

Wall tiles

Variants of the plain, colored tile are single tiles with an individual pattern to break up an expanse of a single color, and tile murals, which are used in groups to make up a complete pattern or motif. In addition to the range of design effects, the different practical properties of each type of tile are listed.

Modern ceramic wall tiles consist of slabs of clay, decorated on one side with a colored glaze. They are fired to produce a durable, stain- and water-resistant surface. Cork tiles are manufactured from pressed layers of tree bark. They are available either sealed or unsealed and come in a variety of natural colors, sometimes with a slight grain direction. Cork is warm to the touch and a good heat and sound insulator, but the surface must be sealed with a polyurethane varnish if it is to be cleaned easily. Some cork tiles are also treated with a washable and steam-proof finish.

Mosaic tiles consist of tiny ceramic tiles, about 1 inch square. They can be square-shaped or interlocking, and are supplied mounted on a mesh or paper sheet. They are laid and grouted in the same way as ceramic tiles and have the same qualities, but are more expensive. Mirror tiles are square or rectangular pieces of clear or tinted mirrored glass. They are easier to work with than mirror sheets, but the wall surface must be perfectly smooth before the tiles are laid, or the reflection will be distorted.

Thin slices of real brick or man-made brick construction are available in several colors and cut to the same size as real bricks to give the wall an authentic appearance. Metallic tiles, usually colored gold, silver or copper in a matt or shiny finish, provide a heat-proof surface. They are washable, but any splash marks must be cleaned off immediately. They can be cut to shape with scissors, or bent around corners, and are fixed with self-adhesive. Since metal conducts electricity, these tiles should be trimmed around light switches.

Vinyl and plastic tiles are made from thin plastic or vinyl sheet. They are easily maintained, warm to the touch and help to reduce noise. Like metallic tiles, they can be cut with scissors; many are self-adhesive.

Floor tiles

Ceramic floor tiles are slightly thicker than ceramic wall tiles (above) and fired at a higher temperature, so that the particles fuse, making the tile almost unbreakable when laid. They may be bought glazed or unglazed in a variety of earth tones. Glazed tiles may be cold and noisy underfoot, but the slip-resistant types are less dangerous when wet. Unglazed tiles may be sealed or left unsealed. Quarry tiles are unglazed and therefore rougher in finish and cheaper than ceramic tiles, but they have the same properties. They are laid on a mortar bed, sealed before grouting and polished. Colors are restricted to earth reds and browns.

Solid vinyl tiles (see resilient flooring page 117) are durable and comfortable, but can be slippery when wet. They are easier to lay than sheet flooring and less wasteful, especially in awkwardly shaped rooms. A choice of colors and patterns is available, some imitating other materials, such as stone and wood. Vinyl-coated tiles are smooth and easy to clean. They are much cheaper, but less comfortable and durable than solid vinyl tiles.

Rubber tiles are quiet and comfortable. Although expensive, they are hard-wearing. The color range is limited, but various embossed patterns can create a "hightech" style. Marble tiles, durable and luxurious, come in slabs of the natural marble colors – pink, green, gray and black – and are laid on a bed of mortar.

Stone tiles, like marble, are enduring but expensive floor coverings. Slate is available in gray, green and blue squares or rectangles and is laid on a mortar bed. Cork tiles are comfortable to walk on but not very durable. Some types are supplied with a polyurethane or thin vinyl finish; others have to be sanded and sealed after laying, to prevent water from penetrating between the tiles.

SUITING THE WALL TILE TO THE ROOM			
Type	**Qualities**	**Room**	**Adhesive**
Ceramic	Hard-wearing, waterproof and stain-resistant	Kitchens and bathrooms	Ceramic wall-tile adhesive – waterproof adhesive in areas likely to be splashed by water
Mosaic	Hard-wearing, waterproof and stain-resistant	Kitchens and bathrooms	As for ceramic tiles
Cork	Warm, reasonably hard-wearing and stain-resistant .	Anywhere except excessively wet areas, e.g. showers	Cork wall-tile adhesive. Nonflammable latex types are safest. Contact adhesive is an alternative
Mirror	Hard-wearing and stain-resistant. Ideal for small feature areas. Gives a feeling of space	Anywhere except excessively wet areas	Many are self-adhesive. Others use mirror mastic
Brick	Hard-wearing. Ideal for complete walls or feature areas such as fireplaces	Any room, but avoid areas where bricks could be affected by grease, excessive steam or water splashes	Brick wall-tile adhesive
Vinyl and metallic	Fairly easy to clean, but some can be damaged by abrasive cleaners. Reasonably hard-wearing	Kitchens and bathrooms, but avoid using plastics near heat, and metallics near steam	Many are self-adhesive. Others use vinyl adhesive
SUITING THE FLOOR TILE TO THE ROOM			
Ceramic	Hard-wearing, waterproof and stain-resistant, but cold and noisy	Kitchens, bathrooms and halls	Ceramic floor-tile adhesive
Quarry	As above	Kitchens, bathrooms and halls	Ceramic floor-tile adhesive or (for thicker types) mortar bed
Cork	Very comfortable, warm and quiet. Not very durable. Reasonably able to withstand water	Any room	Cork floor-tile adhesive as recommended by manufacturer
Vinyl	Very comfortable, warm and quiet. Durable on well-laid sub-floor. Reasonably able to withstand water	Any room but mostly kitchens and bathrooms	Some are self-adhesive. Others are laid with vinyl adhesive
Marble	Hard-wearing and waterproof	Kitchens, bathrooms and halls	Mortar bed
Rubber	Comfortable and quiet. Hard-wearing, waterproof and nonslip	Any room, but mostly kitchens and bathrooms	As recommended by manufacturer

Decorative effects with tile

Tiles offer countless opportunities for individual style and pattern, since they are laid individually and come in a vast array of colors, shapes, textures and patterns. They provide an interesting alternative to plain paint or wallpaper when a room needs something a little different, particularly in kitchens and bathrooms where tiles have a practical as well as a decorative value. The best effects are usually created with the clever combination of plain or textured tiles in one or two colors. In most cases patterned tiles should be restricted to a single wall in a room otherwise tiled in a single color, or interspersed individually or in rows among complementary solid-colored tiles.

Murals can be effective if the style and scale are well chosen. In a small room, use a single background color to avoid dividing the room into disparate blocks of color.

Decorative tiling is as effective on floors as it is on walls. A shrewd choice of floor tiles can completely change the character of a room or hallway. Beware of overdoing the effect, however. For example, a bold, black-and-white floor needs to be offset by low-key walls, as in the picture on the right.

Reducing the space
Warm, advancing colors help to make a large, airy bathroom feel more cozy (above). The cherry floor color taken a short way up the walls helps to reduce the height of the room, and blue tiles interspersed in the tiled area help to break up the spread of color. Colored grout can also relieve the effect and complement or contrast with the basic color.

Increasing the space
An over all mosaic design (right) on the floor and the walls adds a touch of class to a simple bathroom and gives a feeling of space. Changeable accessories create a splash of color.

A bold effect with patterned floor tile

Black and white vinyl tiles can look striking, especially if laid diagonally (far left). Offset such a bold effect with subdued walls. A border of black tiles adds emphasis.

Soft and sophisticated hallways

Cool to the touch but warm to the eye, quarry tiles (left) set off the soft, neutral colors of an entrance hall and the natural pine finish of a kitchen, giving a warm continuity to the entire area.

The range of tile shapes

Most ceramic tiles are either square or oblong, but a range of interlocking circular, hexagonal and Provençale-shaped tiles are also to be found. The most common type of tile, known as a "field" tile, has square edges and is glazed on the top only. "Trim" tile is glazed on the top and one or more edges. Quadrant tiles are round-edged slivers for use as border tiles on corners. Ceramic wall tiles usually come in 4 or 6 inch sizes; ceramic floor tiles come in a wide variety of sizes.

Estimating quantities

The same method of calculating the number of tiles required can be used for all types of standard tile. First make a plan of the area and measure the length of each edge, then work out how many tile widths will fit into each. For example, a 13 × 10 foot room using 12-inch tiles will need 13 × 10 = 130 tiles. For large areas with obstructions, divide the area into smaller squares, then add up a total. Since tiles are usually sold in boxes of a set amount, this may allow for wastage. If you are buying them loose, however, you should add an extra 5 percent for accidental damage.

Remember that, depending on the area to be covered, you may also need quantities of trim tiles for internal and external corners, and also cap and base tiles. One pound of grout, after mixing with water, will cover approximately 18 square feet.

One gallon of waterproof wall-tile adhesive will cover about 50 square feet.

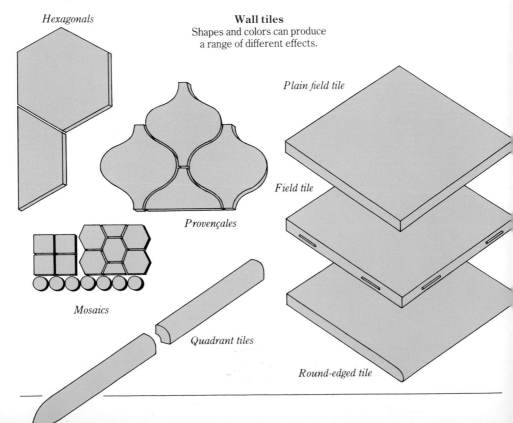

Hexagonals

Wall tiles
Shapes and colors can produce a range of different effects.

Plain field tile

Field tile

Provençales

Mosaics

Quadrant tiles

Round-edged tile

Preparing the surface

Strip off any wall or floor covering material and flaking paint. Sandpaper painted surfaces to key the surface for tile adhesive. If a layer of old ceramic tiles is flat, firmly attached and well keyed, new tiles can be applied on top using epoxy or latex thinset adhesive.

If you choose to remove existing ceramic tiles, use a wide-blade masonry chisel and hammer; cut away hardened grout with a grout saw. If necessary reline the surface – plaster or wallboard on walls and ceilings and plywood or tile backer board on floors.

It is difficult to align tiles unless the wall or floor is perfectly flat. Hold a long, flat piece of wood or level against the surface vertically, horizontally and diagonally to test.

CALCULATING NO. OF TILES				
Area to be tiled (sq ft)	**Number of tiles needed**			
	4×4	**6×6**	**4×6**	**12×12**
3	27	12	18	3
6	54	24	36	6
9	81	36	54	9
12	108	48	72	12
15	135	60	90	15
18	162	72	108	18
21	189	84	126	21

ESTIMATING QUANTITIES OF SHAPED TILES

The method of estimating quantities of standard tiles will not apply to hexagonal and Provençale shapes. As a guide, for 6 × 6¾-inch hexagonal tiles, you will need 45 tiles per square yard. For 6 × 8¼-inch Provençale tiles, you will need 36 tiles per square yard. Again, buy extra tiles for later repairs.

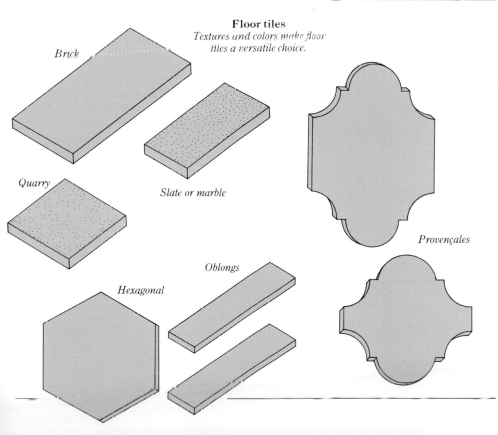

Floor tiles
Textures and colors make floor tiles a versatile choice.

Brick

Quarry

Slate or marble

Hexagonal

Oblongs

Provençales

Planning a tile job

Planning is very important for any type of decorating, but is particularly so when you are using tiles. Not only does good planning result in a neater and more symmetrical finish, it also cuts costs and avoids waste, which can prove expensive.

Marking out a center point

A well-planned room will have equal-sized tiles at edges and corners, to give the area a symmetrical look. To achieve this effect, you should start in the center of the area to be tiled. If you simply begin from a corner, you may end up with whole tiles on one side and narrow slivers on the other. So the first task is to find the center of each side of the square or rectangle to be tiled, then snap a chalkline between both pairs of sides, to form a cross (page 64). Where the two lines intersect is the central starting point.

If the work area is of an irregular shape, it is usually better to line up the first row of tiles parallel with the wall opposite the main door. Snap a chalkline parallel with this wall, then, snap a second at right angles to the first. Finally, snap a third at right angles to the second, in the center of the room. This cross gives the position of the first tile.

Working out the tiling sequence

It is best to tackle an area by dividing the job up into four segments sketched out by the chalklines. Lay the tiles diagonally across the square, to ensure that an equal number of cut

tiles of the same size will be needed at each of the borders.

Work outward in both directions from the first tile, to form a right angle and fill in the gaps as you go. If, however, the area is irregular, you may need to use a piece of wood to mark off the tile widths.

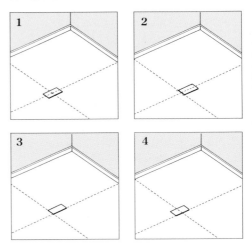

Where to place the first tile
The first tile may be laid in one of four positions:
1 Centered on the cross, 2 Centered on a chalkline,
3 In the right angle, 4 Centered on the other line.
Before applying adhesive, plan out two rows of tiles at right angles to each other.

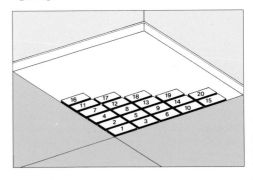

Tiling sequence
Work outward in squares from the center point, forming a right angle. Make sure that an equal number of cut tiles will be needed at each border.

INSTALLING FURRING STRIPS

For 12-inch acoustic tiles, the furring strips are cut to size (usually 1 × 2 inch), installed in parallel rows 12 inches on center and nailed to' the joists with 2½-inch nails. Use a 10½-inch long strip of wood as a spacer between furring strips. When all the strips are in place, you should check that they are level, and pack them with shims if necessary.

Installing acoustic tiles

Acoustic tiles can be cemented directly onto a wallboard or plaster ceiling if it is level, dry, and stripped clean of paper or flaking paint. The normal starting point is in the center of the ceiling, so find the mid-points of the opposite walls and snap a chalkline in both directions. Use special ceiling tile cement and position the first tile so that its corner aligns with the crossing chalklines. Lay remaining tiles by butting the edges to adjacent tiles, working progressively from the center to the perimeter of the room. Ceiling tiles are lightweight and will stick firmly within seconds.

If the ceiling is not in perfect condition or if the joists are exposed, it is best to install furring strips to support the tiles as described below left.

If you want color on the ceiling the tiles can be painted with latex paint, but this should be done a few days before installation as it is difficult to paint into the tongue and groove joints once the tiles are on the ceiling.

Never use oil-base paint – it will constitute a fire risk.

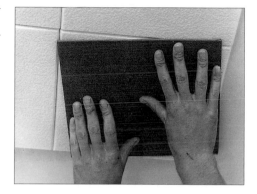

Cementing tiles on to a sound surface
Use a hardboard square, slightly larger than the tile, to press it into position. This will prevent your fingers from leaving small dents in the surface.

Always remove acoustic tiles from their packaging 24 hours before you start work; they need time to adjust to the temperature and humidity of the room.

Border tiles

Unless your ceiling is an exact and even number of feet in both directions you will need to allow for border tiles. To ensure a symmetrical result, it is important to plan out the job carefully, so that the border tiles are the same size at opposite ends of the ceiling; this means that the edge furring strips are positioned to accommodate them. Border tiles are fitted first, so that the work begins in a corner and continues first along one wall, then along the adjacent one. Before you start, you will need to snap one chalkline down the second furring strip and another at right angles to it, a border tile width away from the wall. These provide guidelines to ensure that the border tiles are positioned accurately. The tiles are then cut to size, allowing a fraction of an inch next to the wall for edging trim. Placing the cut edge toward the wall, the border tiles

Cutting border tiles
Place the tile to be cut over the last full tile in the row. Holding a marker tile on top, pushed against the wall, trace a line along its opposite edge, then cut the tile with a sharp utility knife.

are then nailed (using 1½-inch nails) to the furring strips.

Installing polystyrene and cotton-fiber ceiling cove

Ceiling cove, fitted to the angle between the wall and the ceiling, will complement a tiled ceiling. It helps to take the squareness out of a room and hides cracks caused by the normal movement of a house.

There are three types of cove: plaster, polystyrene and cotton-fiber. Polystyrene cove is usually supplied in 3¼ foot lengths, with special corner pieces for both external and internal corners.

Start by ensuring that the area to be covered is dry, clean and free from flaking paint and wallpaper. Then snap a chalkline on the wall as a horizontal guide line for the base of the cove. If you need to remove only a small strip of wallpaper from a papered wall, use a utility knife and scrape off the paper dry. Do not use water, since it may loosen the remaining paper.

Brush the recommended adhesive onto the back of a corner piece and stick it in position. However, if either the wall or ceiling is uneven, use a thick, ceramic-tile adhesive, to ensure that the cove grips firmly and to fill any gaps between cove and wall or ceiling.

Continue fitting the straight pieces all along the wall, butting up the edges firmly. When cutting a length to fit, use a utility knife against a steel straight-edge.

Working out from the corners

1 *Snap a horizontal chalkline on the wall for the lower guide line and trace the top line on the ceiling by holding a straight piece in position. Then secure a glue-backed corner piece into place, following the guide lines. Let it dry.*

2 *Apply adhesive to the straight pieces and push the first carefully into position against the corner piece to form a neat butt joint. Continue fitting corners, then straight pieces, and use a utility knife or fine-tooth saw to cut smaller lengths to fit.*

Installing plaster ceiling cove

Prepare the wall and ceiling as for polystyrene cove. Go around the room, cutting lengths to fit, and tap nails above and below each piece for temporary support. Corner pieces are available, but if these are not used, the end of the cove must be mitered at internal and external corners. A paper template is usually supplied with the cove. This is placed on the cove and the angle of the cut line marked out for an internal or external corner. Use a fine-tooth saw to cut the cove and a saw or utility knife when mitering corners. Any rough edges can be smoothed off with sandpaper.

Mix up plaster cove adhesive to a creamy consistency, and lay it thickly on to the back of the cove. Press the piece into place. Immediately use any squeezed-out adhesive to fill gaps at the edges or between the pieces and clean away the rest of the adhesive with a wet brush before it starts to dry. When the adhesive has set properly – usually after about 24 hours – the cove can be painted with latex paint.

Mitering corners

1 *Use the template supplied with the cove to mark off a corner miter. Cut it with a utility knife and smooth off the edge with sandpaper.*

2 *Spread a thick layer of adhesive on to the cove and push it into position. Tap in a support nail. Fill gaps with adhesive and wipe away the excess.*

Marking out a wall for tiling

It is unusual to be able to tile a wall without having to cut some tiles for the edges of the work. So, to ensure equal-sized border tiles, plan out the job carefully. The simplest way is to mark out your tile widths on a piece of wood, say 6½ feet long. By holding the wood horizontally and vertically on a wall, you will quickly see how the tiles will line up and be able to adjust your plan, if necessary.

Since few rooms can claim to have perfectly true corners, window and door frames, these cannot be used as a guide for the first row of vertical tiles. Likewise, baseboards cannot be used as a horizontal base. Instead you must establish a vertical pencil line, using a plumb line (page 64), and set up a true horizontal, using a carpenter's level, by nailing a wooden batten to the foot of the wall. This will form a base for the first course of whole tiles. Cut tiles should fall along the baseboard. Try to avoid using cut tiles for the top row of tiles, unless the ceiling is crooked.

Applying mirror tiles

Before applying these tiles, check that the surface is sound, dry and level. If it is of porous material, such as plaster or wood, seal it with a coat of alkyd paint, but do not use a high gloss. Leave it to dry for 72 hours. Remove any wallpaper from the area to be tiled, and if the walls are cold, heat the room first to ensure that the adhesive adheres firmly; newly plastered walls must be allowed to dry out. The tiles must be perfectly aligned to achieve a good result, so mark chalklines. If the adhesive tabs used to secure the tiles are not already attached, they will have to be bought separately. Avoid other adhesives: they may cause discoloration. Mirror tiles do not need grouting.

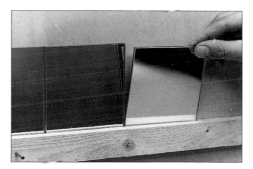

Applying the tiles to the wall
Use a sheet of particleboard or plywood to ensure that the wall is flat before starting: an uneven surface will distort the reflection. Place the tiles in horizontal rows from the bottom of the wall up. Try to align them accurately, leaving a narrow gap between each one.

How to apply ceramic wall tiles

Once you have established vertical and horizontal guide lines, the outlined area can be filled with whole tiles. The tiles are applied in horizontal rows from the bottom up, working in areas of 10 square feet. When the tiles have been in position for 24 hours, the horizontal batten can be removed and the borders filled with tiles cut to size. If tile spacers have been used, remove them at this stage. After 24 hours the joints between the tiles are grouted. Finally, the tiles are sponged clean and, when dry, are polished with a clean cloth.

Laying the first block of tiles

1 *Begin at a lower corner. Smooth a layer of adhesive over about 10 square feet of wall with a trowel. Draw the notched edge horizontally over the area.*

2 *Place the first tile on the batten, lined up against the vertical line, and press it firmly into the adhesive with a slight twist. Lay the tiles in horizontal rows.*

3 *If the tiles are self-spacing, butt them up closely so that the spacers are touching. If not, insert plastic tile spacers for uniform grout lines.*

4 *Check that the tiles are straight, using a carpenter's level, and adjust as necessary. Spread adhesive over the adjacent 10 square feet area and repeat.*

Cutting ceramic tiles

You may need to cut tiles for the borders. There are various tile-cutting gadgets available, some incorporating a measuring and marking gauge. A tile cutter has a sharp tungsten-carbide tip, which scores through the glaze so that the tile can be snapped in half along the score line. Another type of tile cutter contains a small cutting wheel to score through the glaze, and jaws to hold and then break the tile evenly.

When cutting tiles for borders, line the tile to be cut up against the wall and measure it against the gap, then mark it with a pencil. Score a line through the glazed side. If using a tile cutter, put two matchsticks beneath it (right). Press down firmly on each side. With the clamp-like wheeled cutter, simply squeeze the tile between the jaws. Smooth down the rough edges with a tile file.

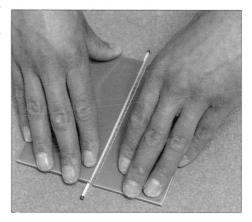

Breaking the tile
Having scored the glaze, place the tile on a flat surface and position two matchsticks under the tile, one at each end of the scored line. Press firmly down on each side until the tile breaks evenly. If you are using a clamp-like cutter, squeeze the tile between the jaws.

Shaping ceramic tiles

Where a specially shaped tile is needed, make a cardboard template of the shape you want and then transfer it to the tile. To cut out an L-shape (around a switch, for example), a pattern of the shape is traced on to the tile. The tile is then scored deeply and evenly along the cutting line. To break up the glaze, criss-cross shapes are scored through the waste portion of the tile. These can then be chipped away with tile nippers or ordinary pliers. A wet saw will almost certainly be needed if slivers of the tile less than ½ inch have to be cut. To cut around pipes, the tile is split in two and an arc is nibbled from each half. Alternatively, use a wet saw.

Cutting an L-shape

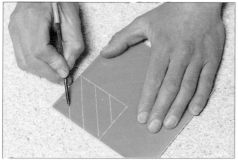

1 *Either use a wet saw or make a template of the shape and trace the lines onto the tile. Score deeply along the lines with a tile cutter, to pierce the glaze.*

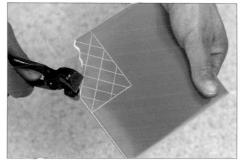

2 *Then score criss-cross lines through the segment to be cut and clip it off in small pieces. Trim to the deeply scored lines, then smooth the edges.*

Grouting ceramic tiles

When the tiles have been in place for about 24 hours, fill the joints with grouting cement. Grout is sold premixed, but it is more economical to use powdered grout to which you add water and mix until it forms a creamy consistency. Colored grout is also available – premixed, as a dye to be added to the powder, or as a paint to be applied to the joints over old grout. Use waterproof grout where appropriate and for tiled counter tops, which need to be washed regularly. Prepare only a little at a time; it dries quickly.

Applying the grout

1 *Use a small piece of damp sponge and work the grout down into the cracks between the tiles.*

2 *When the area is covered, run a small, rounded stick into each joint for a neat finish.*

Fitting accessories

Tile accessories, such as towel rings, soap dishes and toothbrush holders, are either screwed or glued to the wall. Those with a ceramic base the size of one or two tiles are attached using standard tile adhesive.

Put one or two tiles (the size of the accessory base) lightly in position. After 24 hours remove the tiles, "butter" adhesive on the back of the accessory and push it into place. Secure it for 24 hours, using masking tape (below left). Finally, remove the tape and fill the joint around the edges with grout.

To screw into ceramic tiles, use a masonry drill bit in an electric drill. Do not attempt to drill straight into a tile, as the bit may slide around. Stick masking tape over the hole position, then drill (below right).

Finishing off

To prevent water from seeping behind baths and sinks, run a bead of silicone rubber caulk along the edges. This will remain flexible and so keep the gap permanently sealed despite any movement.

At external corners, on a window sill, for example, plastic molding forms a neat, rounded finish to the edge tiles. The molding is bedded down into the adhesive with the larger lip resting on the sill edge. The last course of tiles on the sill then butts up against the rounded lip. Cut tiles should lie at the back of the sill.

If a wall has been half-tiled over existing tiles, the top rim needs to be smoothed off. The gap between wall and tiles can be filled with hardwood molding – either plain or L-shaped – which will need varnish.

 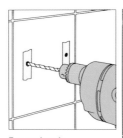  

Adhesive attachment
Glue the accessory to the substrate and secure it with tape until set.

Screwing in
Using a masonry bit, screw holes through the tape to avoid slipping.

Smooth edging
Caulk around baths and sinks to produce a waterproof seal.

Over-tiling
Add plastic molding to external corners for a neat finish.

Applying mosaic tiles

Ceramic mosaic tiles are supplied as a sheet on a mesh backing and applied to the wall with normal tile adhesive. Since the sheets may be as large as 13 × 19½ inch, the main area of wall should be completed quickly, leaving borders and awkward shapes until last. As with individual tiles, meticulous planning and preparation are essential, and horizontal and vertical guide lines should be marked (page 86). Having spread adhesive on the wall, press the sheets firmly into place, ensuring that any arrows on the back face the same way. To fit into corners and around obstacles, cut pieces to the required shape and fit them to the gap. If protective paper covers the face of the tile sheets, leave it on until they are secured, then finish the job by grouting neatly between the joints. Any remaining small gaps may also be filled with grout.

Fitting border pieces

1 *When the main area of the wall is covered, smaller pieces can be cut for the borders and to fit around obstacles. Measure the area to be filled, then turn the sheet over and mark cutting lines on the back. Using a knife, slice through the mesh backing.*

2 *Apply adhesive to the wall and secure the strip in place. Make sure that the border piece is perfectly aligned with the adjacent sheet. If any small gaps remain at the edge, break off individual tiles from the sheet with a tile cutter and slot them into the space.*

Applying cork wall tiles

Check that the wall is flat, smooth and dry before applying cork tiles. You should unwrap the tiles 24 hours before use to allow them to acclimate. Nail a horizontal batten to the wall as a guide for the first row of tiles, draw a vertical guide line and proceed as for ceramic tiles (page 90).

Using a special cork-tile adhesive, press the tiles firmly onto the wall and butt joint them closely. If you find that a tile has to be cut, make sure that you place it on a completely flat surface and use a very sharp utility knife held against a steel straightedge.

If the tiles are not prefinished, apply several coats of wax or polyurethane varnish before the room is used to leave an easy-to-clean surface. Allow the first coat to dry before adding the second. Where cork tiling is taken up to external corners, such as fireplaces, the exposed edges can be protected from scuffing and chipping with wooden molding.

Applying brick wall tiles

The secret of success with brick tiles lies in the careful planning of a realistic running-bond pattern. The easiest way to plan the first few courses of brick is to draw them onto the wall. Spread the adhesive on the back of each tile, using a trowel or putty knife, and press the tile firmly onto the wall. Insert spacers.

To achieve an authentic look, you will probably have to cut several bricks. Use either a diamond blade mounted in an electric grinder or a circular power saw fitted with a masonry disk, or a tungsten-carbide rod saw fitted into a hacksaw frame.

When the tiles have been in place for 24 hours, remove the spacers and fill the joints with mortar or pointing compound. Use a small brick jointer, taking care not to stain the bricks. If you prefer to avoid the labor of pointing, paint the wall with gray latex paint before installing the brick tiles. Make sure that the paint is thoroughly dry before tiling.

Arranging the tiles

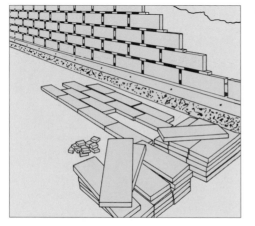

1 *Lay out several rows of tiles on the floor to work out the most realistic running-bond pattern and pencil the pattern on the wall as a guide. Stagger the joints to imitate a brick wall, and, where available, use L-shaped corner tiles for authenticity.*

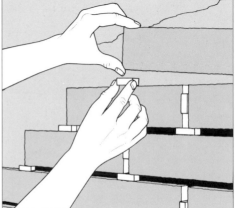

2 *To prevent the tiles from slipping, insert small pieces of wood, about ⅓ inch thick, between courses. Alternatively, saw up slabs of foam packing material into small blocks. After 24 hours remove the spacers and fill the joints with pointing compound.*

How to lay ceramic floor tiles

The floor must be flat, dry, clean and stable before ceramic tiles are installed. Wooden floors should be well ventilated below and strong enough to support the tile. The easiest way to provide a sound surface is to install ½ inch exterior-grade plywood or ½-inch tile backer board over the existing subfloor. To ensure a good bond between the tiles and the floor, brush a primer over the whole floor and allow it to become "touch dry" before laying the tiles. For information on where to start, see page 86.

Always start in the middle of the room and work outward. If you begin tiling against one baseboard, the tiles running along the adjacent wall will not run square. So mark the center point, adjusting it to leave at least half-tile widths at each baseboard. Test the height of the tiles against the door. If thick tiles are to be used, the door may not open. Either remove the door and trim its lower edge, or fit rising butt hinges so that the door rises as it opens.

Prepare according to the manufacturer's instructions the tile adhesive you select – some are premixed but most types require mixing. Apply it as directed, spreading it with the straight edge of the trowel, then combing the ridges with the notched edge.

Press and twist each tile into position so that it is well bedded down. When the first square yard is complete, clean away any excess adhesive from the face of the tiles and clean out the joints, ready for grouting later. Grout when the tiles have been in place for 24 hours.

GROUTING TILES

Grout the tiles after they have been laid about 24 hours. If you grout before the adhesive has set, you may dislodge the tiles. Remove the spacers first. You can fill in any gaps, but wait at least another 24 hours before doing so. When the grout has set – it takes a couple of hours – wipe the new floor with a damp cloth or sponge. Do not walk on the freshly laid tiles for 48 hours or you may dislodge them. Rinse the floor when the grout is thoroughly dry, if necessary.

Laying whole tiles

1 *First ensure that the subfloor is clean and level, and if it is wooden, apply a coat of primer. Spread waterproof adhesive on the floor and follow your planned order of working (page 86).*

2 *Bed each tile firmly into place with a pressing and twisting movement. Use chalklines for positioning and work outward in both directions. Use tile spacers if the tiles are not self-spacing.*

Cutting and laying border tiles

1 *Lay the tile to be cut exactly over the last whole tile and half-cover them both with a marker tile butted up against a spacer at the wall. Trace the non-wall edge on the tile.*

2 *Using a steel straightedge, score along the line with a utility knife, then snap the tile with a snap cutter. Smooth off rough edges with a tile file.*

3 *Comb adhesive onto the back of the cut tile and carefully slot it into the gap. Continue cutting and fitting until no gaps remain, then grout between the spaces.*

Laying vinyl floor tiles

Most vinyl tiles are self-adhesive. The protective paper covering the adhesive on the backing should not be removed until the tile is ready to lay. If the tile is not self-adhesive, spread vinyl-tile adhesive over about 9 square feet of the floor and cover it with tiles before applying adhesive to the next area. Always lay the tiles in the correct order (page 86) and butt up the edges closely, taking care to press down each tile firmly all over to ensure that it is well secured in the adhesive. Do not use the twisting movement as for ceramic tiles (page 90) or the adhesive will be squeezed up between the tiles.

At borders, mark and cut the tiles, taking care to match the design of any patterns. Cut edge tiles in the same way as border ceiling tiles (page 87). Place the tile to be cut over the last full tile in the row, then put a marking tile on top, with its edge hard up against the baseboard. Using a marker, draw the opposite edge of the marking tile on the tile to be cut. Then cut along the line with scissors or a utility knife held against a straightedge.

For awkward shapes, such as around door architraves or pipes, make a cardboard template and transfer the shape onto the tile. When cutting a hole for a pipe, make a slit from the cut-out hole to the tile edge; it will then run

Preparing vinyl floor tiles
When you are ready to lay the tile, peel off the protective paper backing.

from the back of the pipe to the baseboard and be barely visible. If the outline is curved, use wire solder to trace around the curve. Then transfer it to the tile to be shaped.

With marblized or grained vinyl tiles, lay them so that the pattern in adjacent tiles runs in opposite directions. This gives variation and emphasizes the tiling itself. Align the tiles correctly the first time. If they are re-laid, the adhesive weakens.

Cutting an L-shaped tile

1 *One side of the L-shape will need to be the same width as adjacent border tiles. Use a marker tile to trace the gap between the baseboard and the last whole tile.*

2 *Then move the tile around the corner and, in the same way, scribe the outline of the gap to be filled on to the tile. This line represents the second "leg" of the "L."*

3 *Cut along the scribed lines, then apply adhesive to the floor and fit the tile into place, so that it aligns accurately with neighboring tiles. Alternatively, use a template.*

Laying cork floor tiles

Ensure that the surface is free of dust and dirt. Cork tiles are laid in the same way as vinyl tiles (opposite) but they need a cork adhesive. Spread the adhesive over an area of about 9 square feet at a time. If the tiles are to be taken up to exposed edges, they should be protected with wooden beading.

To cut cork tiles, use a straightedge and a very sharp utility knife, otherwise the cork will crumble. Some cork tiles are supplied presealed and waxed or coated with protective vinyl film and need no further treatment. Those sold without a protective finish need to be sealed with wax or polyurethane before the room is used. Several coats are needed. When applying the finish, make sure that you keep the room well ventilated.

Shaping cork tiles
Use a template to trace the shape of architraves and other awkward areas.

Planning patterns with floor tiles

A patterned tiled floor is a versatile and easy way of adding color and variety to a room (see also pages 82–3). Creating patterns with floor tiles is easy, and the resulting effects can be very striking. A simple arrangement of black and white tiles, for example, can make a bold statement. However, bear in mind that solid colors such as black and white can be more difficult to maintain, since they show stains and marks more clearly. With vinyl tiles, some colors – including many pale pastels – have a tendency to fade if they are constantly exposed to strong sunlight.

To plan a simple, two-color chess-board pattern, estimate the number of tiles as for a single color (page 84), divide by 2 and buy equal amounts of each color.

For more complex patterns, use graph paper to plan the tile arrangement – each square on the paper being equivalent to one tile. Shade in the different colors, then count up the amount of each color needed.

SOME FINAL TIPS FOR LAYING TILES

- Be careful not to apply too much adhesive when laying any sort of vinyl tiles.
- Do not leave gaps between vinyl tiles, make sure that you butt them up together.
- Grouting material must be compatible with both the tile and the setting material.

- Use a suitable grout for wet areas such as kitchens and bathrooms.
- Allow new plaster to cure for at least a month before laying any tiles over it.
- Seal weak parts in a plaster wall with shellac.
- Support wallboard and sub-

floors firmly, so that there are no loose or springy sections.
- Clean sound walls with a strong detergent and sand them to aid adhesion before tiling.
- If tiling over plywood, use the exterior, waterproof grade, the interior grade is not strong enough.

Chapter Four

Flooring

New flooring is a major decorating decision. The type of flooring you choose will depend upon the function of the room, the durability of the materials used, the look you want to achieve and the price you want to pay.

Wooden floors have a warmth, color and subtlety of texture that cannot be matched by imitations. They look rich, are hardwearing, blend with both traditional and modern furnishings and are comparable in price with other floor coverings. A sanded floor is a cheap alternative to a new wooden floor. With a stained and sealed finish, it can add a touch of style to any room in the house.

Wooden floors of all types are best for areas where there is little exposure to water. While hardwood floors can be laid in kitchens and bathrooms, they may be difficult to maintain.

Resilient floor coverings come in sheets and tiles of vinyl, rubber, cork and wood. A variety of surfaces – textured, grained, inlaid and no-wax – are not only good-looking, but durable and easy to maintain. With the exception of cork and linoleum, they make excellent waterproof barriers and can be installed anywhere in the house, including the basement.

Carpeting provides luxury underfoot – it is warm, comfortable, sound-proofing and comes in a wide range of colors, patterns and qualities to suit most rooms in the house. Matting is a budget-priced alternative to carpets – useful for rented apartments and if you are planning to move to a new house soon.

Wooden surfaces

Wood forms a warm, smooth and attractive surface. It is extremely durable, has acoustic and insulating properties and is easy to maintain. Much wooden flooring is solid hardwood strips or planks, which is laid over an ordinary subfloor, such as plywood. Some types, however, consist of a hardwood layer bonded to a plywood backing. Flooring comes as long, wide planks, long strips of wood (wood strip) or blocks arranged into patterns (wood block or mosaic panels). Wood blocks can be arranged into a variety of patterns, and basketweave parquet panels can be laid square or diagonally across the room.

Comparing types of wooden flooring

Wooden flooring receives a lot of wear and tear, and the wood needs to be durable. The availability of lumber for different floor types varies. Many manufacturers offer a wide range of styles and species – from oak to ash and beech.

Prices vary, and teak, the most durable, costs a little more than maple and birch. Oak and ash are less expensive. In wood block flooring, all woods cost the same, but ordinary wood block costs a third of the price of pre-finished wood block. In the parquet panel range, teak again is the most costly, followed by mahogany; maple is about three-quarters of the price of teak. However, all reputable brands of flooring are hard-wearing, so do not hesitate to buy a cheaper kind if the color and grain are right for your needs.

Protecting hardwoods

Everyone knows about the threat to the world's rainforests, but we do not always realize that our own consumption of hardwoods can make a difference. A large proportion of hardwood is imported from tropical countries. Much of this is valuable timber such as teak, mahogany, iroko and ramin. Only a very tiny proportion of these woods come from plantations which are managed in the proper way. At the present rate, less than one-third of the rainforests will be left by the year 2000.

Until there is an agreed policy about the production and use of hardwoods, it is better to avoid them altogether. A small but increasing number of importers and retailers are using hardwoods from ecologically sound sources. Look for the Good Wood seal of approval. A list of approved sources of hardwoods is available from Friends of the Earth.

TIPS ON BUYING WOOD FLOORING

- Many homecenters and hardware stores sell wooden strips, blocks and sheets, pre-cut in packs, complete with a coverage guide. Always check that there is a good mixture of light and dark grains.
- Lumber merchants sell wood planed and precut to standard sizes, and most will cut hardwood to a special size if you give them a few days' notice.
- Lumber yards are often cheaper than homecenters, especially for larger quantities, and will usually give good advice.
- Before buying, check boards for defects and avoid any that are bowed, cupped, twisted or heavily knotted. It will be impossible to straighten a distorted board.
- Prices vary according to the outlet and the availability of wood, so shop around.

Tools and equipment

For most jobs you will need at least one hammer and one saw. A number of other items will be required, depending on the job you are doing. As well as the tools illustrated, a masonry chisel is invaluable for levering up floorboards. For sanding wooden floorboards, you need to rent specialized equipment. If you are unfamiliar with any of the tools, you should practice first on scrap wood, to avoid making expensive mistakes.

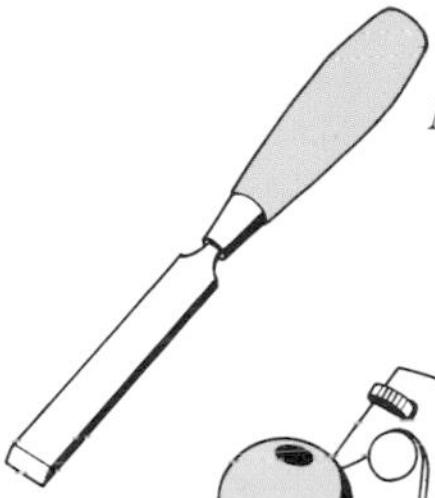

Masonry chisel

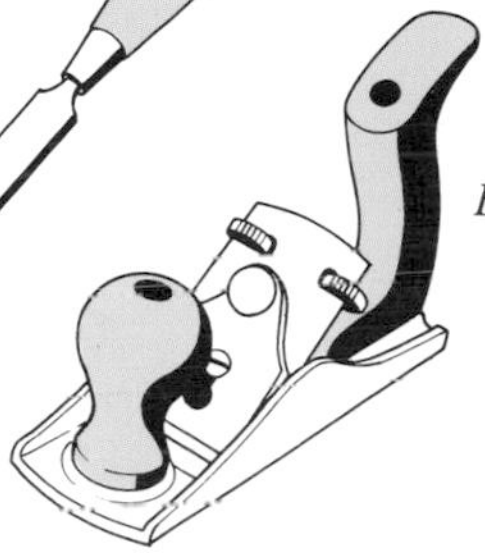

Block plane

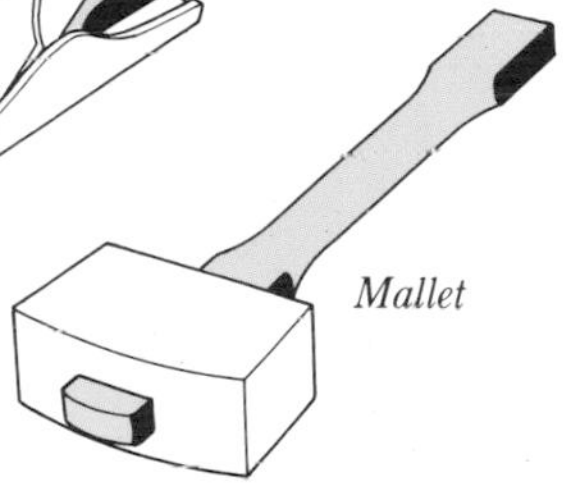

Mallet

Saws

For cutting along the tongue before lifting floorboards, you will need a circular power saw. A hand saw, designed specifically for floorboards is also available. It has a blade with a curved end to make it easier to start the cut. A circular saw with a tungsten-carbide blade should be used for cutting particleboard, which blunts normal blades quickly. A power saber saw is useful if you want to cut across floorboards, but you can use a keyhole saw. You will need a drill to make starting holes before using these saws. Most need a hole about ³⁄₈ inch in diameter. For intricate cuts – for example, when you are laying flooring around obstructions – use a coping saw, while you can use a back saw for trimming by hand.

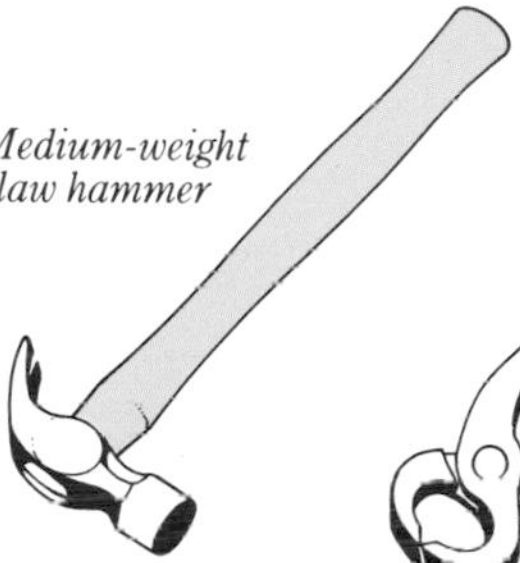

Medium-weight claw hammer

Pliers

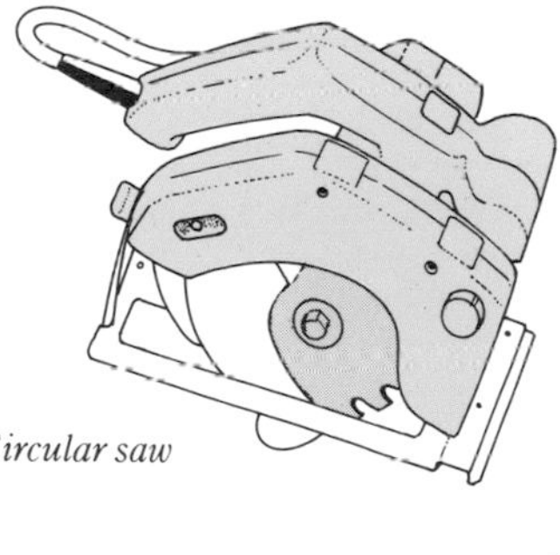

Circular saw

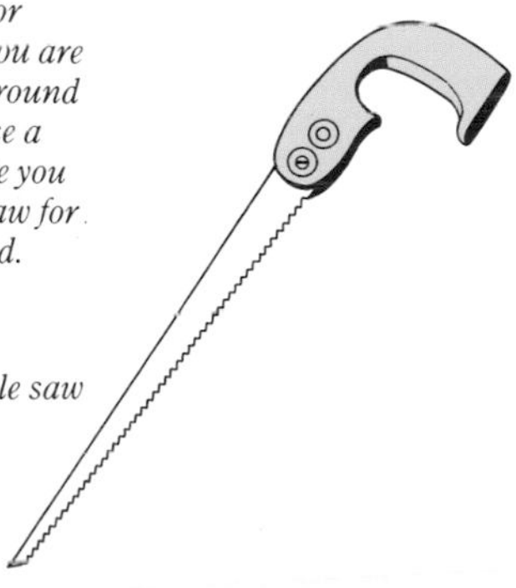

Keyhole saw

Other equipment

A pair of pliers is useful for removing old carpet tacks and nails. You will need a medium or light-weight claw hammer for most flooring work. For hammering down nails, use a nail set. Some form of lever is needed for taking up floorboards. A wide-bladed masonry chisel is good for this, and you may also find a strong length of steel useful. Use a block plane when filling gaps between floorboards with thin strips of wood. A mallet and chisel can be used to chip away wood from the underside of a new floorboard, so that it matches older surrounding boards, and for jobs like taking out damaged blocks in a wood block floor.

Power saber saw

Wooden subfloors

Subfloors are usually made of plywood, which is composed of thin sheets of wood (veneers) glued together. Wood strip and plank flooring can be installed directly over a plywood subfloor, but wood block, parquet, vinyl tiles, cork and carpet often require the use of a second layer of material (underlayment) over the subfloor, if the subfloor is in poor condition. This is usually a layer of ⅜-inch thick underlayment plywood, ½-inch thick particleboard or ¼-inch thick hardboard.

Hardboard is made from pulped wood fiber, hot-pressed into thin sheets and, since it bends easily, may be used as an underlayment over a

wood-plank subfloor. Standard hardboard has one smooth face and a textured back. Medium hardboard has a softer surface for lining walls and ceilings. Double-faced and plastic-coated hardboards are also available.

Fitting new floorboards

You may have to cut new boards along their length to make them fit a long, narrow gap in a floor. A table saw or radial-arm saw is useful for making these long, straight cuts.

The new boards may not be exactly the same thickness as those that make up the rest of the floor. If they are slightly too thin, use pieces of wood as packing between the boards and joists. If the new boards are too thick, make them thinner at the joist positions. Make two parallel saw cuts in the joist and chisel out the wood between them.

You can secure most of the boards with 2½-inch cut floor brads or finishing nails. Screw down any boards that may have to be lifted in the future.

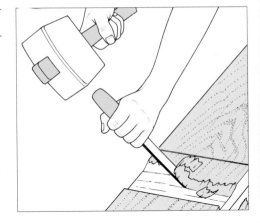

Chiseling away thick boards
Chisel away the wood between the two cuts until the boards lie at the same height as the original ones.

STAINING WOODEN FLOORS

There are three basic types of stain: water-based, oil-based and alcohol-based.

Oil-based stains are applied with a rag or brush. Rub them in both with and across the grain. If the color is too light, wait a little longer before wiping it off (but do not let it dry out). Apply a second coat after about 24 hours. If an oil-based stain does dry out, use turpentine and a rag to wipe it off.

Water-based stains are applied by spraying or with a sponge or rag. They dry quickly. Apply the first coat a shade lighter than you want the finished result. Then apply a second coat to darken it to the required shade. Mix enough to complete the whole job, since matching a second batch to the first will be difficult.

Alcohol-based stains are not as long-lasting as the other types. They can be diluted with solvent if required. Spray, brush or wipe them on. Wear protective gloves and do not smoke when using them.

Wood strip flooring

The most common varieties of strip flooring are hardwood and plywood. Hardwood strip flooring consists of solid narrow tongue-and-groove boards about ¾ inch thick and in random lengths which slot together. They are laid at right angles to the joists and come in a range of solid woods to form a luxurious floor. Some strip floors are made from plywood overlaid with hardwood. The flooring strips are either slotted together into panels with tongues and grooves, allowing them to "float" on the subfloor as one piece, or the plywood has interlocking "ears" which are nailed to the floor. The floor thickness can vary from ¼ inch to ½ inch overall.

Wood strip flooring is quicker and easier to lay than wood block. However, it may shrink when underflooring heating is used, so always check with the supplier first.

Wood block flooring

The most popular types of wood block flooring are wood parquet tiles. Parquet tiles are made up of five or seven hardwood "fingers" in four parts (20 or 28 pieces overall), which are glued together. The tiles are usually either 12 inch or 18 inch square and the individual "fingers" in each panel are arranged to build up a basketweave pattern. This type of floor usually requires sanding and sealing after laying. Some hardwood parquet floors are supplied tongued-and-grooved, presealed and finished in rigid panels, which are strengthened with soft aluminum pins or a plywood backing.

A wood block floor consists of thin hardwood blocks which are interlocked with tongues and grooves into panels, to create a flat, solid surface. Traditional blocks can be laid in a variety of patterns – usually basketweave, but also traditional herringbone, brick-pattern and others. Unlike parquet panels, wood blocks are prefinished. Untreated parquet and wood block floors must be both sanded and sealed after laying.

Teak wood block

Hardwood strip flooring (light oak)

Straightedged parquet tile (teak)

From the center:
Particleboard
3-ply plywood
Hardboard

Tongue and groove parquet tile (red oak)

How to remove and re-lay floorboards

If a wooden floor is badly damaged or unsound, it is best to lift and re-lay the whole floor. Floorboards can have either square or tongue-and-groove edges, which are harder to lift up.

Before you begin to lift either type, look for any screwed-down boards; these are easy to lift and will tell you what types of board make up your floor. Re-laying boards is straightforward. The main problem is getting them as close together as possible. Use a pair of wooden shims to press together the floorboards before nailing them down.

Removing square-edged floorboards

1 *Insert a wide-bladed masonry chisel or a prybar into the gaps between the boards. Pry up each one, starting close to a convenient board end. Providing it is strong, a long prybar is easier to use.*

2 *Lift up the board until you can insert another chisel or prybar on the opposite side. Then work both tools along the board until it is free. If the board is very stiff, enlist a helper at this stage.*

3 *To help loosen the board, place another prybar under the floorboard, resting it on the adjacent boards. Press down on the free end and this will force it up. Move the prybar along and repeat.*

Removing tongue-and-groove boards
Start by cutting through the tongue by sawing along the length of the board. Use a circular saw, set to cut about ½ inch deep. This will leave a small gap which will need to be filled later. Alternatively, you can use a floorboard saw.

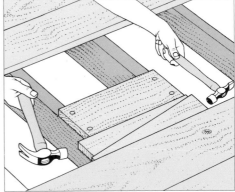

Re-laying floorboards
To ensure that you press the boards tightly together, use a pair of shims made by cutting two pieces of board to a tapering shape. Lay four or five adjacent boards in position and nail a length of wood temporarily to the joists a short distance from the boards. Hammer the shims into place between the boards and the fixed length of wood. This will tighten the boards. You can then nail them in place before removing the shims and the temporary piece of wood. Repeat the process until the floor is completed.

Removing boards by cutting

If you want to lift only a short length of floorboard, or release a long board that is trapped under the baseboard, it may be necessary to cut across the boards before prying them up. This may also be a helpful method for taking up tongue-and-groove boards. First locate the joists which support the floorboards by inserting a knife blade between the boards. Avoid cutting through the joists – cut alongside one of them. They will extend 1 to 1½ inches on each side of the nails. Mark a line to one side of a joist, cut through the board with a saber saw and lift it out.

Cutting and lifting square-edged floorboards

1 *Find the joists, then drill a ½-inch hole to take the saw at a position close to the joist edge. Draw a line along the joist edge.*

2 *Cut along the line with a power saber saw or a hand keyhole saw, tilting the top of the blade slightly toward the center of the joist.*

3 *This will create a beveled edge, so that the board is supported when you replace it. Lift up the board, using a masonry chisel.*

Replacing baseboards

If you need to replace baseboard, you should use the method that was employed when the original boards were fitted. If the wall is made of solid bricks, the baseboards may be attached directly to the wall with masonry nails or nailed to wooden blocks screwed to the wall. Nails should be long enough to penetrate the wall by ¾ inch. On a hollow partition wall fasten the baseboard with nails that pass through the wallboard to the studs of the frame. In older buildings baseboard is often nailed to wood blocks. These may be set into the mortar joints between the bricks or simply nailed to the wall surface. With this type of construction you should attach new blocks to the wall using screws. You can then nail the baseboards to the blocks.

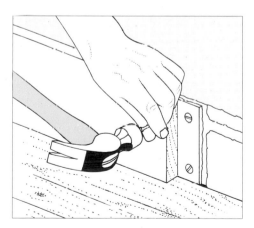

Attaching baseboard to a masonry wall
Attach wooden blocks to masonry walls with screws and nail the new baseboard to these with masonry nails, avoiding the screws.

Sanded floors

A sanded floor is a cheap alternative to other types of wooden flooring. Stained and sealed, it can transform a room by giving it a rich, warm, yet polished look, which can perfectly complement a wide range of decorations and furnishings.

Make sure that all the boards are securely attached. Look for split, damaged or badly patched boards and replace them. If the floor is badly damaged, or if there are a lot of gaps between the boards, it is better to take them up and re-lay them. Remove any nails or carpet tacks with pliers. If the nails that secure the boards to the joists protrude, hammer them well in, or they will tear the sanding belt. Use a nail set to drive them well in.

Sanding equipment and abrasives

The main item that you will need for sanding floorboards is an industrial drum sander. This will enable you to sand the main part of the floor. You will also need a smaller sander (edging sander) for the edges. You can rent both from tool-rental shops, which will also supply abrasives. One day's rental should give you plenty of time to prepare a large room. You will also need a dust mask, a nail set and hammer, pliers for pulling out protruding tacks and nails, and a hand scraper for corners. Use a dust mask even if the sander has a dust bag.

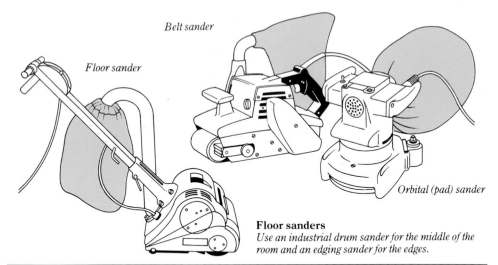

Belt sander

Floor sander

Orbital (pad) sander

Floor sanders
Use an industrial drum sander for the middle of the room and an edging sander for the edges.

Securing loose floorboards

Squeaking floors, caused by loose floorboards, can often be corrected from above by nailing through the board into the joists, so that the board cannot move; use 2½-inch cut floor brads or finishing nails driven at an angle. In other cases, loose boards are best secured from the basement, where there is access to the undersides. If, for example, a board has moved away from the subfloor, you can screw through both thicknesses from below; use wood screws with washers to draw the board back down into position. If, as often happens in older homes, a board has shrunk away from the joist, a wooden shim driven into the gap will secure it.

Decorative effects with sanded floorboards

Even the simplest of wooden floors can have a powerful influence on the character of a room. Floorboards that have been sanded, sealed and polished can give a room an atmosphere of luxury, especially when combined with other polished wood surfaces and matching rugs and carpets. A natural-colored stain can bring out the richness of color in the wood.

But floorboards can also blend well with a simple decorative scheme. Because they wear well and are easy to clean and maintain, they are especially appropriate for living rooms, halls, foyers and other areas of the home that have to stand up to heavy use.

Rich, warm tones
In this children's room the natural wood colors of the door, window frame, cornice and floor harmonize to create a warm atmosphere. A wooden floor has other advantages — it is hard-wearing and easy to clean. Use only nonslip rugs on wooden flooring.

Sanding a floor

After you have prepared the floor, sand the main area with a drum sander. Start with medium or coarse abrasive on the machine's drum, to strip away the surface, before changing to a finer grade to get a smoother finish. You will not be able to get right up to the edges of the room with the drum sander, so use a hand sander for these areas. With both machines, work in a direction parallel to the boards, overlapping each pass by a few inches. Even a hand sander cannot get right into the corners of a room, so you will have to finish off these small areas, together with places where there are other obstructions to the sander, using a simple hand scraper.

Although sanders have dust-collecting bags, these are not capable of picking up all the dust. So when you have finished sanding, vacuum the floor thoroughly. Then clean it carefully with a damp cloth and leave the surface to dry completely before sealing it.

Using sanding machines

1 *Before you switch on a sander, tilt it back so that the drum is raised off the floor. Then switch it on and gradually lower the spinning drum onto the floor. Restrain it so that it travels slowly. But be careful or it will continue to sand the same area and gouge out a depression.*

2 *Work the machine forward and backward in the same direction as the floorboards. Overlap each pass by about 3 inches. Keep the cable out of the way by running it over your shoulder. If the floor is very uneven, make the first few passes at 45° to the boards.*

3 *Start working parallel to the boards when you switch to finer paper. Never run a sander at right angles to the boards – it will not even out the bumps. When you have sanded the main floor area, finish the edges with a hand sander and corners with a hand scraper.*

SEALING FLOORBOARDS

When you have sanded a floor, you need to protect its surface so that it will resist wear. Make sure that the floor is perfectly clean and dry, then apply the first coat of finish. Use a pad made from lint-free cloth, rubbing it well into the floor. As soon as the surface has dried (which will take about 12 hours), apply another coat. Do not spread it too thickly, and brush it out well. After another 12 hours apply a third coat, and, within a further 24-hour period, perhaps a fourth. Applying the finish at these intervals will ensure that each coat bonds with the previous one.

TIPS FOR SANDING

- Hammer all nails well below the surface before you start, to avoid damaging the sander.
- Use only sanders designed for floors – an electric drill with a sanding attachment is not sufficient.
- Let the drum sander move along the floor as soon as you lower it into position – if you do not let it move, it will quickly make an indentation in the floor.
- For floors in poor condition, start by sanding at 45° to the floorboards before sanding parallel with the boards.
- Do not sand at right angles to the floorboards – the sander will not even out the surface and serious scratching will result.

Laying hardboard

Hardboard creates the ideal underlayment for many floor coverings. Use standard hardboard, ¼ inch thick. In kitchens and bathrooms, use tempered hardboard. Before installing, it is important to condition the boards. Separate them and stand them on edge for 72 hours in the room where you are going to put them down. In kitchens and bathrooms they should be sprinkled with water. Secure the boards with flat staples, hardboard pins or ring-shank nails.

Securing hardboard sheets

1 *Sprinkle the rough sides with water and stack the boards flat, back to back, for 48 hours (tempered board for 72 hours). Cut each sheet in half to provide for more expansion and cut some in half again.*

2 *Use these pieces at the start of alternate rows, to give staggered joints. Secure the boards smooth side down. The fastenings should be 4 inches apart at the edges and 6 inches apart over the rest of the board.*

Laying particleboard

Particleboard is normally used in non-structural situations and can, like plywood and hardboard, provide a useful form of underlayment. Either straightedged or tongue-and-groove sheets are available, ¼ to ½ inch thicknesses being best-suited for underlayment. Although particleboard is normally quite strong, care should be taken when handling it, to avoid damaging the sheet-edges. Use 2-inch nails to fix the sheets, staggering them so that four corners never meet at the same point – this will add to the strength of the surface.

If a final floor-covering, for example tiles or linoleum, is not to be immediately placed over particleboard underlayment, then steps should be taken to ensure that its flat, grainless surface is protected. Regular exposure to dampness can, in particular, seriously weaken particleboard – for this reason, it should not be used as an underlayment in bathrooms.

Particleboard blunts saw blades, so if you are going to cut many sheets, use a circular saw with a tungsten-carbide-tipped blade, or a hard-point handsaw. A power saber is best for intricate cuts.

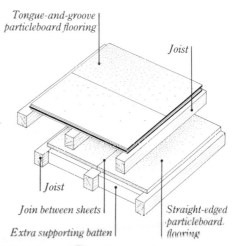

Tongue-and-groove particleboard flooring

Joist

Join between sheets

Extra supporting batten

Joist

Straight-edged particleboard flooring

Decorative effects with hardwood floors

Wooden floors can look effective in both traditional and modern homes. The most luxurious effects are usually obtained with hardwood floors, whether they are woodstrip or woodblock types. Narrow woodstrips can help to emphasize the length of a small room, while parquet tiles, laid in basketweave form, will provide an attractive yet subtle and unobtrusive pattern.

This type of flooring gives a room unity. Wooden floors set off a wide range of furnishings, from antique to ultra-modern, and help them to look good together. An expanse of wooden flooring, for example, may echo the color and grain in wooden furniture while it offsets brighter fabrics. A selection of rugs will add softness and comfort and can help to coordinate the color scheme.

A patterned effect
Parquet flooring creates a subtle pattern that does not dominate a room (below).

Strongly patterned rugs can be placed on parquet without creating disharmony. The contents of this room encompass a wide variety of styles.

Antique chairs, a modern table, and rugs of widely differing patterns are all included. But none of these items seems to clash, because they all harmonize with the neutral wall color and the rich wood of the basketweave pattern in the parquet floor.

A modern interior
The large windows and empty central area of this modern room (left) would look stark and cold if it were not for the polished woodstrip floor, which is easy to maintain, a bonus in modern life. Its color adds warmth, the polished surface reflects a rich light, and its lines guide the eye from the furniture at one end to the rug and chair at the other, making it seem less empty. This type of floor is available in many different woods, so it is possible to get a good natural match, as here, between the colors of furniture and the floor.

Preparing a floor for woodstrip or blocks

If your existing floor is made of wood, make sure that any loose boards are secured (page 106). If necessary, lay hardboard underlayment rough-side-up to give an even surface (page 109).

For better insulation, and to give a sound-deadening effect, lay rigid foam insulation under the hardboard. In kitchens and bathrooms, use a polyethylene vapor barrier. Secure rigid insulation board using the same method as for hardboard. Use ring-shank nails long enough to penetrate the floorboards by at least ½ inch. Attach the hardboard to the insulation board with a contact or PVA adhesive. Make sure that the joints in the hardboard do not align with those in the insulation board: the floor will be less firm and the insulation less effective if the joints are directly in line.

If you are laying hardboard on a concrete floor, the original surface must be clean, dry and level before you start. If a concrete floor is uneven, use a leveling compound, or smooth and insulate the surface using rigid foam insulation and hardboard. Always use a polyethylene vapor barrier with concrete floors, for protection against dampness and water seepage.

Laying woodstrip flooring

Woodstrip flooring consists of narrow pieces of tongue-and-groove-edged wood which come in random lengths. The grain color can vary considerably, so it is a good idea to open the packs and check that the colors are consistent before you start to lay the floor.

Woodstrips often look best if laid in line with the doorway. But they can make long, narrow rooms seem wider if you lay them across the width of the room. Put a few boards in position before you start, to see what looks best.

It is best to condition woodstrip flooring for at least 48 hours before laying it. Open the packs in the room where you are going to install the flooring and let the wood acclimate to the temperature and humidity levels of the room.

Prepare the existing floor so that it is clean, level and dry. You can then lay insulating material to conserve heat and deaden noise. The woodstrips are then attached using brads.

Underfloor heating can make woodstrip flooring shrink. Consult the manufacturer before laying the strips.

If the room is square, lay the first strip parallel to the wall and ⅜ inch away from it, to allow for expansion. If the room is not square, use a chalkline to position the boards. If the strips are sealed, finish off the surface by polishing with an electric drill fitted with a lamb's-wool buffer.

Installing woodstrips

1 *Fit the first strip, groove to the wall, at right angles to the floorboards. Attach it with brads through the tongues.*

2 *Butt joint the strips and nail them down. Add the next row, hammering it into place, protecting it with an offcut.*

3 *Nail the strip through the shoulder of the tongue. Stagger the joints between strips. Saw the last strip along its length to fit.*

Laying parquet flooring

Parquet tiles consist of small pieces of hardwood much shorter than those used in woodstrip flooring. They are glued to an underlayment, a wooden subfloor or a vapor barrier over a concrete floor. The tiles are usually grouped together to make up a larger panel of basketweave pattern, although they can be separated so that you can use individual tiles to fill small gaps and work around obstacles, such as fireplaces.

With parquet flooring, the conditioning of the tiles before laying and the preparation of the floor itself are the same as for woodstrip flooring (page 111). Leave an expansion gap of ½ inch around the edge of the floor area. Use a cork strip to help maintain the gap. Start by fitting the whole panels. Leave gaps where you have to trim and fit smaller pieces. Cut parquet panels with a back saw, a power saber saw, a radial-arm saw or a handsaw. To go around pipes and similar obstacles, separate individual tiles from panels and cut these into even smaller pieces if necessary.

Fitting parquet panels

1 *Apply adhesive directly to the floor with a notched trowel. Once you have laid the first row of panels, spread the adhesive in blocks of about 20 inches square and lay the next row.*

2 *Cut some panels to fit the gap. To make them less obvious, put them at the side of the room farthest from the door, or where a large piece of furniture will stand; and away from the light of a window.*

3 *Tap the panels down firmly using a mallet, and make sure that the edges butt tightly together. For the small edge pieces, it is usually best to split up the large panels into sections to fill the gaps.*

4 *To mark a panel for cutting, place it on top of the last complete panel in a row. Place another panel on top of this with its edge ½ inch from the baseboard. Draw a line along its edge onto the lower panel.*

Laying woodblock flooring

Wood blocks are assembled in a basketweave pattern and look rather like parquet panels. But unlike parquet, they usually have tongue-and-groove edges so that they interlock and form a very flat, good-quality floor. Also unlike parquet panels, wood block does not require sanding.

Woodblock flooring needs a good underlayment. You can use hardboard (page 102) or special underlayment plywood.

Wood blocks are usually loose laid, without nails. In other words, the panels simply "float" on the floor surface, and the interlocking tongues and grooves hold them all tightly together. When you are fitting the final edge pieces, knock them into place with a hammer, protecting the edge of the flooring from its blows with a scrap of wood. Do not forget to leave an expansion gap of ½ inch. To fit the last corner block, you will have to cut off the tongue and the lower part of the grooves so that it will simply drop into place. This will give you a good place to start if you ever have to dismantle the floor. Woodblock flooring normally comes ready-finished, so there is no extra work to do once you have laid the blocks.

Installing wood blocks

1 *Make a basketweave pattern, using cork strips to hold the blocks in place. Hammer the pieces together, protecting them with an offcut.*

2 *Measure the remaining gaps. Plane the tongues off edge blocks and drop the final corner pieces into the gap. Hammer them into place.*

Finishing off a woodblock floor

To work around a door, saw horizontally through the base of the architrave at the height of the finished floor surface. Then push the flooring underneath. If you cannot do this, make a template and cut out the shape with a coping saw. Across the width of the doorway, finish off the edge with metal edging or a hardwood strip that matches the floor.

Presealed woodblock floors require no further treatment. Untreated types should be sanded smooth and sealed (page 108) to make the floor easy to clean and wear-resistant. A polyurethane-based finish forms a clear gloss or matt coat; a penetrating-resin finish soaks into the wood to give a scratch-resistant, lustrous surface. Both finishes will darken the wood slightly.

If there is a large area to sand, rent a floor-sanding machine and use it with fine-grade abrasive paper. But usually only a light sanding is needed, and an electric belt sander, or even a smaller finishing sander, will be suitable unless the floor is very large.

Floor coverings

Carpets are available in a variety of materials and are constructed in one of three ways. Woven carpets such as Axminster and Wilton are made from tufts woven in with the backing; tufted types have the tufts inserted into a pre-woven backing; and non-woven carpets are bonded, not woven, onto the backing.

Manufacturers produce carpet in roll form (broadloom), in strips (body), in large squares or rectangles (square), or as carpet tiles. Carpet squares, for example, may have unbound edges if they are remnants from rolls, and will be most suitable in a small room. Squares with bound edges are intended for

laying in the center of a room with a large area of floor visible around the edge. Carpet tiles are easy to lay and trim, and, of course, to clean and replace. They can be moved around a room to ensure even wear, and are easier to transfer to a new home than carpet.

Unlike its predecessor, linoleum, sheet vinyl is relatively easy to lay. And although it takes longer to put down than vinyl tiles, it involves fewer seams and has the added advantage of offering a wider choice of patterns. The name vinyl derives from polyvinyl chloride (pvc), the flexible plastic from which it is made. Other materials are added, but the best-quality vinyls contain a high proportion of pvc.

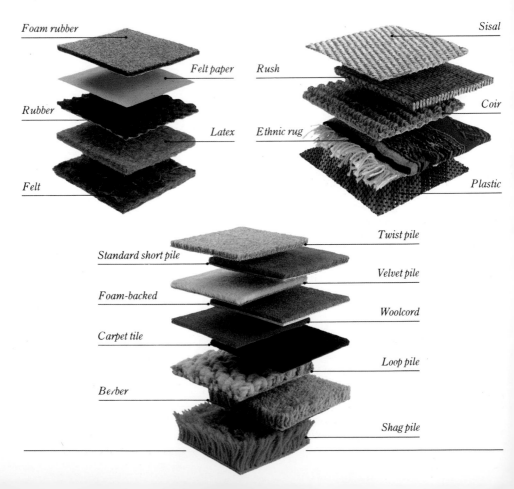

Foam rubber
Felt paper
Rubber
Latex
Felt

Sisal
Rush
Coir
Ethnic rug
Plastic

Standard short pile
Foam-backed
Carpet tile
Berber

Twist pile
Velvet pile
Woolcord
Loop pile
Shag pile

Carpets

Carpets can be broadly divided into the following categories. There are tufted, woven and bonded types, which refers to the construction method; there are cut, looped cord and twisted types, which refers to the pile; and there are jute-backed and foam-backed, which refers to the backing material.

A standard pile carpet is available in either a woven form (such as Axminster and Wilton carpets, named after the looms on which they are woven) or in a cheaper, tufted form. The pile is cut short. Loop pile carpet has fine or coarse yarn woven into it, but this is left uncut to make a series of loops. Sculptured pile carpet is a woven or tufted variety that is a mixture of cut and looped pile. Some loops are cut and some left looped, to produce a three-dimensional result, which, though attractive, can be difficult to clean. Hair and woolcord carpet has the yarn woven into the backing, pulled tight and left uncut, to give a hard-wearing surface. The yarn in twist carpet is twisted before the carpet is woven, to give the carpet a textured, springy and very hard-wearing surface. Velvet pile is extremely dense, deep and smooth and is cut to produce a luxurious finish, with a definite right and wrong way. It will shade and track when walked on.

Shag is a luxurious carpet with a long-cut pile of 1 inch. The pile treads down easily and needs to be raked and cleaned regularly. Berber carpets have a dense, looped pile and are made from undyed sheep's wool.

Foam-backed carpet is usually a tufted carpet with a foam backing. It is easier to lay than jute-backed types, but normally it does not wear as well.

Rugs and matting

Rugs and mats can be a relatively inexpensive way of covering floors, or of adding a touch of color to an expanse of plain carpet.

Rugs
Ethnic rugs are available in cotton and wool. Oriental, African, European and American rugs are generally flat-weave. The price varies according to the fiber content and the intricacy of the design. Cotton rugs may "bleed" if laid over a pale carpet, so it is best to line them with fabric or paper and dry-clean.

Greek Flokati rugs, which have a luxurious, deep pile, are made from woven wool fleece. They are machine washable.

Mats
Rush matting is usually woven in 12 inch squares and can be sewn together to form larger pieces. It is available in a variety of designs, can be loose laid directly onto wood or concrete without an underlayment and is easily rolled up to take with you when you move. However, it collects dirt and should be regularly lifted to sweep away the dust. It can be gently scrubbed with a soapless detergent.

Coconut matting is the coarse matting found at front and back doors and is available in a variety of sizes for use in areas of heavy and dirty traffic. Coir matting is a more refined form of coconut matting. Coir comes in a variety of thicknesses, colors, textures and weaves, from simple crossweave to a heavier, tighter loop with a nonslip backing. Split cane matting is similar to rush matting, but more rigid. It is inexpensive and hard-wearing, but attracts dust. Sisal matting is tough with a naturally white fiber that makes a good floor covering in halls and passageways.

Plastic matting is useful in kitchens and bathrooms. It is cheap, easy to clean and comes in a range of bright colors.

PADDING
The traditional type of felt underlay has been largely replaced by jute-backed latex (rubber) padding. Other commonly used types of carpet padding are sponge-rubber foams, soft- and hard-back vinyl foams, and felted-cushion paddings. Of all types, the latex and vinyl foams are generally considered the most practical. Jute-backed and paper-backed latex are the best quality paddings for most carpets and are essential under stairs. Most carpet padding comes in a standard 4½-foot width.

Suiting the floor covering to the room

Before choosing a floor covering, it is important to consider the demands that will be put on it – whether it will be subject to splashing, scratching, spills or heavy traffic. The first decision is the type of floor covering – carpet, vinyl or matting; the next is the quality. Price will naturally be a controlling factor, but when selecting carpet, it is essential to choose a grade that will withstand the wear it is likely to be subjected to. Once you have chosen the most appropriate type of flooring, it is worth buying the best quality you can afford because it will last longer.

Short-pile nylon or synthetic for easy cleaning, or loose-lay carpet tiles can be used in kitchens. However, sheet vinyl is most suitable and can be set off with rugs or matting. For bathrooms, sheet vinyl is again the most suitable, being water-resistant. Although carpet has a luxurious feel in a bathroom, it should only be selected if it is polyester and has a waterproof backing.

A hard-wearing grade of carpet is suitable for the living room; add rugs to brighten a large expanse or to hide worn areas. A light, soft grade of carpet is a sensible choice for bedrooms. Strew rugs as a way of adding color and whimsical designs. For hallways, carpets need to be very hard-wearing to withstand heavy traffic, and sheet flooring may make more sense, particularly if you have pets or children. Mats and rugs can make bright, cheap coverings over sheet flooring, tiles, or plain carpet.

Types of carpet construction

There are three different ways of connecting the carpet fiber to its backing: by close interweaving; by stitching and gluing; and by simple glue bonding. Woven, tufted and bonded carpets are all available in a variety of fibers, pile lengths and roll widths. When you are looking at carpet samples, bend them back to see how dense the pile is and how it has been connected to the backing. Then tug at a few tufts to check that the fiber is securely attached to the backing. If the pile seems to be uneven or the weaving method insecure, the carpet will probably not wear well.

Axminster

Tufts woven by row

Wilton

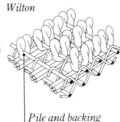

Pile and backing interwoven

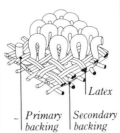

Latex

Primary backing | *Secondary backing*

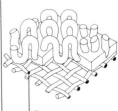

Pre-woven backing

Woven carpet
All woven carpets are made by either the Wilton or the Axminster method. These are two different weaving techniques, not brand names. Axminster carpets are woven one row of tufts at a time, so that the loom anchors the U-shaped tufts into the

backing material as it weaves each row. Wilton carpets are woven in one continuous length, and the pile and backing are closely interwoven for extra strength and thickness. Wilton backings are usually flatter and denser than Axminster.

Tufted carpet
The yarn is stitched into a "primary" backing to give a looped or cut pile. The primary backing is then coated with latex to secure the tufts and a second backing is added in order to make it stronger and easier to handle.

Bonded carpet
This is a newer manufacturing process in which the pile fiber is bonded on to a pre-woven backing. Bonded carpets will not fray when cut. They are available in plain colors only, but in a number of different types of fiber.

Suiting the padding to the carpet

Padding plays an important part in the life of your carpet. It increases its heat- and sound-insulating properties and gives it a softer tread, so be sure to choose the right one. Carpets with a woven backing need to be laid over a good-quality latex padding with a paper or jute backing or over felt padding. Foam rubber paddings are also available, but are only advisable in areas of light wear. They need a layer of paper underneath to prevent them from sticking to the floor. Most cheaper carpets have a built-in foam backing and should be laid over felt paper padding. Use felt padding where there are gaps between floorboards, to improve insulation.

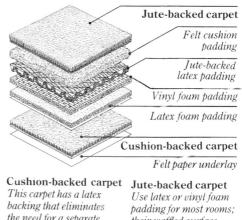

Jute-backed carpet

Felt cushion padding

Jute-backed latex padding

Vinyl foam padding

Latex foam padding

Cushion-backed carpet

Felt paper underlay

Cushion-backed carpet
This carpet has a latex backing that eliminates the need for a separate underpadding; it is non-skid and holds the carpet in place without tacks.

Jute-backed carpet
Use latex or vinyl foam padding for most rooms; their waffled surface tends to hold the carpet in place effectively.

TYPES OF CARPET FIBER

The three basic types of carpet fiber are wool, synthetics and mixtures of both. The fiber content should be clearly labeled together with other details on every carpet.

Wool, the traditional carpet fiber, is expensive but warm, hard-wearing, dirt-resistant, naturally fire-resistant and easy to clean.

Synthetics include acrylic, which is closest to wool in feel and appearance; nylon, which is cheap and hard-wearing, but attracts dirt and dust; and polyester, which is soft and reasonably water-resistant for bathrooms, but less hard-wearing. Mixtures are a blend of two fibers to combine the best properties of each. The most popular combination is 80 percent wool and 20 percent synthetic, since it reduces the price of the carpet, but looks like wool.

Types of resilient flooring

The quality of sheet flooring is determined by its construction. Sheet vinyl consists of an outer "wear" layer, a filling and a backing. The most comfortable vinyl has a "cushioned" filling layer; in the more durable solid vinyl the design is integrated in the material. Rubber flooring consists of layers of natural and synthetic rubber, compressed under high pressure and temperatures into a strong sheet. "Wood tiles" consist of a fine layer of wood, usually oak, on a foam base, protected by a special finish. These are laid in the same way as vinyl but with a special adhesive.

Rubber

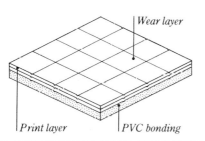

Wear layer

Print layer

PVC bonding

Sheet vinyl

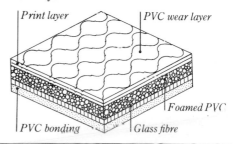

Print layer

PVC wear layer

PVC bonding

Foamed PVC

Glass fibre

Carpets

Choosing a carpet is an expensive decision, so it is tempting to "play safe" and settle for a plain carpet that will not "date" and will not need replacing with every redecoration. Nevertheless, a carpet can help to unify and bring life to a room; it can play visual tricks; it can suggest and reflect style; and it can bring interest to the flat expanse of the floor. But a carpet must be made to "work" with the decorating scheme. Its most important role is to coordinate with the walls, furnishings and accessories. For good color balance, a room should be divided into three: 60 percent covered in a basic color (usually the walls and floor), 30 percent in a second color (often furnishings) and 10 percent in a third, accenting color (accessories). A fourth, neutral color can form a useful link. When choosing a carpet, remember that the carpet color intensifies wall and ceiling colors.

Traditional designs

The rich colors of oriental carpets create an appropriate, dignified backdrop for a traditional setting (left). Warm reds and golds breathe life into a subdued room and bring a luxurious, cozy feel to a study. Smaller oriental carpets and rugs laid in simple rooms often reflect Islamic or Far Eastern culture and lend an ethnic touch.

A winding stair

A diagonal stripe on a winding stair (left) creates an intriguing network of angles with the lines of the banisters and harmonizes with the conflicting shapes. If the wallpaper is patterned, make sure the carpet is of a suitable design to go with it; don't overdo the effect. A plain background color will usually set off a strong design to advantage.

Modern design

Geometrics are cool, clean and allow you to play games with shapes. A carpet with parallel stripes, for example (above), draws the eye from wall to wall and appears to elongate the room. If you have stripes or geometrical designs elsewhere in the same room or area, ensure that they harmonize with the carpet pattern: use a sample to make sure.

An integrated effect
The carpet acts as a neutral base, blending subtly with the paintjob. The same color is picked up in the patterned wallpaper, and the whole scheme is set off by the cool grays and warm oranges of the accessories and furnishings.

Tools and equipment

The number of tools required depends on the type of carpet being laid. Foam-backed carpet simply demands cutting and installation equipment, and carpet tiles may only need trimming. Jute-backed carpet, however, needs specialist tools to ensure that it is stretched and securely attached – a knee-kicker (which can be rented), metal edging and carpet tacks, a masonry chisel and carpet adhesive. Upholsterers' tacks, which have a bright, domed head, are not suitable for use when laying carpets.

Other essential tools are a hammer and nail set for putting down tackless strips, a straightedge and a cutting board. If necessary, use a shim of wood to push the carpet behind the tackless strips.

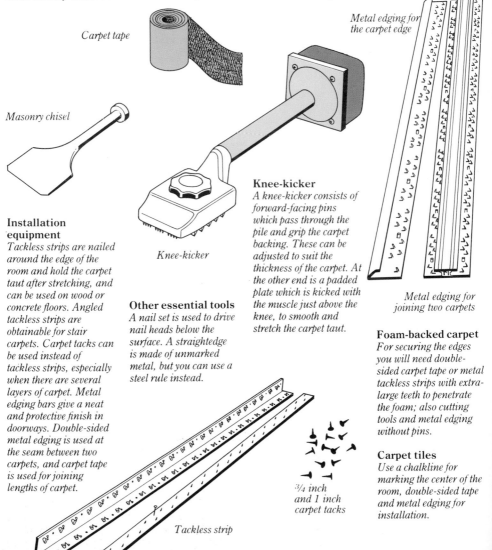

Carpet tape

Masonry chisel

Knee-kicker

Metal edging for the carpet edge

Metal edging for joining two carpets

Installation equipment
Tackless strips are nailed around the edge of the room and hold the carpet taut after stretching, and can be used on wood or concrete floors. Angled tackless strips are obtainable for stair carpets. Carpet tacks can be used instead of tackless strips, especially when there are several layers of carpet. Metal edging bars give a neat and protective finish in doorways. Double-sided metal edging is used at the seam between two carpets, and carpet tape is used for joining lengths of carpet.

Other essential tools
A nail set is used to drive nail heads below the surface. A straightedge is made of unmarked metal, but you can use a steel rule instead.

Knee-kicker
A knee-kicker consists of forward-facing pins which pass through the pile and grip the carpet backing. These can be adjusted to suit the thickness of the carpet. At the other end is a padded plate which is kicked with the muscle just above the knee, to smooth and stretch the carpet taut.

Foam-backed carpet
For securing the edges you will need double-sided carpet tape or metal tackless strips with extra-large teeth to penetrate the foam; also cutting tools and metal edging without pins.

Carpet tiles
Use a chalkline for marking the center of the room, double-sided tape and metal edging for installation.

¾ inch and 1 inch carpet tacks

Tackless strip

Dealing with dampness

If water problems are not detected and cured at an early stage, you risk ruining any newly laid carpet. If you have noticed "tide marks," or if you suspect that the room is damp, test the area to see if the problem is caused by superficial condensation or water seepage. You *must* cure water seepage. Before treating the problem, ensure that the surface is clean and dust-free. When painting the floor and wall with waterproof sealing compound, take it up the wall a short way.

Testing for water seepage (left)
Tape a square of plastic over the affected area. Droplets on the underside indicate water seepage.
Curing water seepage (right)
Remove the baseboard and paint the floor and wall with waterproof sealing compound.

Estimating quantities for floors

Many retailers will measure and estimate free. If this service is not available, or if you wish to estimate the cost in advance, mark the measurements on a plan of the room. Then choose a suitable carpet width for the minimum of waste and calculate the length required. If your room is 15½ × 12½ feet and if a 13-foot roll is not available, you would need a 12-foot width with a 6-inch strip. Alternatively, you will have to use a 15-foot width and waste a 2½-foot strip.

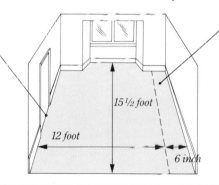

Drawing up a room plan
Sketch an outline of the room, including doors and windows. Measure the length and the width of the room, allowing for alcoves and doorways, then mark the maximum measurements on your plan. You can then calculate the most economic arrangement of lengths.

15½ foot

12 foot

6 inch

Where to position seams
If a standard carpet roll width will not fit very conveniently into your room, or if you are using carpet squares, you will have to make at least one seam. Run the pile to face away from the light and position seams by a wall at right angles to the main window. Do not lay strips in a doorway.

Estimating quantities for stairs

Either make an accurate plan for the supplier, or if you do an estimate yourself, follow these instructions. Assume that the landing carpet will overlap the top riser. Then measure from the top tread over each tread and riser to the foot of the stairs. Add 1½ inch to the total length of each tread to allow for the padding and for tucking into the tackless strips. Add a further 20 inches to allow the carpet to be moved up or down occasionally to even out the wear. To establish the width of your carpet, measure the width of the treads, and if the treads have one open side, allow ¾ inch for turning under at the edge.

On winding staircases measure along the outer edge for the longest length. Then allow 1½ inches extra for tucking in the padding and an extra 20 inches for moving the carpet, as with straight stair carpets. The pile should always run down the stairs.

Preparing the floor

Before laying carpet you should check that the floor is smooth, dry, clean and firm. Repairs undertaken at this stage will save taking up the carpet later. For repairs to wood floors, see pages 104–5. Some concrete floors slope toward a drain, others may be concealed beneath another surface, so ensure that the floor is dry and level. Undertake minor repairs where possible, but if the floor is uneven, apply a floor leveling compound. This is mixed with water until creamy, then poured on the floor.

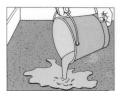

Applying leveling compound
Spread it roughly with a trowel, working toward the door. The compound sets quickly and can be covered by carpet after 24 hours.

Minor repairs
Scrape away flaking or crumbling sections. Vacuum the floor to remove dust and fill indentations with mortar or leveling compound.

Fitting tackless strips

Before installing padding, secure tackless strips around the edges of the room with the nails angled toward the wall. Leave a gap of about ¼ inch between the tackless strips and the wall to allow the edge of the carpet to be tucked down neatly against the baseboard. The strips should form a continuous line and shorter lengths can be butted together.

On wooden floors, tackless strips can be nailed into position, but on concrete, use either masonry nails or an adhesive recommended by the manufacturer. The alternative to using tackless strips is to use carpet tacks.

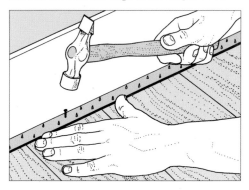

Nailing tackless strips
On wooden floors, nail tackless strips around the edges of the room, using a hammer and nail set. Position them ¼ inch from the baseboard and angled to the wall.

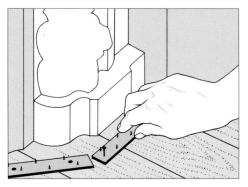

Fitting strips around awkward areas
Around curving places, such as door architraves, fireplaces and recesses, saw a strip into several short lengths and nail the pieces at each end.

TACKLESS STRIPS

Tackless strips hold the carpet taut and are invisible after installation. They consist of plywood strips through which a series of angled nails protrude toward the baseboard. The strips, about 1 inch wide and ¼ inch thick, are usually available in 4 foot and 5 foot lengths and can be cut to size with a saw. They come with ordinary nails for attaching to solid wooden floors, or with masonry nails for attaching to concrete floors.

Laying padding

A good-quality padding will improve a carpet's heat- and sound-insulating properties and will increase its life-expectancy. The two chief types of padding are latex (rubber) foam and felt (page 117). They are installed in different ways, and the method is determined by the type of floor.

In most cases it is best to move the carpet into the room before fitting the padding. In this way, the padding is not disturbed when the carpet is dragged into the room. The carpet is then rolled back a section at a time to allow the padding to be installed.

If you are laying carpet over existing vinyl tiles, or if you are laying foam-backed carpet, always use felt paper instead of a latex or vinyl foam padding.

Securing latex padding

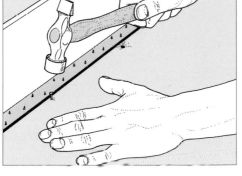

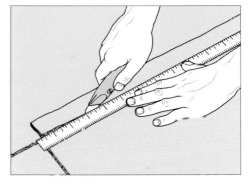

1 *Lay it rubber side down. Cut it roughly to size and install it first in one corner of the room, with the carpet half rolled back. Fasten it just inside the tackless strip running along an adjacent wall. On a wooden floor, secure it with rustproof staples or tacks.*

2 *Fold back the other half of the carpet, then unroll the rest of the padding and fix it down at the far wall. If two pieces of padding need to be joined, overlap the edges and cut both layers, then secure the edges with adhesive, staples or tacks to form a neat seam.*

Securing felt paper padding

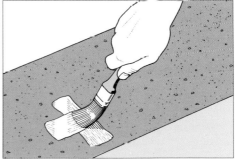

1 *To form the padding, first join strips of felt paper with heavy-duty carpet tape. Then secure it to the floor. On a wooden floor, fix down the paper with staples or tacks, which should be inserted into the padding at 12 inch intervals.*

2 *Use adhesive on a concrete floor. The padding should stop 2 inches from the baseboard so that double-sided carpet tape can be used to secure the carpet edges. There is no need to allow for extra layers of padding in areas of heavy wear.*

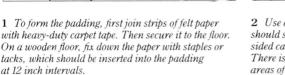

How to lay and stretch jute-backed carpet

When the padding is down, the carpet can be rolled out onto the floor. It should be placed so that the pile leans away from the light, to prevent uneven shading. It will save trimming the carpet along all four walls, if it is positioned so that only about ½ inch of material turns up against two adjoining walls. The carpet is then fixed to the tackless strips or tacked on one side, stretched across the room and hooked on to the rest of the strips or tacked before trimming and finishing. The correct method is described in detail below.

Fixing the carpet on to tackless strips

1 *Bring the carpet to a corner and line it up so that it overlaps the tackless strips by ½ inch on each wall. Push down the edge to hook the backing onto the tackless strips, for about 12 inches on each wall.*

2 *Then run along the tackless strip covered by carpet with the side of a hammer or mallet, to ensure that the teeth of the tackless strips engage with the carpet backing for a firm grip.*

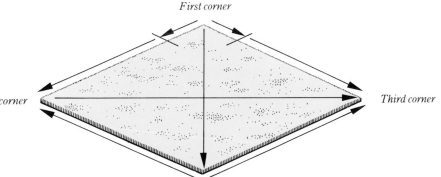

First corner

Second corner

Third corner

Fourth corner

Stretching jute-backed carpet

First hook the carpet onto the tackless strips in one corner for 12 inches on each wall.

Next, stretch the carpet across the room to an adjacent corner, using the knee-kicker, and hook it on. Then complete the wall between the two corners.

Stretch the carpet across to the corner and secure it on the tackless strip along the diagonally opposite wall

to your first corner. Finally, stretch and smooth the carpet right across the room to the last corner. Hook it into the corner and complete the last two walls.

If using carpet tacks, insert temporary tacks about ½ inch from the baseboard. When the carpet has been stretched, fold the edge under and drive tacks through the double thickness well down into the pile, at 6 inch intervals. Remove temporary tacks.

Stretching the carpet
Place the head of the knee-kicker on the carpet and adjust the pins so that they engage in the backing without tearing the pile. Then kick the pad with the muscle just above your kneecap (not the kneecap itself), while smoothing the carpet with your hands.

Trimming off excess carpet
Crease back the carpet at the baseboard and mark a cutting line along the back. Then fold the carpet right back and cut along the line, with a cutting board protecting the carpet beneath. Roll back the carpet to test that the fit is correct, and retrim if necessary.

Finishing off edges
Once you have cut off excess carpet at the borders, trim it carefully against a straightedge so that only ½ inch rests against the wall. Press a paint scraper into the gully between the tackless strip and the wall, until the carpet is neatly tucked against the baseboard.

Laying carpet tiles

The technique for planning out carpet tiles and the working sequence are the same as for floor tiles (page 86). The first tile should be secured in place with double-sided carpet tape, while subsequent tiles can be loose laid. If, however, the tile manufacturer recommends securing the tiles at random intervals to prevent them from moving and creating gaps, use a flooring adhesive or double-sided carpet tape. Working from the center, butt up the tiles tightly against each other and ensure that the arrows on the tile backs point in the same direction, unless you prefer to lay them in alternate directions for a checkerboard effect.

Always cut border tiles on a cutting board to avoid accidents, and secure them in doorways with a metal edging strip.

Fitting around problem areas

To allow the carpet to fit snugly in alcoves or around projections such as fireplaces, you must make vertical release cuts from the carpet edge to the floor. If the carpet has a tendency to fray, first coat the back with latex adhesive. To fit around pipes, cut a slit in the carpet from the front of the pipe to the edge of the carpet behind it. Ease the carpet around the pipe, making small release cuts where necessary, then trim to fit the wall.

Door architraves
Make cuts in the carpet until it lies flat. Trim until ½ inch rests against the architrave. Push behind tackless strips.

Fireplaces
Allow an overlap of 1 inch and cut. Press down and trim, allowing ½ inch to ride up against the fireplace. Secure edges.

LAYING FOAM-BACKED CARPET

Foam-backed carpet needs no stretching. You simply lay it on the floor, butt up two adjacent edges against the baseboard and trim the other two edges to fit.

Trim the carpet in position, or as for jute-backed carpet (page 124). Tackless strips with extra large teeth are available for foam-backed carpet, but it may prove easier to secure the edges with double-sided carpet tape or with carpet tacks.

Joining carpet pieces

However carefully you plan, seams may be necessary. If seams are unavoidable, the options are to seal the edges with 2 inch-wide carpet tape and latex carpet adhesive, or, if the seam falls in a doorway, to use an edging strip with twin grooves (page 120). These aluminum strips have angled grippers to hold the carpet taut and a protective edge to prevent the carpet from fraying. Trim the edge of the carpet, tuck it into the edging strip and press it down flat. Then, using a piece of softwood to protect the strip, hammer down the lip to meet the carpet surface.

Using carpet tape

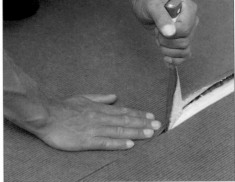

1 *Brush a 1-inch band of adhesive along a half-width of the tape, and along the back of one edge of one of the pieces to be joined. When the adhesive is dry, press the glued tape on to the glued carpet, leaving the other half of the tape free.*

2 *Coat the remaining half-width of tape and the back of the other carpet. When the adhesive is nearly dry, join the glued surfaces, taking care to ensure a tight seam without marks. When laying carpet squares, tape the entire border.*

Preparing the stairs

Before laying carpet, it is wise to examine the stair surface and make any minor repairs. Loose nails should be pulled out or set below the surface, and any suspicious holes treated with insecticide. Any rotten treads or risers can be replaced by knocking out the glued wedges, removing the old board and sliding in a new one.

A creaking stair will be silenced by gluing and screwing a wooden block into the angle between the front of the tread and the riser below, working from below the stairs. If the stairs are boarded in, screws driven through the front of the tread into the riser below should cure the squeak. Finally, the stairs should be vacuumed and, to avoid taking up the carpet later when you wish to redecorate, the entire staircase should be given a fresh coat of hard-wearing paint.

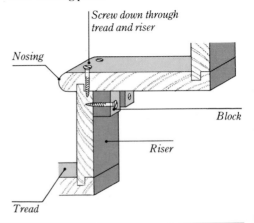

Fitting padding on stairs

There are two ways of fitting stair carpet: with tackless strips or with tacks. The method used will determine how the padding is to be installed. If the carpet is to be tacked, the padding must also be tacked.

If angled tackless strips are to be used to secure the carpet, a piece of padding is placed over each tread and half-way down the next riser, then tacked into place. Angled strips are then fixed on top of the padding. If normal strips are to be used, these are nailed directly on to the stairs in pairs, with the nails pointing into the stair angle. The padding butts up to the edges of the strips, leaving a gap between each pair for tucking in the carpet. Whichever method is used, guide lines must be marked for the position of both carpet and padding. However, if the carpet is to be fitted to the full width of the stairs, fit the tackless strips ¾ inch from the banister edge and ¼ inch from the wall.

Marking guide lines

1 *On the top tread, mark with a pencil where the edges of the carpet will fall, taking care to ensure that the borders are equal. Then make a second pencil line ¾ inch inside each mark as a guide line for the padding. Repeat this procedure on the bottom tread.*

2 *Suspend two stringlines from the two inner points on the top tread, pull them taut, form a straight line and secure them to the two inner points on the bottom tread. Mark pencil guide lines for the position of the carpet and the padding on each tread.*

Carpeting a winding staircase

The treads of corner stairs in a winding staircase are triangular, so it is best to use a separate piece of carpet for each individual tread with its riser.

To ensure a good fit, it is a good idea to make a paper template of the stair shape. If tackless strips are to be used, two strips are fitted as for straight treads, to allow the carpet to be tucked down firmly. But, in addition, a third is nailed along the wide, wall edge. Leave a small gap between the tackless strip and the baseboard. Always cut the carpet slightly larger than you think will be necessary, to allow for mistakes.

Ensuring a good fit
Use a third gripper along the wall edge of the tread, and two at a corner.

Carpeting a straight staircase

Once the padding is in position, the stair carpet can be laid on top. The carpet *must* be securely held, or accidents may occur. The carpet can be installed using either tacks or tackless strips, and this decision must be made *before* fitting the padding.

If the padding is tacked, the carpet must also be tacked. If you have chosen to use plain tackless strips, the carpet is inserted into the gap between them; the "teeth" hold the carpet backing. If angled tackless strips have been installed, the carpet is inserted between the

two rows of teeth on each strip. If the carpet is to be fitted to the full stair width, the strips are fixed ¾ inch from the banister edge, to allow the cut edge to be turned and tacked. Although foam-backed carpet is not generally recommended for stairs, some types of foam-backed carpet are hard-wearing enough. Special tackless strips, without nails to tear the backing, are available, but tacks provide a firmer attachment.

If you are also carpeting the landing it should be treated the same way as a floor carpet (pages 124–5). On an open landing, the edge bordering the stairwell should be turned under and held with tacks or metal edging.

Using tackless strips

1 *Arrange the carpet with the pile running down the stairs and align the edges with the guide lines on the top tread. Push it on to the teeth of the tackless strip and tuck the edge into the stair angle. Tacks at each side ensure that the edge will not move while you fit the carpet.*

2 *Draw the carpet tightly across the tread, down over the riser below and on to the next tread. Push the carpet securely on to the tackless strip by hammering a wooden shim or a thin, flat masonry chisel into the gaps between tackless strips.*

3 *Continue drawing the carpet over the stairs, fixing it firmly on to the teeth. Check the alignment, ensuring that a row of tufts in the pile runs across the nosing in a straight line, and that uncarpeted borders are of equal width.*

4 *At the bottom, turn under a 3–4-inch hem of carpet and neatly tack or staple it to the bottom riser. Working from the center out, attach it at 2¾ inch intervals. This surplus will allow you to move the carpet up later should this be necessary.*

Using carpet tacks

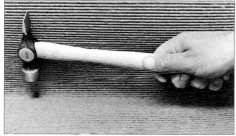

1 *With the top edge turned under by about 3 inches, align the carpet and tack it down on the top tread at 4 inch intervals. Check that the carpet is correctly aligned and the pile runs downward, then begin fitting. Pull the carpet tightly over the first tread and down to the base of the riser below.*

2 *Tack down one corner into the base of the next tread down, stretch the carpet across the tread and tack the other corner. Insert tacks at the back of the tread at 4 inch intervals between the two holding tacks. Repeat this process of securing, stretching and tacking down, until you reach the bottom stair.*

3 *Pull the carpet taut over the last tread. Fold under a 3–4-inch hem of surplus carpet, so that the crease in the carpet lies in the angle between the bottom riser and the floor.*

4 *Then fold the inner vertical edges under to give a neat single thickness. Finally, tack or staple through both thicknesses on the bottom riser to encourage the hem to lie flat.*

Carpeting an open-tread staircase

Since these stairs have no risers, each tread should be individually wrapped in carpet. When measuring, allow 1½ inches for hemming. The padding is flapped over the tread and tacked or stapled to the underside, 2 inches from the edge of the stair. The carpet is then laid on top so that the tufts in the weave line up with the nosing. The edges are then folded under by about ¾ inch and tacked at the center of the tread on the underside.

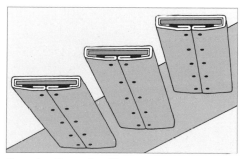

Securing the underside
Lay the carpet over the tread and tack down the folded edges under the tread, at the mid-point.

Resilient flooring

Most resilient floor coverings come in roll widths of up to 13 foot and in virtually unlimited lengths. This means that all but the largest rooms can be covered in one sheet.

Most of the vinyls are available in an easy-to-match pattern, so that if smaller widths are used, and they are laid carefully, the seams will not be obvious. Tiles are also available.

Tools and equipment

For laying resilient flooring, you simply need cutting, measuring and adhesive equipment and a ballpoint pen. Other useful items include a small block of wood for making trimming lines and some thick paper if you are going to make templates. Remember to clean any dirty equipment after use and store rolls of vinyl on their side. Never stand unsupported rolls on end, as the vinyl may distort and crack.

Measuring tools
A steel rule, ideally 3 foot long, is useful both for measuring and to provide a straight cutting edge when trimming.

Thick felt paper for templates

Vinyl flooring adhesive

Strong adhesive tape

Cutting tools
You need a utility knife with some curved blades for roughly trimming the vinyl and a set of heavy-duty straight blades for accurate lines. A pair of large, sharp, unserrated scissors is also useful for cutting and trimming edges, and a large scraper for pushing the vinyl into corners.

Adhesive equipment
Use either vinyl flooring adhesive or double-sided adhesive tape for sticking down at doorways and along seams. Only use tape approved by a flooring manufacturer, since some types damage the vinyl with time. A plastic adhesive spreader may come with the can, but durable metal spreaders are available for large jobs.

Extra equipment
A metal edging will make a neat finish in doorways.

Metal edging strip

Preparing the floor and vinyl

Clear the room of all movable furniture and remove the doors. If you are fitting out a new bathroom, lay the vinyl before installing baseboards or bathroom equipment. Screw down loose floorboards (page 106), and sand uneven areas (page 108). If the floor is colored by wood preservative or insecticide and smells strongly, let it dry out for several months, otherwise, cover it with foil-backed building paper and hardboard (page 102).

Leaving the vinyl to adjust to normal room temperature makes it more supple and easier to lay. Lay the vinyl on its side, loosely rolled with the pattern facing outward, and leave it for 24 hours in the room where it is to be installed. In cold weather, heat the room to a comfortable working temperature.

Sheet vinyl

Sheet vinyl

Sheet vinyl is a durable, easy-to-clean and attractive floor covering, particularly suited to kitchens and bathrooms. It needs little attention except for sweeping and occasional washing and polishing. If a glossy vinyl fades, it can be recoated. Vinyl comes in a range of qualities, textures, patterns and colors. Most have a cushioned backing which makes them comfortable and quiet. The easiest type to lay is the "lay flat" variety. It needs no adhesive except at doorways and seams. Any large areas of damage can be patched with an offcut. The new patch will need to be cut larger than the tear and adjusted to match the pattern. Having chosen a suitable line of pattern for the edge of the patch, you cut through both pieces of vinyl, using a sharp utility knife. The old piece is removed and the new patch coated with adhesive and pressed into place.

Rubber is a hard-wearing type of flooring which is quiet and waterproof. It is more

Linoleum

Rubber flooring

difficult to lay than vinyl, and marks more easily. Linoleum is hard-wearing, but rots if water gets underneath.

Making a room template

The best material for making a template is thick paper felt sold as carpet padding, which can be taped together to form the room shape. If replacement vinyl is being fitted, the old sheet can serve as the template. Outline the walls on the template, mark the position of any doorways and cut out holes to allow for awkward areas. Lay out the template on the vinyl in a larger room or outdoors and centralize the pattern, then stick the template to the vinyl with adhesive tape. Transfer the outline of any obstacles from the template to the vinyl and cut a hole within the outline to allow for trimming. Then cut the vinyl about 2 inches larger than the template.

Tracing obstacles on to the template

1 *Cut a line from the edge of the template to the back of the pedestal and cut a rough hole around it. Then, using a 1-inch wooden block to trace the contour, pencil a line, 1 inch larger than the object.*

2 *When transferring the shape to the vinyl, use the block to make the hole 1 inch smaller than on the template, so that the cutting line falls within the template outline, allowing a generous margin.*

How to lay and trim sheet vinyl

If you have used the template method (page 131), lay the cut-out vinyl sheet on the floor, taking care to align the pattern with the walls and allowing the surplus to rest against them. Smooth out the main area, eliminating any bubbles. Fit the vinyl around any obstructions by making release cuts at the edges. If possible, follow the natural lines in the pattern to disguise the cut marks. When the sheet is in position, trim and fit the internal corners first, then the external corners and finally the borders. Pull the vinyl back at doorways and seams, spread a band of adhesive on the floor and smooth down the vinyl over it. If the room is too large to be completed with a single sheet, cut several lengths and join them. For joining sheets, see next page. Never remove old vinyl by sanding or grinding; harmful asbestos fibers may be released into the air – they can be dangerous to your health.

Fitting internal corners

1 *Gently push the vinyl into the corner, allowing a 2 inch surplus. Fold it back and mark the position of the corner on the back. Make a release cut down to the point of the corner.*

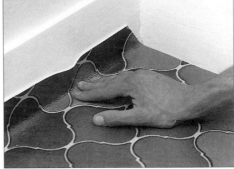

2 *Then cut away small pieces to remove the surplus until the vinyl lies flat along one wall, but work carefully to avoid overcutting. The vinyl will then need to be trimmed against the other wall.*

Trimming with scissors

1 *Having fitted the corners, the remaining edges need to be trimmed around the baseboards. The easiest way is to use scissors. Press the vinyl into the baseboard with a large scraper, fold back the surplus material and mark dots along the fold line.*

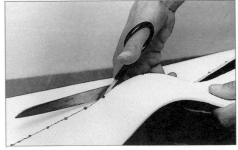

2 *Pull the vinyl right back until it lays flat, join up the dots with a rule and cut along the line with scissors. If the vinyl buckles slightly at the wall when it is replaced, re-trim the edges until it lays flat. Always cut off too little, or you may be left with a gap at the baseboard.*

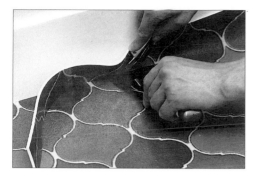

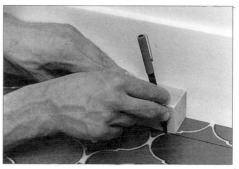

Trimming with a knife
The fastest way to trim the edges is to cut freehand, but this may need some practice to ensure a good fit. Press the vinyl firmly into the angle between the floor and the baseboard with a broad paint scraper and cut to fit with a sharp utility knife, held at an angle. Continue working all the way around the room and cut off the remnant strips.

Marking trimming lines with a scriber
Another method of trimming vinyl is to use a block of wood and pencil to mark a cutting line. Pull the vinyl slightly away from the wall, keeping the line of the material straight. Lodge the block firmly against the wall and trace the contours of the room on to the vinyl. Cut and fit, then repeat the sequence along the remaining walls.

Joining sheets of vinyl

Where more than one sheet is to be used, and seams are inevitable, add 3 inches to each sheet for trimming on the overlap. You should mark a chalkline across the floor for the first length and try not to position seams in heavy-traffic areas.

Fit the sheets to the edges of the room, ensuring that the pattern matches at the overlap. Trim the edges, and secure the vinyl to the floor with adhesive. At this stage, if the vinyl is not the "lay flat" variety, it can be secured to the floor with an overall coating of adhesive. Where the two sheets meet in the main area of the room, make a cut through both sheets at the seam along a suitable pattern line. Remove the offcuts and press the edges down on to a band of adhesive to form a neat seam. Subsequent sheets are joined in the same way, and when the last sheet is in place, any loose edges can be secured with adhesive. Wipe off any surplus adhesive with a damp cloth.

To protect the material from scuffing, or to hide a bad seam, install metal edging in doorways or at seams. These aluminum bars come with pre-drilled holes and are held down with screws.

Making the first seam

1 *Overlap two sheets and, using a knife held vertically, cut through both layers.*

2 *Remove the top offcut strip, then fold back the edges of both sheets and remove the other.*

3 *Spread an 8-inch band of vinyl adhesive on the floor along the seam line. Replace the edges and press down firmly.*

4 *If necessary, use a wallpaper seam roller to ensure a firm bond. Finally, wipe off any surplus adhesive.*

CHAPTER FIVE

SHELVING

Well-placed shelving helps to maximize
the space in a home and can either conceal
or display its contents to their best
advantage. It can be built into alcoves and
corners, or the space created by a sloping
attic roof, enhancing the architectural
features of a room while housing a
multitude of books and assorted objects.
There are three basic types of shelving:
built-in or fitted shelving, adjustable
shelving systems and prefabricated
shelving kits that can be assembled at
home. Ideally, all shelving systems should
be versatile so that they can be moved to
another room, extended, enlarged or
adjusted to store different contents.

Tools and equipment

If you are buying an adjustable shelving system, you may find that you need a saber saw to cut the metal strips to the right length. If you have not bought your shelves precut, or if you are building a wood framework, you will need a small hand-held power saw. For boring holes, use a hand-brace and drill bit, or a power drill with a masonry bit for solid walls, and a twist drill bit for wood. Use 2 inch, 2½ inch or 3 inch countersunk screws of the correct gauge and wallplugs of a corresponding size for solid walls, and cavity dowels or toggles for hollow walls. You will also need a measuring tape, steel tape and carpenter's level.

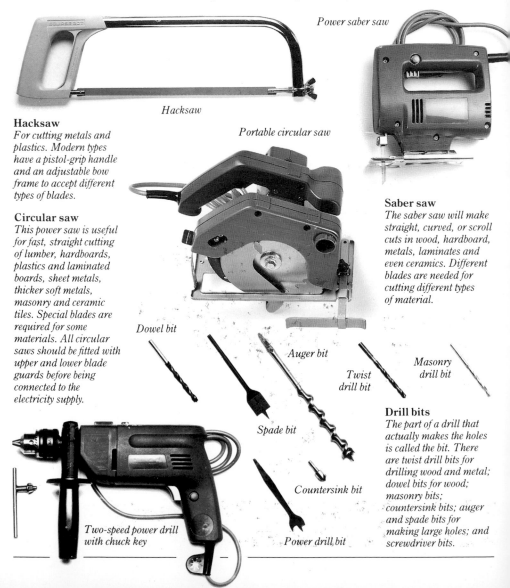

Power saber saw

Hacksaw

Portable circular saw

Hacksaw
For cutting metals and plastics. Modern types have a pistol-grip handle and an adjustable bow frame to accept different types of blades.

Circular saw
This power saw is useful for fast, straight cutting of lumber, hardboards, plastics and laminated boards, sheet metals, thicker soft metals, masonry and ceramic tiles. Special blades are required for some materials. All circular saws should be fitted with upper and lower blade guards before being connected to the electricity supply.

Saber saw
The saber saw will make straight, curved, or scroll cuts in wood, hardboard, metals, laminates and even ceramics. Different blades are needed for cutting different types of material.

Dowel bit

Auger bit

Twist drill bit

Masonry drill bit

Spade bit

Countersink bit

Drill bits
The part of a drill that actually makes the holes is called the bit. There are twist drill bits for drilling wood and metal; dowel bits for wood; masonry bits; countersink bits; auger and spade bits for making large holes; and screwdriver bits.

Two-speed power drill with chuck key

Power drill bit

Wallplugs
Used in brick, concrete and masonry. There are different types for solid and hollow walls.

Toggles
Spring toggles are pushed through a predrilled hole and spring apart in the cavity. Use gravity toggles for vertical surfaces only.

Hand-brace
To drill large-diameter holes in wood. Fitted with the appropriate bit it can also drive and withdraw screws.

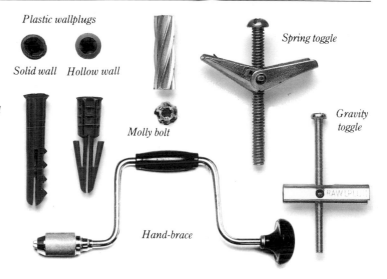

Plastic wallplugs

Solid wall   *Hollow wall*

Spring toggle

Gravity toggle

Molly bolt

Hand-brace

Fitted shelf supports

For wall-hung shelving, brackets or wooden battens can be fitted. L-shaped brackets fit standard shelf widths and are fixed to a flush wall if there is a suitable width of shelf. Wooden battens are only suitable in a recess, since there is no supporting arm. For a long shelf, fit an extra batten on the back wall. Triangular brackets and angled metal strips are also used in alcoves. Cantilever brackets are inserted into the back edge of the shelf at each end.

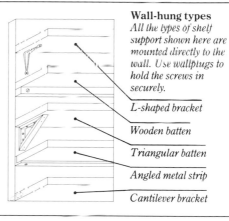

Wall-hung types
All the types of shelf support shown here are mounted directly to the wall. Use wallplugs to hold the screws in securely.

L-shaped bracket

Wooden batten

Triangular batten

Angled metal strip

Cantilever bracket

Adjustable shelf supports

For lightweight, adjustable shelving, pegs, dowels, plastic studs, clips and wire can be inserted into holes in wooden uprights. Metal or plastic studs come in various shapes and sizes. They slot into holes in wooden uprights at each corner of the shelf. There are special ones designed for glass shelving. Wooden dowels can be cut to length and tapped into holes at the corners. In addition, invisible wire supports and metal clips are neat and unobtrusive methods.

Peg for glass

Plastic peg

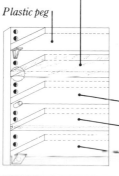

Panel-mounted types
Metal studs for glass either grip the glass or have a felt pad as a buffer. Wire supports fit into a groove at each end of the shelf. Two-part clips consist of a socket and supporting arm.

Dowel

Invisible wire

Two-part clip

Choosing and fitting storage systems

Storage space is at a premium in most homes, and whether you choose storage units or shelving will depend both on the space available and the use to which it will be put. Always measure precisely before choosing your storage system, since a fraction of an inch too large or small can make a crucial difference. The choice includes three basic types of storage system: fitted built-ins, free-standing and modular arrangements. A full fitted unit will provide good insulation against cold and sound and maximizes existing wall, floor and ceiling space, while free-standing systems can be disassembled and reinstalled in a different room or house. Modular units may be fitted or free-standing, built up from cubes, shelves, drawers and cabinets that can be easily adapted or enlarged to suit your needs.

Storage units and shelving kits can be bought prefabricated to be assembled at home. This is the quickest way to create storage space.

Loft space
The existing room shape will often suggest storage space. Alcoves and corners can be transformed into attractive and useful storage. Cellars and attics need to be warm and dry for storage, so insulate them first.

Grids and hooks
Hanging racks and hooks provide convenient storage in a kitchen (above) and make an attractive frame for herbs and utensils.

Window space
Objects displayed on window shelves and sills make an attractive arrangement (right) but the window must be sealed first.

Using storage space

Every room offers more storage space than meets the eye. Storage units can be built around corners, to span alcoves and overhang beds; closets can be fitted to the full height of the wall, and extra shelves can be added. Choose units with sliding, folding or hinged doors and trays or bins that swivel out; these help to increase the working or living space in a small area.

Shelves and drawers can be specifically arranged to provide interior storage for stereo equipment, cassettes, games, and other items you want up and off the floor. Conceal inner storage areas with sliding or louvered doors or drop-flap desk tops. Practical storage ideas can also be decorative, and it is worth improvising for individual effects.

Modular and built-in units
Modular units that can be lined up along a wall, or stacked to form staggered storage offer flexibility and choice. Two modules can be spaced apart to allow a shelf or desk top to rest on top. Free-standing units can be used as room dividers but must be weighed down at the bottom to prevent toppling. Built-in units may be designed to fit into fireplace alcoves or to bridge a gap between kitchen appliances

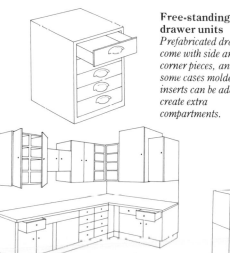

Free-standing drawer units
Prefabricated drawer kits come with side and corner pieces, and in some cases molded inserts can be added to create extra compartments.

Securing shelving to walls

Most shelf supports need to be secured to a wall or panel by means of screws. The weight of the load will determine the size and strength of the screw; select a screw long enough so that at least two thirds of its length is in the base material to which you are fastening.

Always attach shelving supports securely to a stud so that the shelves can carry a reasonable weight without pulling loose from the wall. Shelf brackets can be fixed almost anywhere, but the position of the studs in a plaster or wallboard partition will govern placement of the supports. Screws will not grip on their own in solid or hollow walls, so in most cases some sort of wallplug must be used (page 137).

Screwing into solid walls

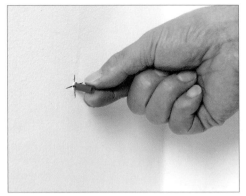

1 *Drill a hole into the wall to the depth of the wallplug. To prevent the drill bit slipping before you begin, make a small indentation in the wall by turning the drill manually. Plaster is not strong, so be sure to penetrate deeper into the masonry. To avoid drilling too far, however, wrap some adhesive tape around the drill bit, the length of the wallplug away from the tip.*

2 *Insert the wallplug into the hole and drive in the screw. The plug will then expand and the screw will be held securely in the wall. Take care, however, not to tighten the screw so hard that it breaks through the end of the plug. Do not drill holes near electrical switches or outlets or where you think pipes may run behind the wall; it could prove dangerous.*

Screwing into hollow walls

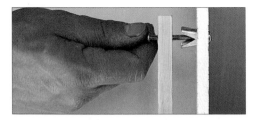

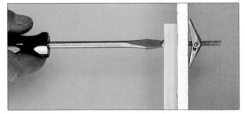

1 *A plasterboard wall is too thin to allow a screw to grip sufficiently. Drill a hole and insert the toggle into the wall. When it no longer meets the resistance of the wall its "wings" open and anchor the fixing in position. Only drill a small hole, just wide and deep enough to take the plug or toggle.*

2 *Drive in the screw, maintaining tension by pulling back the fitting. This will cause the plug or toggle to open. If you have a stud wall, drill and screw directly into the studs. To locate the framing studs accurately, tap the wall and where it makes a dull sound, make your drill holes.*

Screwing into wooden surfaces

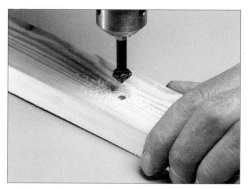

1 *To ensure straight fixing holes, drill right through the wood and into the wall using a twist drill bit slightly smaller than the screw you are using. In the wood that is to be mounted redrill the pilot hole with a twist drill bit slightly larger than the screw, then countersink this hole.*

2 *Drive in the screw with a screwdriver until it lies just below the surface. For larger holes, use a hand-brace or a power drill.*

Putting up a fitted shelf

When you have decided how much weight the shelf is to bear, choose a suitable thickness and width of shelving and sufficiently sturdy brackets and screws. L-shaped brackets are the best for fitted shelves. For small shelves or if your wall is even, it is worth screwing the bracket to the shelf before mounting it to the wall. If your wall is uneven, or if the shelf is very long, it may prove easier to put the brackets on the wall first, then screw the shelf to the brackets. If the shelf is to bear a heavy load, use cantilever brackets.

Use a level to mark the position of both brackets (right). Drill two holes in the wall for the first bracket, and when it is in position,

Fitting brackets to the wall
Hold the shelf up to the wall with a level on top, and when you have it at the correct height and level, mark the position of both brackets on the wall with a pencil.

insert and tighten the screws. Then repeat for the second bracket. With the two brackets in position on the wall, put the shelf on top, center it over the brackets and push it firmly against the wall. When it is in position, screw the first bracket to the underside of the shelf. Check that the shelf is straight, then screw the second bracket to the shelf.

FITTING ALCOVE SHELVING

Recessed shelving can be supported by wooden battens, angled metal strips or triangular brackets, which are fitted to the wall in the same way as L-shaped brackets. If, however, the walls are very uneven, it may be best to make two wooden side uprights to fit against the walls and mount the shelves to them.

Cut three battens to length, one to span the back wall and two for the side walls, each slightly shorter than the width of the shelf. Drill holes in the battens every 18 inches, then drill corresponding holes in the wall, along the horizontal line. Insert wallplugs and screw the battens into position. Rest the shelf in the alcove on the battens. No further fixing is required.

CHAPTER SIX

CURTAINS AND SHADES

By day, window hangings and shutters are simply decorative, but at night they afford privacy, conserve heat, and muffle outside noise. Even if privacy is not a problem, at night glass becomes a cold, black, reflective surface, and drawing curtains or pulling down a shade will make the room seem much more cozy and hospitable. When choosing curtains or shades, remember to check what they will look like from the outside as well as from within. Try to unify the decorative scheme from the outside, so that different windows on the same side of the house get a consistent treatment.

Sewing equipment

Sewing your own curtains, shades and other home furnishings is both economical and practical. Most curtains and shades are not difficult to make, and you can choose the style and fabric that best complements your décor. When buying fabric for household use, your first consideration before design and color should be its practicality – will it stand up to daily wear and routine laundering? The most important point to remember when sewing window coverings is to make sure that the seams are strong enough. Always finish them off securely, backstitching to strengthen and finishing any raw edges that could fray. Adding a lining will greatly increase the life of curtains, and heavier draperies.

Sewing machines

An electric machine with straight-stitch and zigzag settings is efficient and adequate for work on home furnishings. A machine with these relatively limited functions is called a zigzag or swing-needle model.

A semi-automatic machine is more sophisticated, including facilities for blind-hemming, buttonholing and a few simple embroidery stitches. A fully automatic model has all the above and a stretch-stitch capacity that is ideal for knit fabrics. This offers additional embroidery stitches and a more efficient method of working buttonholes.

Electronic or computerized machines have exceptionally easy, push-button or touch-control selection for a wide range of stitches, often with a "mirror" facility that allows any pattern to be worked in reverse, so that the pattern direction can be alternated. Other functions include an automatic technical adjustment that allows equal needle penetration at all speeds on all types of fabric. There may also be stitch-by-stitch control for accuracy in areas of intricate work, and a memory that stores a selection of stitches and repeats them as required at the touch of a switch. It is also possible to work lettering and border motif repeats.

Threading the machine

Machine stitching is formed by the interlocking of an upper and lower thread; the upper thread comes from a spool of thread placed on the machine, the lower from a bobbin loaded with thread and positioned under the needle plate. Most machines are threaded in a similar way – the upper thread is taken across from the reel, down into the tension disks, up through the take-up lever, down again and through the needle. Thread the machine with the take-up lever and presser foot raised: the instruction booklet will explain this and how to wind thread on to the bobbin and insert it below the needle.

In straight stitch the needle creates a single line of stitching. In zigzag and decorative stitching the needle swings from side to side as well as moving forward. Stretch stitches include a backward movement which allows "give," so that stitches do not break as the fabric itself – stretch or knit fabric – gives with use. Some of the stretch stitches provide useful extra strength in stitching heavy fabrics. Professional-type machines also have the facility for twin-needle work, which creates a double line of stitching.

The presser foot of a machine controls the feed-through of the fabric. There are usually several types supplied with the machine and one of the most useful is the zipper foot. This allows you to stitch very close to the teeth of an inserted zipper and works equally well for seaming alongside a bulky piping cord.

Sewing-machine needles are available in all points, as for hand-sewing needles – *sharp* for woven fabrics, *ballpoint* for knits, *wedge-point* for leather, suede and vinyl. Correct size is important; the wrong needle puts a strain on the thread, and if it is too thick it can leave ugly holes in the fabric, or split the seams of fine fabrics such as voile and organdy. Be guided by the sewing-machine manufacturer's instructions.

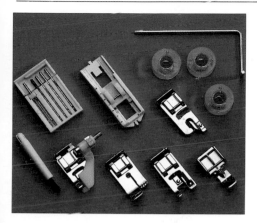

Overlocker

An overlocking machine can be a worthwhile investment if you are serious about sewing.

Accessories

Left to right top row: needles including a twin needle, buttonhole foot, roll-hemming foot, bobbins, quilting guide bar. Bottom row: cleaning brush with bobbin extractor, blind-hemming foot, straight-stitch foot, zigzag-stitching foot, zipper foot.

Upper thread tension dial

Needle bar thread guide

Feed dog

Needle clamp screw

Snap-on presser foot

Extension table with accessory box

Handwheel

Pattern selector

Zigzag width dial

Stitch length dial

Power and light switch

Foot control plug hole

Cutting equipment

Cutting out fabric with poor scissors is hard work and leads to inaccuracies which will ultimately show up in the hang or fit of the finished item. Have two pairs of good scissors – one used only for cutting out fabric and the other for close cutting when sewing. Keep these separate from household scissors so that the blades are not blunted by general use.

When choosing scissors, take along fabric pieces of different weights and ask if it is possible to test before buying. If the scissors are sold in sealed packaging, a sample pair may be available for testing. Check that they not only perform the task of cutting efficiently, but also are well-contoured and feel comfortable in your hand, when you are straight cutting, and cutting curves and corners.

Dressmaking (sidebent) shears are large and suitably weighted for cutting out fabric. Eight to 10 inches is a suitable length. Left-handed and "ambidextrous" models are now available.

Embroidery (needlework) scissors are small, about 5 to 5½ inches long. They are sharp at the point and cut with a clean, quick action for trimming or clipping threads and seams, for cutting into confined areas or for following intricate shaping. Electric scissors plug into the wall or are battery operated. Test them before buying, as some types are not useful for fine or bulky fabrics, although they deal efficiently with medium-weight materials.

Pinking shears are more useful for dressmaking than for home furnishings but can be used on small items, to trim seam allowances on non-fraying fabric as an alternative to overcasting. The shears should be used for neatening seams after sewing, not for initial cutting out. A seam ripper is indispensible for quick ripping out of seams. It has a small, sharply curved blade with a long and short point fixed in a narrow plastic handle, and a protective plastic cover.

Sewing aids
There is a wide range of modern, well-made and attractively designed equipment available which is suitable for both the amateur and the professional. Most of the items are inexpensive.

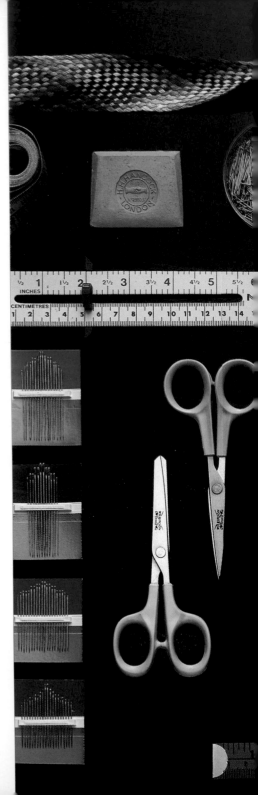

Types of needle

Although sewing machines have taken away much of the slow and tedious work of hand sewing, some stages of any job will involve hand sewing nevertheless. You will need a range of needles, therefore, for fine and heavy fabrics. Basting, finishing and embroidering decorative details also need different types and sizes of needle.

Sharps are used for general domestic sewing. They are long and have oval eyes, which make them suitable for a wide range of fabrics. Milliner's needles are similar to sharps, but are longer. They are used for jobs such as basting, where their extra length is an advantage. Betweens are also similar to sharps, but are shorter and used for medium and heavyweight fabrics.

A bodkin is used to thread cord, elastic or ribbon through a casing. It is blunt and thick since it does not go through the fabrics. Ballpoint needles are used with knit fabrics. They push the fibers aside, thus leaving the texture itself undamaged. Tapestry needles, used for embroidery and tapestry work, can also be used for threading ribbon or elastic.

Marking and measuring equipment

Curtains and shades rely for their effect to a great extent on accurate cutting and measuring. Curtains in particular should have hems and heads of equal length, or they will have an amateurish look. Inaccurate measuring can lead to a waste of expensive material.

Tailor's chalk is sold in various colors. Ideally you should have at least two, to mark light- and dark-colored materials. It comes in pencil form and in flat pieces. An alternative is to use a water-soluble marker. The coloring can be rinsed out with water.

There are various measuring implements, the most common of which is the tape measure. Use a fiberglass or linen one if possible, since these hardly stretch at all and thus give greater accuracy. The yard stick is useful for measuring curtains. It will not stretch and is easier to handle than a tape measure over large amounts of fabric.

Sewing aids

If you find it difficult to thread fine needles, a threader is a useful, inexpensive investment. A fine metal, looped filament passes through the needle eye; the thread is slotted into the loop and drawn back through the needle. The thimble is a useful but often ignored sewing aid, invaluable when you are dealing with a tough fabric or with several heavy layers.

Pins
You can choose the plain stainless steel type, or the larger plastic-headed pins which come in several colors. These are more easily seen when they are embedded in the fabric. Color ball pins are available for use with knit fabrics. Don't use pins on leather or suede; keep the edges together with small pieces of adhesive tape on the wrong side.

Pins
The smaller types are available in plain stainless steel, while the larger ones have plastic heads in various colors, making them easy to see against the fabric.

Make sure you have sufficient pins when starting a big project. Keep them together in a box and don't use any that are rusted or bent. Don't leave them too long in the fabric, as they may cause marking. A pincushion makes them more accessible while you are working; a magnet is a handy device for picking up spilled pins.

Special fabric adhesive, which is usually sold in stick form, is a quick and easy way to turn up a hem on lightweight fabrics before you finally stitch them in place.

Pressing equipment

Pressing is an important part of home-sewing projects – to flatten and smooth out seams and hems as you go along and to give a crisp, professional look to the finished item. Equip yourself with a steam or steam-and-spray iron; it is not the weight of the iron but the heat and moisture which take out the creases. Ask for pressing instructions as well as washing and cleaning advice when you purchase fabric. Match any symbol markings on the fabric label to the settings on your iron. A non-stick coating on the soleplate of the iron gives easy movement over the fabric; take care not to press any pinned areas, as the pins could damage the coating.

Choose an ironing board or table of suitable height and width – a pull-out sheet rail, available on some models, is very handy for pressing large items, keeping them flat and clear of the floor.

A cheesecloth or soft cotton cloth, slightly dampened, protects the surface of the fabric while it is pressed, although some steam irons can be used without a pressing cloth. A piece of light, firm woolen cloth, again made lightly damp, prevents the flattening of woolen fabric. Wash out the cloth before use to remove any sizing. It can be kept damp during pressing by sprinkling with water – a plant-mister spray

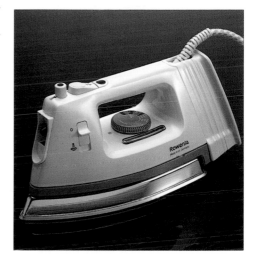

Steam-and-spray iron
The heat and moisture, rather than the weight of the iron, take the creases out of fabrics.

bottle is an invaluable accessory for this purpose. When pressing pleats, use brown paper under the folds to prevent depressions from pressing into the fabric underneath.

If the soleplate of the iron picks up a deposit from sizing in fabric, periodic use of a commercial brand cleaner, usually sold in stick form, helps to restore "slide" to an iron that has developed a tendency to drag on the fabric.

Choosing the right thread

Thread should be chosen individually for each project to suit the weight and type of fabric. Use cotton thread for natural fabrics, such as cotton, linen and wool. Synthetic threads are made for use with man-made and synthetic fabrics, for example acrylic, polyester and nylon. Silks and fine fabrics should be stitched with silk thread or a fine cotton filament. Special basting threads are available, or you can use up left-over spools for basting, but do not make do with what you have for finished stitching: an unsuitable thread is likely to break or cause puckering. If you use the same thread

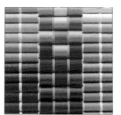

Shades of thread
Try to match thread and fabric as closely as possible. If the match is not precise, a darker rather than a lighter shade will blend better with the material.

as you will be using for finished stitching, you risk running out of thread later on. When buying thread, if you cannot get a precise color match between thread and fabric, choose a slightly darker shade, which will blend in more evenly than a lighter color. Secure the loose ends on the spools after sewing, and keep them together in a box.

Curtains

When choosing fabrics for curtains it is important to select color, pattern and texture to suit the style of the room. The price, of course, will also be a significant consideration, and it is always better to buy a slightly cheaper fabric and use it lavishly than to skimp on a more expensive material. Curtains need to be about two to two and a half times the width of the window, and they will never look good if they are not full enough. Also, you should allow for wastage and for pattern repeats where necessary.

Hanging curtains

The method you choose for hanging curtains may affect the way they should be made, so you must consider the type of track or rod that will be used when you are deciding on a suitable heading tape for the styling you have in mind.

Rods and tracks

A basic track supports the curtains directly; the hooks attaching the heading tape function as both hook and runner and are threaded over the track.

A traditional track is designed to have runners or gliders hanging from the track. Hooks are inserted in the curtain heading and then attached to the runners. Any standard or decorative heading tape can be used.

A decorative metal or wooden rod can be of any thickness you wish, providing it will support the curtains adequately and you can find rings large enough to thread over it. Large curtain rings are fitted with a smaller ring at the base to which the curtain hooks are attached. The rod is fitted on brackets screwed into the wall or the ceiling.

Expandable or sprung-tension rods are ideal for lace or sheer curtains. They are fitted between flat facing walls, in a narrow bay or across the window inset. Fine rods and curtain wire can support a lightweight curtain directly through a cased heading on the curtain which threads over the rod or wire. Narrow metal and plastic rods are available. Curtain wire is a coiled length in a plastic sheath, slightly expandable and fixed by means of eyelets screwed into the wire at either end, which can be attached to simple cup-hooks.

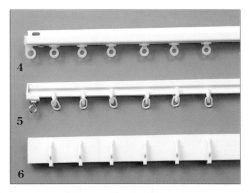

Rods and tracks
Curtain tracks were traditionally hidden by a cornice or valance but the modern streamlined tracks are unobtrusive when curtains are drawn back, and rods are a decorative feature. Some are flexible, making them suitable for bay windows.

1 *Light wooden rod with concealed runners*
2 *Metallic-finished rod with rings*
3 *Polished wooden rod with rings*
4 *Track with concealed runners*
5 *Track with exposed runners*
6 *Basic track with combined hooks and runners*

Choosing the hanging method

Whichever type of track or rod you choose, make sure it is available in long enough lengths for your windows; joins are impractical. It must also be strong enough for the type of curtain you want. If you have curved or bay windows, choose a track that can be bent around corners. Check also whether a cording set can be fitted to the track. Most types of straight track accept pull cords, so that you can close and open the curtains from one side. But some types of curved track will not take pull cords. The traditional brass curtain track has been largely superseded by nylon, plastic and aluminum track, and wooden rods. As well as the traditional brass tracks, those used with a cornice include aluminum and plastic types with nylon runners.

Attaching curtain tracks to a wall

Most curtain tracks are sold with the brackets you need to put them up, and sometimes with the screws and wallplugs as well. Putting up rods involves the same technique as putting up curtain tracks. True rods only require brackets at either end, so they may not be the best choice for long windows, unless they are strong enough to take the weight of the curtains without sagging. Imitation rods can be fitted with brackets at intervals.

Curtain tracks can be fitted to the window frame itself, but it is unlikely that there will be enough space in the recess for anything except lightweight sheer curtains. So the best solution is to fit the track to the wall above the window. Drilling the wall and inserting wallplugs should be simple with a hammer drill and a masonry bit unless there is a concrete lintel above the window. In this case, the best solution is to fit a batten above the window.

Fitting brackets to the wall
Drill holes in the wall at regular intervals to take the screws and wallplugs. When you mark the positions for the holes, always use a carpenter's level to make sure that they are level.

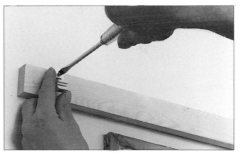

Fitting brackets to a batten
Remove any paper from the wall. Then attach the batten at either end with screws and wallplugs and secure the central part with contact adhesive. Paint or paper over it.

FIXING CURTAIN TRACKS TO A CEILING

If the top of the window is very close to the ceiling, it may be easier to mount the brackets to the ceiling. Hollow wallplugs in the ceiling itself will not be strong enough. Find the positions of the joists above the ceiling and screw into these. They are usually about 16 inches apart. On lower floors, the easiest way to pinpoint joists is to lift a floorboard in the room above and make a tiny marking hole through the ceiling next to the joists. On top floors, find the joists by going into the attic. If the joists run at right angles to the wall, mount a bracket to each one. Use screws that are long enough to go through the full thickness of the ceiling plaster and into the joists themselves.

Visual effects

It is possible to use fabric to alter the appearance of less-than-perfect windows, to make them seem larger or smaller, of better proportions, or simply to make them look more interesting or unusual. To block a dreary view, hang full-length lace or sheers that will admit enough light into a room that is in permanent daytime use.

To preserve your privacy without cutting out all the light, place café curtains over the lower half of the window. This also draws attention away from peeling paint or less-than-perfect window frames.

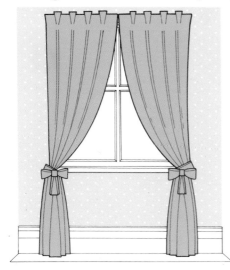

To make a large window look smaller
Hang curtains to meet at the top of the window, but loop them up at the sides with tie-backs.

To avoid covering a radiator
Hang long "dress" curtains, but keep them drawn back, and use a shade to cover the window.

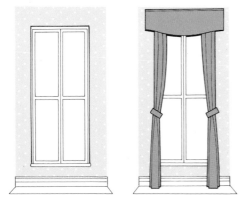

To lower the height of a tall window
Use a cornice or valance across the top, or above the window to make it seem lower.

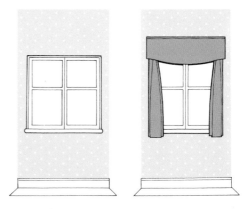

An illusion of width
Extending the curtain track at either side of the window improves the proportions of a narrow window.

Other effects with curtains

For a dramatic effect, or if paired curtains would overpower a narrow window, a single, asymmetrical curtain can be very effective. A flat curtain suspended from hooks through eyelet holes in the fabric can be attractive, and tie-backs can create interesting shapes. Other interesting effects can be created with sheer curtains. While their main purpose is to prevent people seeing in, you can use them more imaginatively, by draping them elaborately, using them to diffuse light, or gathering them on the type of headings used on conventional window curtains.

Matching fittings
Curtains, tie-backs, cornices and pillows made of the same fabric create a harmonious effect in this spacious bay window.

Curtains and shades
The combination of curtains and shades gives great flexibility – the translucent shade lets in some light, while the curtains act not only as light shields but also as decorative features to enhance the view.

Sheer curtains can diffuse light
You can diffuse bright sunlight with full-length sheer curtains. In this room the striped and textured effect of the full sheer curtains is picked up by the reflective glass surface of the coffee table.

Curtain fabrics

Curtain fabrics are available in an almost endless variety of colors, textures and patterns, ranging from lightweight sheers to heavyweight velvets and patterned weaves. There isn't any particular restriction on the type of fabric you could use – as long as it suits your purpose and is reasonably practical from the point of view of cleaning and rehanging. Loose-weave and open-textured fabrics can be a problem, tending to sag dismally soon after hanging, but you can get around this by supporting them with a firm, medium-weight lining. Of course, as the fabric must hang permanently in the window, choose a type that does not fade or discolor in the sun.

Lightweights, such as sheers, voiles, laces and synthetics, are primarily used to provide some privacy while allowing light to come into the room, so they are often hung under heavier curtains. These fabrics are usually sold in light colors – white, cream, beige and pale pastels – although some stores stock deep-colored laces which create an unusually dramatic effect. If you are given to browsing around antique shops and flea markets, you may be lucky enough to come upon an undamaged length of old lace which will enhance a period décor or disguise a stained table.

Medium-weights are available in a variety of fibers and in a wide range of patterns and finishes. These are the most popular and versatile curtaining fabrics. Medium-weights can be used almost anywhere and are particularly useful if you want the slip covers and pillows in the room to be made to match.

Heavyweights include brocade, linen and velvet, suitable for traditional and formal styles of curtaining. It is usual to line heavy fabrics, and they have excellent draping qualities for floor-length curtains, hanging evenly by their own weight. They also have good insulating properties, although medium-weights can also be given insulating linings which can be just as effective.

Choosing fabrics

Fabrics are made from different fibers, come in a range of weights and textures, and are found in hundreds of different colors and patterns. The fabric you choose should be appropriate in its use as much as in its appearance. Many shops now helpfully indicate suitable uses for the various materials, and sales staff should be able to give sound advice. Always read the label on a roll of fabric, to check its fiber content and any special properties. Be sure of instructions for care and cleaning; whether or not a fabric is washable may be the most important thing you need to know about it.

Check that fabrics are fade-resistant; this, obviously, is very important for curtains, shades and curtain linings.

Do not skimp on the amount of fabric you buy in order to afford your most expensive choice; it is a false saving and you will get a better effect from being generous with a less expensive material. But do choose good quality fabric, whatever the price range: it is not worth spending time and effort on sewing up an item which soon appears worn and lifeless. If your budget, or the effect you want, seems to dictate a choice of inexpensive light- or medium-weight fabric, rub it between your hands to see if any sizing comes off, leaving the cloth itself rather limp. Check for flaws in the weave or pattern; these should be indicated by a contrast thread marker at the selvage. Be sure to buy sufficient length to complete what you intend to make; it may be difficult to color-match fabric from a different roll later on.

Some fabrics have a shrink-resistant finish. If not, shrinkage must be generously allowed for, as it can make a considerable difference to the calculation of the amount needed: there may be 6 percent or more shrinkage on untreated cottons. Certain synthetics require this allowance, too, particularly loose-weave types. When thinking about trimmings, such as ruffles, ribbons or tassels, make sure that they are compatible with the fabric and the lining for easy laundering.

Color and pattern

The design on a fabric goes a long way toward setting the style of a room. It is a message about your personality and way of life, so your instincts and natural preferences are important when it comes to choosing colors and patterns. Color creates impact, and many people find it difficult to visualize color effects on a relatively large scale. This often leads to a choice of "safe" or neutral colors for basic décor, with small areas of contrast or bold focus. Although color may be the strongest feature of a design, it is never an independent factor. Two colors always affect each other.

If you intend to use patterned fabrics, your thoughts on color become further complicated by the style and scale of the pattern design. Coordinated fabrics may solve the problem, but it can be more exciting, and a far more personal choice, to mix and match from the full range available. Think about mixing large and small patterns, using the same fabric in reversed colorways, opting for a monochromatic or harmonious scheme, or a riot of rainbow colors.

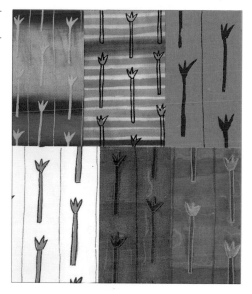

The effects of colors on each other
The variations of color in this basic pattern show how colors affect each other, producing warm, cool, exotic or simple effects. If you are mixing patterns, take a key element such as shape, color, scale or direction to make a link between them.

PATTERN AND TEXTURE CHECKLIST

• Patterned fabrics are more practical than solid, as they do not show soiling as readily.
• Texture affects the "seen" value of color, and this varies with change of light.
• Viewed from a distance, subtle coloring can merge and pattern detail may disappear.
• Light colors suggest an expansive effect, whereas dark shades tend toward intimacy.
• Fabric patterns should be printed on the straight grain of the fabric, to give the correct effect at seams and hems.
• A large pattern repeat will mean that more fabric is required overall.
• When different patterns are combined to make up a single article, the fabrics should have equal weight and "give."
• The mutual enhancement or contrast of colors may be visible between schemes in adjoining rooms, as well as within a single room.

FABRICS CHECKLIST

• Always use washable, easy-care fabrics for articles which need regular cleaning.
• When budgeting for fabric, choose to buy a generous quantity of inexpensive material rather than risk a skimpy effect with a more expensive type of fabric.
• If using two or more fabrics to make up a single item, select similar weights and check that they are compatible for washing or cleaning.
• Allow for shrinkage if the fabric has no shrink-resistant finish and is not pre-shrunk.
• Check fabrics for flaws before purchasing.
• Try to get the full length you need taken from one fabric roll. If two rolls are used, check that the colors match perfectly.
• Test inexpensive fabrics for large amounts of sizing which will wash out at the first laundering, leaving the fabric limp and lifeless.
• Make sure your fabric choice has the finishes – easy-care, shrink-, stain-, fade- and flame-resistance – required for its purpose.
• Don't use flimsy fabrics for home furnishing items, except as trimming or decoration.

Fabric construction

The majority of fabrics used in home furnishings are plain weaves, with the pattern, if there is one, printed on the surface. However, many types of fabrics are also woven to produce textured surface effects, solid color pattern motifs and patterned weaves of two or more colors.

Weave
Most furnishing fabrics feature weaves that it is possible to construct on a basic loom with no special attachments. These provide a surprising range of textures. Plain weave is the simplest woven structure; it may be made in one or more colors and with various types and thicknesses of yarn. When different colors are used for warp and weft, the result is described as "shot" fabric. With satin weave, more warp thread is exposed on the surface of the fabric than in plain weave, resulting in a smooth, unbroken and luxuriously shiny surface appearance. Twill weave is a diagonal, ridged pattern of varying effects according to yarn weight and direction of ridging. Traditional herring-bone is a variation on twill weave; diagonal ridging is reversed at regular intervals to create a zigzag pattern.

Leno weave is a lacy, open weave which may be combined with other weaves. It is made by twisting warp yarns around each other in figures-of-eight as the weft passes between them. Dobby weave has a more intricate texture, such as small geometric motifs woven in at regular intervals. Pile fabrics, such as corduroy and velvet, are produced by the use of two warp threads, one of which forms the base, the other being pulled upward and cut to form the pile.

Texture
The texture of a fabric derives from the fibers and the method of construction. Textural variations are applied to the complete range of fabrics, from the finest sheers to the heaviest of natural-fiber materials. Their visual and tactile surface qualities create the atmosphere of a room design scheme.

Smooth, shiny surfaces give a cool look appropriate to sophisticated schemes. Depending upon the weight of the fabric, this can be designed to complement sleek hi-tech styling, or a formal, traditional style of décor. Rough or soft textures – matt, fluffy, slubbed, loosely woven – create a warmer atmosphere which may be formal or luxurious, with a rich pile fabric such as velvet, for example, or casual and informal, as with a coarsely woven material such as burlap, or a heavily slubbed weave. Fine ribs and inlaid pattern motifs can be used in any type of décor as a balancing factor. The introduction of textural interest is important where solid colors are favored rather than a patterned fabric scheme.

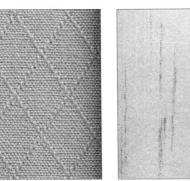

Jacquard fabrics
These are produced on a special type of loom invented in 1801 by Joseph Jacquard for the weaving of patterned fabrics. Solid colored designs or designs of two or more colors can be woven. In damask, flat designs are created by a contrast of satin and matt finishes; in brocade, on the other hand, the pattern is raised from a differently colored background area.

Types of curtain heading

The important thing about your curtains is how they look to you. They can set the style of the whole room, and although they must have the necessary practical qualities, easy-care properties will not compensate for a mistake in styling that you will have to live with day in and day out.

Once you have an idea of the type of fabric you may choose, the next important decision is the heading tape, which can dictate informal or formal styling, the fullness, width and overall effect of this focal point in the room.

There is a remarkable range of heading tapes now available, in different materials to suit different fabrics – special tapes for lightweights and sheers, for example – and with a good variety of interesting design effects. The tape gathers or pleats the top of the curtain by means of cords threaded along the length, which draw up the fabric to a specific style – simple gathers, smocked gathers, narrow pencil pleats, clustered pinch pleats. The tape also has lines of pockets where the curtain hooks are inserted and can be narrow or deep, with one row of pockets or three. Deep tapes allow you to position the curtain hooks to bring the top of the heading level with the track or standing slightly above it. If you are using a decorative rod to hang the curtains, the hooks can be placed on a line which leaves the curtain heading clear of the rod while concealing the hooks and base rings.

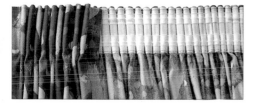

Pencil pleats
Classic pencil pleat heading tape forms crisp, even, upright pleats. The type shown has a special monofilament thread woven in, which keeps the heading upright. This tape requires 2¼ to 2½ times the width of the track. It has two alternative rows of suspension pockets, so it can be used with any type of curtain track or with a decorative curtain rod.

Pinch pleats
An elegant heading tape with groups of three pleats spaced apart. The pleats are pinched in close together at the lower edge of the tape and fan out at the top. This tape requires 2 times the width of the track. The tape has two alternative rows of suspension pockets, making it suitable for any type of curtain track or rod. Special curtain hooks are needed.

Lightweight pencil pleating
This type of heading tape is specially designed for use on lightweight fabrics, sheer fabrics and nets. It normally takes 2¼ to 2½ times curtain fullness, but on static nets, which will not be drawn back, 3 times fullness looks more attractive. This type of tape also has two rows of suspension pockets, making it suitable for any type of track or pole.

Standard heading tape
This is a narrow heading tape, about 1 inch wide, which forms gathers. It is used mainly on small informal curtains and valances, and where the curtain heading will be hidden. It requires 1½ to 2 times the total width of the track. Standard tape has only one row of hook suspension pockets, so the tape should be positioned so it will hide the track.

Estimating quantities

When measuring for curtains, use a wooden rule or a steel tape measure and hold it at eye level. It is essential that you calculate the fabric amounts accurately – guesswork inevitably results in too much or too little, either way an expensive mistake.

When you have decided on the full width, fit the track or rod. Measure with a wooden ruler or metal tape measure to arrive at the width of the finished curtains after the heading is drawn up.

The measured width of the track is the basis of your calculation. Remember to allow a little extra if you are having an overlap at the center. Multiply this measurement by 1½, 2 or 2½, depending on the heading tape (page 157). It may be necessary to join widths of fabric to make up this full measurement.

As well as deciding on the finished drop of the curtains, allow for the heading to cover or stand slightly above the curtain track. If you are hanging the curtains from a decorative rod, they will hang just clear of the rod, so it is visible. Measure from the point where you estimate the top of the curtain should be to the point representing the finished length.

To this measurement you need to add allowances for the top turning and lower hem. The top turning allowance is generally 1½ inches when a heading tape or facing is to be attached, but allow more if you are making a gathered heading with a ruffle standing above the tape. The lower hem is usually 6 inches for unlined curtains – more if shrinkage is likely – and 4–6 inches for lined curtains.

To work out how many drops are needed, divide the total width of both curtains by the width of your chosen fabric. Round up the final amount to the next whole number, which will create an allowance for seams and side hems. Divide the figure in two to find out the number of full-length fabric pieces in each curtain. This will also tell you whether a half-width is needed on either side.

The number of drops multiplied by the cut length is the total amount of fabric you need to buy. Remember to add a little extra material for pattern matching if necessary.

Measuring cross-over drapes

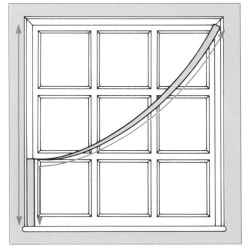 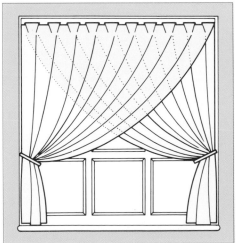

1 *The outer edge of each curtain should equal the window drop. To find the length of the inner edge, drape a tape measure across the window and down to the sill. Cut both curtains to the longer length. Mark off the shorter length down one side.*

2 *Lay the curtains with right sides together and cut diagonally across the bottom from the marked shorter length. Lay one curtain on top of the other, right sides upward. Baste the top edges together. Hang the curtains, tying them back with tie-backs.*

Patterned fabrics

When selecting a patterned fabric for curtains, consider first how large an area they will cover when closed. A large pattern on a large area may be either exciting or overwhelming, according to your personal taste.

If you use patterned fabric, an allowance must be made for matching the pattern at seams and across both curtains. One extra pattern repeat should be allowed for each drop of fabric after the first (so add two pattern repeats if your curtain has three drops, and so on). In a pair of curtains, the pattern repeats should occur in the same place on each length for both curtains.

An easy method for matching the pattern in different lengths is to place a cut length over the next section of the fabric, aligning pattern details and marking them with pins. There will probably be some excess material to cut away between the end of one curtain length and the start of the next; these offcuts come in handy for tie-backs, a valance or cornice, or pillows to match the curtains.

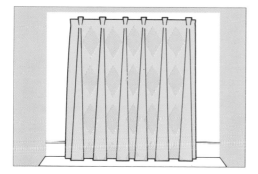

Partial repeats for long curtains
If you cut through a horizontal motif, position the partial repeat at the bottom of a floor-length curtain, where it will not be noticed.

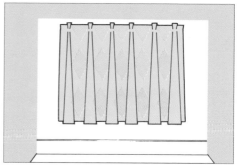

Partial repeats for short curtains
Place the cut-off repeat at the top and a full motif at the bottom, where it will be in the direct line of vision of those seated in the room.

QUANTITIES FOR DIFFERENT CURTAINS

If you are having heavy, luxurious, floor-length curtains, you may wish to allow the full width to be drawn back clear of the window glass. This will take up quite a bit of space, since the heading will not bunch up tightly due to the thickness of the fabric. This means the curtains will have to extend beyond the window area. If you choose lightweight, cotton fabric, on the other hand – for gathered kitchen curtains, for instance – these will not need much extra width beyond the window frame. The type of heading tape will also have a bearing on the width of the curtain. You may want to make an extra allowance for a generously draped effect with full-length curtains, with some of the fabric actually lying on the floor once the curtains are hung.

POINTS TO REMEMBER

- Measure the width of the track or rod. Multiply by 1½ or 2½ (according to your choice of heading tape, page 157) for the finished width of curtains. Round up to the nearest whole figure for the number of drops required.
- Multiply the total number of drops by the cut length to find the total amount of fabric required.
- When measuring for curtains, always allow extra material for hems, headings and pattern repeats. If you find this difficult to calculate, an experienced assistant in a furnishing fabrics department will be able to help you if you provide the basic measurements.
- Make sure that any curtain tracks or rods you want to use are available in sufficient lengths – joins are not usually possible.
- If you are using a batten to support curtain track brackets, mount it securely to the wall using screws and, if necessary, adhesive.

Unlined curtains

Quick and simple to make, inexpensive but attractive and practical, unlined curtains are ideal for the kitchen or bathroom, or other working areas where they may be exposed to dirt and need frequent washing. Printed cottons are definitely the best choice and offer a range of lovely colors and patterns, from quaintly traditional florals to bright, bold abstracts and geometrics.

You will probably need to join several fabric widths in order to make up the total width required for each curtain. If you have to cut a half width as well as full widths, place the half width at the outer edge of the curtain. You can join the panels with a simple flat seam, but a flat fell seam conceals the raw edges.

To make a flat fell seam, place fabric right sides together and pin and stitch a flat seam. Turn the fabric over and press the seam open. Trim one seam allowance to ⅛ inch and turn under ¼ inch on the other seam allowance and press. Fold the larger seam allowance over the trimmed one to enclose the raw edge. Press to the main fabric. Stitch through all the fabric

layers close to the edge of the fold. Only one line of stitching will show.

A gathered heading suits the simple styling of unlined curtains, but you can use a more elaborate pleated or smocked effect; look at the range of available heading tapes and decide on the style when you choose the fabric, so you know how much to buy. With a gathered heading, you can allow for a small ruffle standing above the heading tape, turning over 1½ inches at the top edge of the curtain and stitching the tape 1 inch below.

Calculating fabric amounts

Width: Multiply the width of the track by amount of fullness required for heading. Add 1½ inches for each side hem. Divide the total by width of fabric, rounding up to the next full width. Allow 1¼ inches for each join.
Length: Measure the length of the area you are curtaining; add 1½ inches for the top heading hem and 6 inches for the bottom hem. Multiply the length by the number of widths needed to give the fabric amount.

Making unlined curtains

1 *Along each side of the curtain, turn a ½-inch hem to the wrong side. Press in place. At the bottom of the fabric, turn 3 inches of the hem allowance to the wrong side. Pin and press. Remove the pins.*

2 *To make neat corners at the bottom, measure a further 3 inches from the raw edge of the turned-under hem toward the top of the fabric. Fold over the side hems from this point and press in place.*

3 *From the point of the raw edge of the bottom hem, turn the remainder of the side hem allowance to the wrong side. Pin and press it firmly in place to provide a steep diagonal edge at the bottom. This forms half a mitered corner. Repeat the same procedure at the other side. Although mitering is not absolutely necessary, it results in a neater finish.*

4 *Fold over the other half of the bottom hem, aligning the two diagonal edges of each mitered corner. Pin down and press in place. Slip-stitch down the diagonal joins to secure the corners. Then neatly slip-hem the side hems and bottom hem in place. This completes the bottom hem. (Note that mitering also reduces the bulk of the material.)*

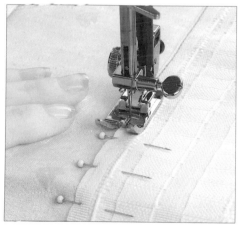

5 *Turn a 1½-inch hem to the wrong side at the top of the curtain fabric and press it firmly in place. Cut a length of the correct type of heading tape to the finished width of the curtain plus an extra allowance of ¾ inch. Place the heading tape on the wrong side of the top of the curtain, just below the top edge. Tuck under the raw ends of the tape level with the side edges of the curtain. Then pin and baste the tape in place, ready for stitching. There is no need for any special sewing-machine attachment.*

6 *Machine-stitch the heading tape to the curtain. Stitch one short edge first, then one long edge and the other short edge. Repeat stitching the other long edge, so that the short ends are stitched twice to secure the ends of tape cord. It is a good idea to stitch the long edges in the same direction to make sure that the tape does not pucker. Gently gather up the fabric by pulling the tape cords from the center. Hold the cords together with one hand and ease the tape into pleats with the other. Finally, loosely knot the cords at the center.*

Lined curtains

A wide variety of fabrics can be used for curtain linings. They protect the face fabric, add body and improve drape, and should be chosen to suit the weight and type of the main fabric and the use – for example, both fabrics should be either washable or for dry-cleaning only. Cotton sateen is widely used as a lining for curtains. Insulated fabric treated with aluminum is available for curtain lining; the metallized side is placed to the wrong side of the curtain fabric. Linings can either match or contrast with curtain fabrics.

Simple-lined curtains

It is often assumed that because curtains are large items and tend to be dominant in a room scheme, they are difficult to make, especially if lined. Simple-lining requires no more sewing skill than making unlined curtains; the lining is simply machine-stitched to the main fabric at the side seams only – forming a "tube" of fabric. The proper finish is achieved by cutting the lining slightly narrower than the full curtain, so that when the tube is turned out to the right side and pressed flat, the main fabric laps around on to the back of the curtain, forming a neatly finished edge at both sides, with the seams and lining invisible from the right side.

With this construction, the raw edges of any seams joining fabric widths on curtain or lining are concealed within the tube. However, as the lining is not attached to the curtain at any point within the width, it can move independently of the main fabric, and tends to separate as the curtains are pulled back, effectively forming two draped layers. This is not necessarily a disadvantage, depending on the curtain width and type of fabric you are using, but if you want absolutely smooth draping, it is preferable to use the locked-in lining method shown on page 164.

Calculating fabric amounts
Curtain fabric: Calculate the width and length as for an unlined curtain (page 160).
Lining: The width should be 2 inches less than the finished width of the curtain; the length should be the same as the finished curtain minus the hem allowance at the top.

Making up simple-lined curtains

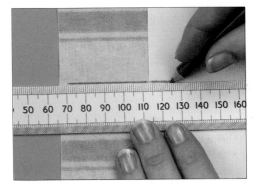

1 *With the right sides together, place the lining on the curtain fabric, carefully aligning the bottom edges. Then, with tailor's chalk, clearly mark the center point of the curtain width on both the curtain and lining fabric pieces.*

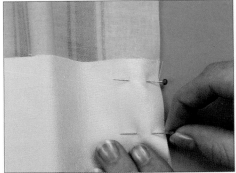

2 *Pin and baste the side edges of the lining and the curtain fabric together. As the curtain fabric is slightly wider than the lining, allow the curtain fabric to form undulating folds beneath the lining while you baste it firmly in place.*

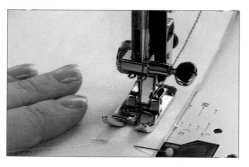

3 Mark the finished length of the curtain together with the hem sewing line on the lining with tailor's chalk; allow for a 6-inch hem. Turn, pin and machine-stitch ⅜-inch side seams from the top of the lining down to within 4 inches of the hem sewing line at the bottom of the curtain.

4 Turn right side out. The curtain fabric should pull over to the lining side at the side edges by 1 inch. Press the curtain and lining. Match the center-marked points on the lining and curtain fabric at the top. Fold over the curtain fabric at the top edge of the lining and press in place.

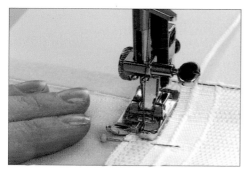

5 Position the heading tape just below the top of the curtain fabric, tucking under the raw ends to neaten. Pin and baste in place. Machine-stitch one short side first. Then stitch each long side in the same direction to avoid puckering.

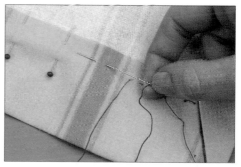

6 Do not pull the cords up yet. At the bottom of the curtain fabric, turn under a double 3-inch hem and press in place. Miter the corners to minimize the bulk in same way as with an unlined curtain. Baste the hem in place to secure it.

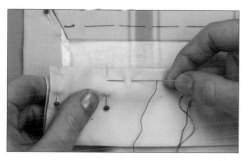

7 Turn up a double hem to the wrong side of the lining fabric. The lining should hang about ¾ inch above the hem level of the curtain fabric. Trim any surplus lining. Baste the hem of the lining in place.

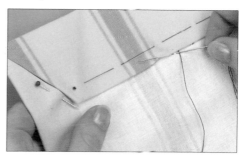

8 Pull up the curtain heading tape. Hang the curtain for several days to allow the fabric to drop. Only then slip-hem the hems and the lining to the curtain down the rest of the sides.

Locked-in curtain linings

A locked-in lining is the most professional finish for lined curtains, especially good for wide and deep curtain styles where fabric widths are joined to make up the full finished width of the curtain. The lock-stitching must be done by hand, but this should not deter you because the stitching method is surprisingly quick.

The lining is lightly sewn to the curtain fabric at regular intervals vertically across the width and right down the length, so that the fabric layers move as one and the lining cannot bunch up behind the drawn curtain, to spoil the smoothness of the drape. If you are using a dense, heavy fabric, the lining adds thickness and improves insulation, as well as making the curtains look well finished from the reverse side; with a looser weave or textured curtaining material, the locked-in construction prevents the main fabric from sagging in an unsightly way when hung.

For the main fabric, choose the traditional formality of velvet, brocade or heavy chintz and team it with a richly colored sateen lining, or a slightly slubbed and sheeny synthetic. For less formal styling, consider a roughly textured, heavyweight fabric such as jute or a tweedy weave.

As the main fabric and lining are locked across the whole construction of the curtain, it is vital that you check the care instructions for both to ensure they can be cleaned in the same way and, if washable, do not shrink at different rates.

Calculating fabric amounts

Curtain fabric: Calculate the width and length as for an unlined curtain (page 160), but allowing only 4 inches for the bottom hem of the curtain.

Lining fabric: The width should be the same as the unmade curtain width; and the length should be the same as that of the required finished curtain length.

Making locked-in curtain linings

1 *Stitch the curtain fabric widths together with flat seams to make up the full curtain width. Press the seams open. Pin and stitch the lining widths together and press the seams open. Trim 1½ inches from the side edges of the lining, and turn and press a ¾ inch hem down the sides, and a ½-inch hem along the bottom of the fabric. Then turn another 1½ inches under along the bottom. Pin and stitch the lower hem firmly in place.*

2 *Next, press a generous 1½ inches turning down each side of the curtain fabric to the wrong side of the fabric. Then turn up a 4-inch hem at the bottom of the curtain and miter the corners neatly. Slip-stitch the mitered corner seams. Then, using a large herring-bone stitch, sew the side and bottom hems. Make sure that you pick up just a thread of the flat fabric with each stitch, so that the stitching will not show on the right side.*

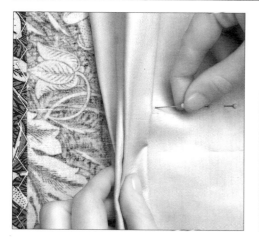

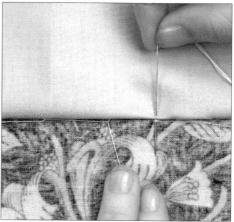

3 *At 12 inch intervals, mark vertical lines on the wrong side of the curtain material with tailor's chalk. Place the lining on the fabric with the wrong sides together so that the side edges of the lining are ³/₄ inch in, and the lower edge is 2 inches up from the curtain edge. Then trim the top of the lining level. Baste the lining and curtain together, following the first vertical line and beginning 6 inches down from the top of the curtain fabric.*

4 *Fold back the lining material along the basted line. Lock-stitch the curtain fabric to the lining fabric, beginning 6 inches from the top of the curtain fabric. Make sure that you pick up only a thread of the curtain fabric at a time so that the stitching will not show on the right side of the curtain fabric. To avoid puckering the fabric, do not pull the stitches tight and make sure that you space them wide apart. Then remove the basting stitches.*

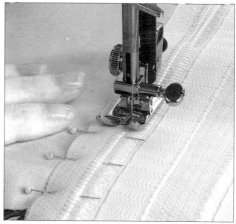

5 *Baste and lock-stitch the fabrics together along the next vertical line, and so on until the lining is lock-stitched in place across the full width of the curtain. Next, pin and baste the sides and bottom edge of the lining in place, and slip-hem the folded-in sides of the lining to the folded-in edges of the curtain fabric. Then slip-hem the bottom hem of the lining to the bottom hem of the curtain fabric, and remove all the basting stitches.*

6 *Turn the hem to the wrong side at the top of the curtain and lining and press it. Cut the heading tape to fit the top edge, allowing an extra allowance to turn under at each end of the curtain. Position the length of the heading tape just below the top edge of the curtain, turning the raw ends of the tape under neatly. Pin and baste the tape in place. Stitch along the short end and then along both long sides in the same direction to prevent the stitching puckering.*

Detachable curtain linings

A detachable lining does not follow the folds of the curtain fabric in the same way as a sewn-in lining, so it does not affect the hang of the main curtaining. It does, however, protect the fabric as much as any other type of lining, and there are various advantages in its construction. Because it is separate, the lining does not have to be as fully gathered as the curtain, so you save on the amount of fabric – one and a half times the track width should usually be ample for the lining width.

The lining can be taken off for washing separately if the main fabric is dry-clean only. This is a further advantage of detachable linings – you do not have to ensure compatibility of washing and care instructions because the curtain fabric and the lining can be treated as separate articles. Detachable linings are also an economical way of lining curtains intended for a short life – if you are putting up temporary furnishings until you are fully settled in a new home, or if the room needs a facelift but you are planning to move in the near future.

A final advantage is that you can add a detachable lining to an existing curtain without fully remaking it, or you can transfer the lining to a new curtain when you are revising a room scheme to give a new look with different patterns and colors.

Calculating fabric amounts

Make up the curtain in the same way as an unlined curtain (see page 160). Attach heading tape to the curtain in the usual way.

Hem the sides and bottom of the lining fabric in the same way as the curtain fabric, but leave the top edge unhemmed. Trim the top edge so that the lining is a little shorter than the finished curtain. Lining tape has two skirts and is fitted so that one skirt falls to each side of the lining fabric.

Curtain fabric: Calculate the width and length of the curtain material in the same way as for unlined curtains (see page 160).

Lining fabric: Calculate the width and length of the lining fabric in the same way as for the curtain fabric.

Making detachable linings

1 *Cut the lining tape the width of the curtain plus another 4 inches. Then knot the two cords together at the end that will be over the inner edge of the curtain. With the lining tape the right side up and the lining fabric the right side up, ease the lining fabric between the skirts as shown. The knotted end of the lining tape should overhang the center edge of the lining fabric by about ³/8 inch.*

2 *Turn a ¼-inch hem on the knotted end of the lining tape. Turn a further ¼-inch hem to the wrong side of the lining fabric, so that the tape is flush with the edge of the lining. Pin the lining tape in place. Make quite sure that the top raw edge of the fabric is slotted right into the tape. This will prevent the fabric from pulling out if the raw edge should fray when the curtain is being cleaned.*

3 *At the other end of the lining tape, pull the cords free, so that about 1½ inches of each cord hangs down. Trim the surplus lining tape, so that only ³/8 inch overhangs the outer edge. Turn a double ¼-inch hem to the wrong side of the lining fabric, as for the end of the lining tape at the inner edge. Leave the tape cords free for gathering the lining, and baste the tape firmly in place.*

4 *Take care to stitch right through the two sandwiching layers of tape. Close to the bottom and side edges, stitch the lining tape in place. Next, remove the basting and gently pull the two loose cord ends, easing the lining fabric along at the same time with your other hand. Even out the gathers until the width of the lining exactly matches the width of the curtain itself, then firmly knot the cords.*

Hemming curtains

Hems are used to finish the edge of fabric. The depth of the hem can vary between ¼ inch and 6 inches and should relate to the size of the item; a narrow hem on a large item will give an oddly unfinished look, while too deep a hem on a small item will look very clumsy.

Hems can be stitched by hand or machine. Hand stitches include blind stitch, hemming and slip stitch, and the choice between these stitches is really a matter of personal preference. Catch stitch is worked over the raw edge of a single hem on lined curtains, and is especially useful on thick fabrics. Straight stitch machined hems are quick to make, especially on large areas. Machine blind stitching is most suitable for thick-pile fabric where the stitches do not show. Zigzag machine stitch is a strong hem used for the decorative effect of the stitch.

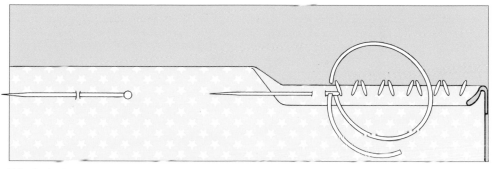

Blind stitch
Work from right to left if you are right-handed. Fold back the hem edge and fasten the thread inside it. Sew a small stitch in the fabric about ¼ inch to the left.

Then sew a small stitch in the hem, ¼ inch to the left again. Repeat the stitches, alternating between fabric and hem, all the way along. You can also work blind stitch with a sewing-machine.

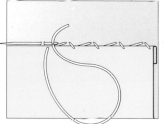

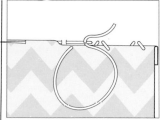

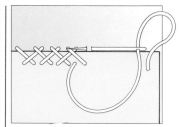

Hemming
This is the most basic and simple stitch. Work from right to left if you are right-handed, with the turned-under edge facing you. Make two stitches on top of each other on the folded fabric to secure the thread. Just above the folded edge pick up a couple of threads of flat fabric. Insert the needle slightly to the left into the two layers of fabric close to the fold and draw the thread gently through. Repeat the stitch to complete the hem.

Slip stitch
Beginning at the right (if you are right-handed), make a couple of stitches in the folded fabric to secure the thread. Do not put the needle through the side where it will show. Catch the flat fabric and then insert the needle inside the folded edge, sliding it along for about ¼ inch. Then bring the needle out of the fold and catch a couple of threads from the flat fabric immediately opposite the point where the needle emerged from the fold.

Catch stitch
With catch stitch, you work from left to right if you are right-handed. Secure the thread in the folded fabric as described before. Carefully pick up a couple of threads from the flat fabric with the needle pointing from right to left. Then pull the thread gently but firmly through. Position the needle further along the fabric to the right, but still pointing it to the left, and take a horizontal stitch through the folded fabric.

Sheer curtains

Fine, translucent fabrics create a light, sunny effect perfect for summer. They mask the window subtly and cut down strong sunlight, but admit enough light during the day. Sheers can be hung as the only form of curtaining, or combined with heavier curtains which can be drawn to block out the light.

Lace serves the same purpose as sheers: protecting privacy while letting in some light. Some are closely constructed to give a sheer, translucent effect; others have a relatively complex pattern repeated regularly throughout, which may give a very open style with a loose, stringy texture.

Sheer fabrics

Some of the more commonly used sheer fabrics are lace, loose-weave fabrics, cheesecloth and net. Lace used to be handmade, but is now almost exclusively made by machine. Available in nylon, cotton or polyester in a range of elaborate designs, lace is expensive and its crisp texture is best suited to gently gathered curtains. Lace and other sheer fabrics can be difficult to sew and may slip on a sewing machine, so put tissue paper under them.

Loose weaves will add texture to lined curtains and filter harsh sunlight through a window. They are made from most natural fibers and come plain or with a simple design woven in. Cheesecloth is a soft cotton or cotton/polyester blend. This gauzy fabric is loosely woven to give a sheer texture. Although naturally cream-colored, it can be dyed any shade you choose and is cheap enough to be used generously.

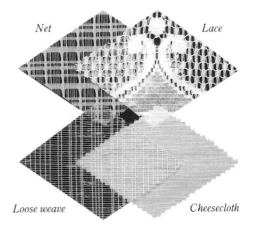

Net *Lace*

Loose weave *Cheesecloth*

The fine fibers in net curtains are knotted or twisted, instead of woven or knitted together like other fabrics, to form a mesh. Usually made from synthetics, such as nylon or polyester, net will diffuse the light coming through the window, and colored net will soften the effect.

CALCULATING FABRIC AMOUNTS

The following calculation applies to all sheer fabrics except lace, which is dealt with separately below.
Width: Multiply the width of your track or rod by 2 to 3, depending on the fulness required. Add ¾ inch for each side hem. Divide the total by the width of the fabric, rounding up to the next full width and allowing for seam allowances for each width join. Divide the total

by the number of curtains needed.
Length: Measure the length of the window area. Add 1½ inches for the top heading and 2 inches for the bottom hem.
For lace:
Width: Measure the width of the window area and multiply by 2 to 3, depending on the fullness required. Add 1 inch for each side hem.
Length: Measure the height of

the window area. Add 2½ inches for the top hem and 2½ inches for the bottom hem.

Making sheer curtains

A finely woven heading tape is available, specially designed for use with sheers and netted fabrics, and if two types of curtain are combined you can hang them on a double curtain track which automatically holds them at the same level and leaves sufficient space between the layers for both curtains to draw easily and separately.

If necessary join fabric widths with French seams: wrong sides together, stitch a flat seam of ¼ inch and trim to ⅛ inch. Turn so that the right sides are facing. Pin and baste two layers together. Machine-stitch ⅜ inch in from the first seam. The raw edges are completely enclosed in the seam and to the back of the fabric; in addition, no stitching line is showing.

Double hems are essential when using sheer fabrics, so that raw edges are concealed in the fold of the hem edge. Turn a ⅜-inch hem to the wrong side along the side edges and press. Turn over again by the same amount. Press and pin the hem in place. Stitch through all the layers.

Next, turn a 1-inch hem to the wrong side at the bottom of the sheer curtain fabric. Turn over again by the same amount to make a double bottom hem. Press the hem, then pin and stitch it in place. When the curtain is hanging, you will find that no raw or uneven

Heading tape
This allows you to draw the sheer fabric into neat pencil pleats. You can then either thread the bars fixed to it onto a narrow rod or elasticized wire, like lace curtains, or hang it like an ordinary curtain by inserting curtain hooks at regular intervals to the pockets, which are also provided.

edge will be visible through the fabric. Finally, turn 1½ inches to the wrong side at the top of the curtain and press in place. Position translucent lightweight net tape wrong side down just below the top of the curtain. Pin in place. Turn under the ends so that they align with the curtain edges and stitch the tape neatly in place.

Making lace curtains

Cut fabric to required size. Avoid joining fabric; rather make separate curtains. If the side edges of the fabric are raw cut edges, turn a double ⅜-inch hem to the wrong side along both edges. Pin and stitch in place.

Along the top raw edge of the fabric, turn under ⅜ inch to the wrong side and press. Turn under a further 2¼ inches and pin and baste in place.

Next, turn under ⅜ inch and a further 2¼-inch hem along the bottom raw edge. Pin and tack in place.

Measure 1¼ inches in from the outer fold at the top of the lace fabric. Machine-stitch

parallel to the top folded edge at this point keeping stitching level. Then machine-stitch 1¼ inches from the bottom folded edge of the lace curtain fabric in the same way.

Machine-stitch parallel to the basting stitches ¼ inch from the inner fold at the top hem. Machine-stitch ¼ inch from the inner fold along the bottom hem. This completes the top and bottom casings. The curtain wire will thread between the two rows of stitching so a self ruffle is formed at the top and the bottom of the lace.

Thread a piece of curtain wire through the top casing and another piece through the bottom casing. The hooks at either end hook on to screw eyes, which are inserted at either side of the window.

Café curtains

Café curtains can be made with an interfaced, scalloped heading and hung from decorative rings which are threaded onto a curtain rod.

Café curtains of this type do not need to be lined, but a lining can protect the main fabric from dirt and exposure to light and helps the curtain to hang elegantly.

Calculating fabric amounts
Curtain fabric: Measure the width of the window. Add 4 inches so that the curtain is not absolutely taut. Add 1¼-inch seam allowances. Measure the length of the area to be curtained. Add 2⅜ inches for the hems.
Facing: The width of the curtain multiplied by 8 inches deep.

Making café curtains
Decide on the size of the scallops at the top of the curtain. Add ⅜ inch to the inner curve for the seam turnings. Using a pair of compasses or a suitably sized plate or bowl, make a semicircular template.

Cut a strip of paper the width of the finished curtain and draw a line to represent the top of the curtain, adding on ⅜ inch for the seam turnings. Fold the paper in half widthways; crease and unfold. Place the template on the center of the strip with the straight edge of the semicircle, aligning with the top line. Draw around the template. Continue along the strip

of paper. Work outward from the center, leaving regular gaps between each semicircle of no less than 1½ inches and finish 1½ inches from each edge.

Cut the semicircles from the paper pattern. Cut out the curtain fabric to the required size. Pin the paper pattern along the top of the curtain fabric on the wrong side. Cut out the scallops and remove the paper pattern. Next, cut out the interfacing. Pin the paper pattern to the top edge of the facing and cut out the scallops, making sure that they match those at the top of the curtain. Turn a double ⅜-inch hem along the unscalloped long edge of the facing. Pin and stitch in place.

Turn a double ⅜-inch hem along the side edges of the curtain fabric. Pin and stitch in place. Turn a double 1-inch hem along the lower edge of the curtain. Pin and stitch the hem in place.

With the right sides together and raw edges matching, pin the scalloped edge of the curtain fabric to the scalloped edge of the facing. Baste along the scalloped edge. Machine-stitch scallops together, ⅜ inch from raw edges. Remove the basting. The raw edges of the facing at the sides will overlap the hemmed edges of the curtain fabric at the sides.

Turn under the raw side edges of the facing and press. Slipstitch the turned-under edges to the hemmed edges of the curtain. Press.

Oversew a curtain ring at the center of the space between two scallops to the wrong side of the curtain. Finish the ends securely.

Cutting out the scallops
Pin the paper pattern along the top of the curtain fabric on the wrong side. Cut out the scallops to match the top edge, and remove the paper pattern.

Neatening the scallops
To reduce the bulk of the material, clip around each curve and across the corners of the scallops. Turn the corners right side out and press them carefully.

Adding the curtain rings
Oversew each ring firmly to the center of the space between the scallops, on the wrong side of the curtain. Finish the ends securely and neatly.

Binding curtain edges

Binding is a simple but effective finish which not only secures curtain edges more firmly, but also gives them a professional look. The bias binding purchased in a millinery shop is made from a fairly lightweight material, and is more suitable for edging smaller items – table mats, napkins and table-cloths – than for use with larger items and heavier materials. For curtains and other large items, it is best to make bias strips out of a fabric which is of a similar weight to the item to be bound, as this will give it a much better finish. If the material is striped or checked, the bias strips, being cut diagonally on the fabric, will create a special effect. A simple method of making these bias strips is given below.

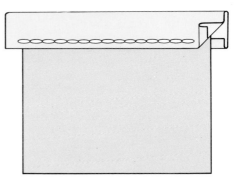

Applying binding with a sewing machine
Fold the bias binding, wrong side down, over the raw edge of the fabric to be bound, and press. Baste in place and then machine-stitch through the fabric and the two folds of binding, close to the edge of the binding. Remove the basting.

Applying binding by hand

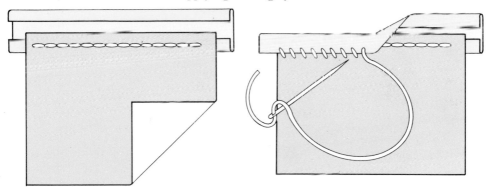

1 *Open one folded edge of the bias binding and match this edge to the raw edge of the fabric to be bound, right sides together. Pin and stitch them together down the fold line of the binding.*

2 *Refold the binding and turn it over to the wrong side of the fabric, enclosing the raw edge. Pin in place and slip stitch the second folded edge of the binding to the fabric along the first line of stitching.*

FINDING THE BIAS OF A PIECE OF FABRIC

Bias binding is used to strengthen raw edges and to add a decorative finishing touch. Because it is cut on the bias, it has more give than binding cut on the straight grain.

To find the bias of a piece of fabric, fold a straight raw edge diagonally so that it is parallel to the selvage of the fabric. This fold line is the bias line.

Mark out 1½-inch strips parallel to the bias line, and cut them out. To join the strips, place two with right sides together and at right angles to each other. The raw edges will be parallel and there will be two triangular corners. Pin and stitch the seam ¼ inch from the raw edges. Open the seam out flat and press. Trim the corners.

Window treatments

A cornice is a stiff, paneled heading to curtains, unlike the valance, which is draped. It must be based on a rigid support for the fabric covering, which may be a sturdy wooden "box" mounted above the windows or a specially made stiffening designed as an interlining to fabric for this type of effect. Self-adhesive backing is available, which makes the work of stiffening the fabric quite simple, or you can use traditional buckram, a woven cloth that is treated to maintain rigidity, in combination with a heavy interlining.

Because the cornice is rigid you can cut the lower edge to any shape – regular scallops or zigzags, or a broad arc at the center of the window, sweeping down to flat panels at either side over the drawn-back curtains. The simplest way to apply trimmings is to stick on braid or fancy edging with a fabric adhesive after the cornice has been made up.

There is a variety of fabric window treatments. They can either take the form of a gathered valance, or be treated with a stiffener. Valance cornices can be hung from a shelf above the window or suspended from a second curtain track in front of the main one. Another type of cornice, sometimes known as a draped swag, is made up of fabric draped across the top of the window and tails decorating the edge. This type of cornice looks very effective on large windows, but takes up a lot of fabric. So before you commit yourself by buying material, it is best to experiment with a sheet to find out approximately how much you will need to get the effect you require.

It is also possible to combine the strength of a wooden or hardboard cornice construction with the elegance of a fabric design to produce a fabric-covered wooden cornice. This can either have a simple rectangular shape or have curved edges to give an effect similar to a valanced cornice. The fabric can either match or contrast with the curtain material.

Cornices
To hide the heading and give interest to the top of the curtain, you can use a cornice. Cornices allow you to fit the curtain track in two pieces with an overlap at the center. They are also useful to give two adjacent windows a unified look.

Hardboard cornice

Valance cornice

Fabric-covered wooden cornice

Draped swag

Cornice trimmings (left)

The simplest way to apply trimmings is to stick on braid or fancy edging with a fabric adhesive after the cornice has been made up.

Fitting the cornice to the window (below)

The fabric cornice is mounted onto a wooden cornice board which has small side boards (returns) attached at each end (below). The cornice board is fitted above the window with angle irons and is positioned so that the top of the board will be level with the top of the cornice. Attach the cornice with touch-and-close tape or with tacks along the top of the cornice and front and side edges of the board.

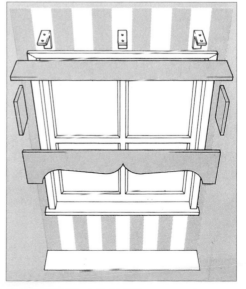

Construction of cornices

Cut all the materials to shape, plus ½ inch for turnings. Stitch the interlining to the fabric. Baste the stiffening to the fabric and interlining. Turn the fabric over the stiffening and glue in place. Stitch the lining to the back of the cornice.

Curtain valances

A deep ruffle of fabric gives a finished look to the top of a window, framing the proportions of the window and curtaining and providing the final disguise for the curtain track. As with the main curtains, the valance can be hung on a track or rod, depending on the weight of fabric, and the fixtures can be mounted on a narrow, shelf-like projection fitted above the window frame to fall cleanly and loosely over the curtain heading. Decide on the depth and decorative treatment of the valance after the main curtains are hung. To create a stylish effect the valance should be of the same fabric as the curtains. A contrast or coordinate will look odd unless well linked to other furnishings.

Calculating fabric amounts

Width: Measure the width of the window area and multiply by 1½ to 3 times, depending on the fulness required. Add 1 inch for each side hem allowance.

Depth: Divide the curtain drop by 6; add 1 inch for the lower hem allowance and 1½ inches for the top hem allowance.

A coordinated finish
A deep ruffle of fabric gives a finished look to the top of a window and disguises the curtain track.

Making a curtain valance

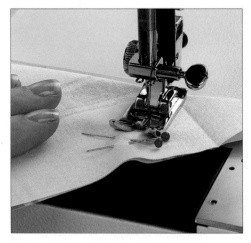

1 *Cut fabric to required size. Press 1-inch hems at sides and lower edge. Unfold hems and fold corners diagonally, right sides together. Stitch at right angles to the fold from the corner crease to ³/₈ inch from the edge.*

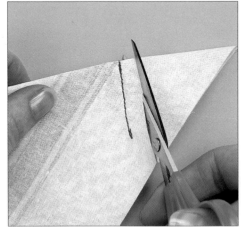

2 *Cut off the corner ³/₈ inch away from the stitching, using a pair of very sharp scissors. Then turn the fabric right side out and carefully poke out the new corner with the closed scissors.*

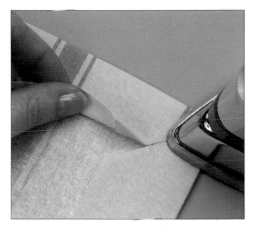

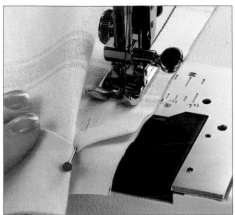

3 Press the seam flat with a hot iron. Repeat the same process for the other bottom corner. Having done this, then trim ⅕ inch from both the side and the lower edges of the lining if you are doing a sewn-in lining, and place the valance fabric and the lining with their right sides together.

4 Next, align the side raw edges of the valance hem. Pin them firmly together. You will find that the lining fabric will overlap the valance fabric at the corners. Machine-stitch carefully down both sides of the valance, approximately ⅜ inch in from the raw edges of the fabric.

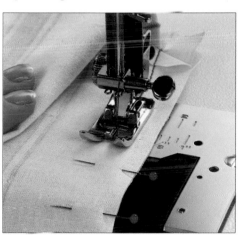

5 Now stitch the bottom edge of the valance lining carefully to the valance hem approximately ⅜ inch away from the raw edges of the fabric, in the same way as you did for the edges. Then snip off the two bottom corners of the valance lining diagonally with a pair of sharp scissors to reduce the bulk, making sure that you do not cut too close to the stitching. Having done that, turn the joined pieces right side out and press the seams. Turn the top of the valance fabric 1½ inches to the wrong side. It should fold over at the top edge of the lining, concealing the raw edge. Press, pin and sew the fabric neatly in place.

6 With the wrong sides facing each other, pin the heading tape firmly to the top edge of the valance. Next, turn under the side edges of the heading tape to align precisely with the fabric. Knot the cords of the heading tape firmly at one end. Then stitch this same short side, and then both long sides of the heading tape. At this stage, leave the cords free at the other end of the tape so that you can gather the valance. When you have gathered the valance to the right width, tie the loose cords neatly together. Finally, insert the curtain hooks at regular intervals along the tape, and hang the valance.

Shades

Practical and economical, shades are often chosen for their functional advantages. Because they do not obstruct the window area in the same way as draped or billowing curtains, they are the ideal choice for windows situated above a desk, countertop or sink, or in a "working" area such as a bathroom or playroom. They are also particularly suitable for rooms which tend to be dark, as they do not cut out as much of the light when they are pulled up to the top of the window. You can add trimmings and decorations as you please.

Fabrics for shades

Roman shades hang flat when pulled down, but draw up into horizontal pleats. They should be made from a reasonably substantial fabric, but not one with a stiffened finish. Any good-quality, curtain-weight cotton is suitable. Austrian and festoon shades have a gracefully swagged appearance. Both types look very pretty if made from fabrics such as lightweight voile, net, lace or fine cotton.

A cottage shade is ruched vertically across the window, covering half the window area. Light- or medium-weight fabrics are suited to this simple effect – attractive printed cottons and lightly embossed or textured fabrics for solid color and pattern; sheers, nets and laces for translucency; broderie anglaise and other machine-embroidered fabrics for a pretty, fancy finish. A roller shade should be made from a firm fabric which hangs smoothly and rolls up evenly. Roller-shade kits are not expensive and easy to make up.

Choosing the right type of shade fabric
Light shining in through a window or darkness outside will alter the look of fabric used for shades. See the effect of light and darkness on an all-over miniprint with a dark background (left), a plain cotton seersucker (center), and a lightweight flocked voile (right).

EFFECTS WITH SHADES

Shades offer a range of stylish and versatile window treatments, whether used as the only window covering or teamed with curtains. The look can vary from plain and simple to exotic, according to the type of shade you prefer and your choice of fabric and trimmings. Choose the most appropriate style for the effect you wish to create – a Roman shade for a smart graphic effect; a ruffled Austrian shade for a pretty look; a festoon shade for sumptuous elegance. For simpler styling, a permanent half-length cottage shade blocks a drab view or protects your privacy if the window is overlooked. A basic roller shade is just a flat length of fabric, but clever choice of color and pattern or an inventive way with trimmings and edgings can enliven the plain construction of the shade.

Measuring and positioning shades

Roman, Austrian and festoon shades are usually attached to a wooden batten, so that the screw eyes holding the cords which draw up the shade can be fixed to the underside of the batten. Roman shades are attached directly to the front face of the batten, but Austrian and festoon shades have a curtain heading tape which can be hung from a curtain track mounted on the batten, giving extra support to the weight of the fabric and making it easy to remove the shades for washing or cleaning. It is also possible to buy a special shade track which incorporates the "eyes" for the cord system, thus making the batten unnecessary.

Shades can be positioned inside or outside the window recess. If the shade is teamed with curtains, hang it inside the recess and make sure that it will not catch on the window fittings. A cottage shade is positioned on the window and need not extend beyond the frame. A roller shade hangs from brackets which you can fix to the frame or outside it.

The way you hang any shade may affect the finished size. Before you measure up and buy fabric, make sure that it is feasible to mount brackets or battens at the position where you want the shade to hang in relation to the window itself.

Calculating fabric amounts

For a Roman shade, add 1½ inches to the width for the side hems and 4½ inches to the length for the bottom and top turnings.

For an Austrian shade, measure the track length and multiply by 1½ to 2½, depending on the type of heading tape you have chosen. Make a small allowance for the side hems and joins in the fabric. For a festoon shade, calculate the fabric width as for the Austrian shade.

For a cottage shade, measure the area of window to be covered and add 1½ inches to the width for the side hems. To the length, add enough to make a casing for the curtain wires or rods on which the shade is threaded.

For a roller shade, add ¾ inch to the width for the side hems (ready-stiffened fabrics that will not fray need no hems) and add 12 to 13½ inches to the measured length to allow for a lath channel and attachment to be fitted to the roller.

Tape requirements

To calculate how much tape is needed, make a scale drawing of the shade and work out how many vertical tapes should be evenly spaced across the width to draw it up neatly. You must make sure that you position tapes down either side of the shade close to the edge; while those in between should be spaced equally across the width of the gathered shade no more than 12 inches apart.

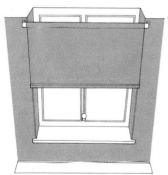

Roller shade
A roller shade can be either mounted inside the window recess, or outside, as shown here, when a batten is not required.

Roman shade
A Roman shade can look attractive when mounted within the window recess, with decorative tied-back curtains mounted outside.

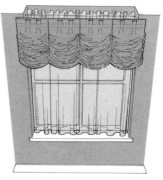

Austrian shade
Fitted outside the window recess, they are effective when used in combination with a lace curtain hung within the recess.

Equipment for roller shades

Fabric stiffener

A roller-shade kit consists of a spring-loaded roller, a wooden lath or plastic bar for the bottom of the shade, a pull cord and the necessary fixings and screws. The roller can be made of either aluminum or wood. The fabric for the shade is often bought separately. Kits are sold in a range of sizes – buy one slightly larger than you need so that you can cut it down to the required dimensions.

Roller

Roller-shade kit
These easy-to-use roller-shade kits can be purchased at home centers. They come in several sizes, and it is best to buy one a little larger than you need.

Brackets

End caps

Pull cord

Cord knob

Assembling roller shades

First check the roller length that you will need. Take into account the projecting brads that fit onto the ends of the roller – they usually take up about 1 inch at each end. Depending on the design of the brackets, you may also need a little space to allow for the fixing screws.

When you attach the brackets to the frame, the one with the round hole should go on the right, the one with the slot on the left. Cut the roller to the correct length at the non-spring end. Make sure that you cut it square by measuring the length in several places, marking it all the way around, and using a fine-toothed saw, such as a back saw, for wood, or a hacksaw for aluminum.

Having cut it to the required length, smooth off the cut end with sandpaper and attach the fixing to the roller. On an aluminum roller this means simply pushing on the end caps.

To prepare the material, cut it to the right size, iron it flat and stiffen it. The easiest and quickest way to do this is to use a spray can stiffener. If you prefer not to use aerosols because of the risk of environmental damage, make a solution of stiffener and water and soak the fabric carefully according to the manufacturer's instructions.

MEASURING FOR ROLLER SHADES

First decide whether you want the shade to hang inside or outside the window recess. If you are going to fit it inside, measure the width of the recess and then subtract an amount to allow for the shade fixings on either side. If you are installing the shade outside the recess, allow for an overlap of at least 2 inches on each side. Measure the length from where you want to fix the shade to the bottom when fully lowered.

Assembling a roller shade

1 *When assembling a wooden roller, carefully drill a pilot hole for the fixing pin, push on the end caps and tap the pin home.*

2 *Mark the bracket positions on the window frame, with a pencil, using a carpenter's level to ensure that the shade will be level.*

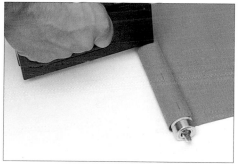

3 *Attaching the bar at the bottom of the fabric is usually simple. Cut it about 3/8 inch shorter than the shade and either glue it to the fabric or fit it into a pocket sewn along the bottom edge. Screw the holder for the pull cord to the center of the bar.*

4 *With aluminum rollers, the material either fits into a slot in the roller or is secured with screw clips. With wooden rollers, the best method is first to glue the fabric to the roller to keep it in the right position and then to set it permanently with tacks or staples.*

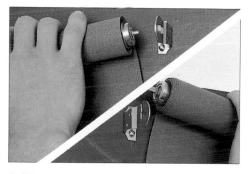

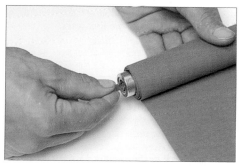

5 *When the fabric is attached, roll it up, put the roller on the brackets, and tension the spring so that it rolls and unrolls properly.*

6 *If the tension is wrong, unhook the non-spring end, turn the roller by hand to increase or decrease the tension, and refit it to the bracket.*

Roman shades

A Roman shade hangs flat against the window when drawn down and folds into deep, horizontal pleats as it is raised. Roman shades give an elegant, tailored look to the room, but are not difficult to make, particularly if you use a shade tape with woven-in loops or rings already attached. This fixes the size of the pleats, so if you wish to create deeper or narrower folds, you can machine-stitch plain tapes down the back of the shade and sew on small curtain rings by hand.

The geometric styling of the shade is particularly suited to strong colors and definite patterns, but when choosing patterned fabrics, bear in mind that the pleating will interrupt any large motifs or one-directional designs. All-over miniprints are ideal and you can find these in good, medium-weight cottons which are firmly woven and will fold crisply when drawn up. Plain, bold colors also create a good effect – clean lines are the essential feature here.

Before cutting out the shade fabric, work out the position for the top batten from which the shade will be hung. Measure the length from the top edge of the batten position to the required finished shade length. Then add the hem allowances to the length before cutting out. The cords are threaded across the top edge and then down the shade.

Calculating fabric amounts

Measure the window drop. Add 5½ inches for hems and a little extra for making horizontal tucks in the fabric. Measure the width of the window area. Add 2⅜ inches for side hems. Allow extra for seams if you are joining widths.

Roman shade
Choose fabric to reflect the mood of the shade. A small, geometric print goes well with the clear, uncluttered lines of the otherwise plain Roman shade.

FITTING TAPES TO A ROMAN SHADE

There are various types of shade tape but they all work on the same principle. The tape has rings or loops placed at regular intervals along it. A cord ties into the lowest ring or loop and threads up through the other rings or loops which pull up to form the back folds of the shade when the cord is pulled. The tape shown on the right has loops ready sewn and these are suitable for both Roman and Austrian shades (page 182).

Measure the width of the shade and divide the amount by 12 inches, rounding up or down

to the nearest whole number. This will give the number of sections between the vertical tapes. Fold the shade into the appropriate number of sections and press in creases at folds as guide lines for the tapes. Cut the tapes to fit over the side hems and creases, making sure that each lower ring or loop is 4¾ inches up from the edge.

Tie the cord firmly to the lowest ring or loop on the first tape. Thread the cord up through the ring or loops, then across the top to the side edge and down the length of the

shade. Make sure that the edge with the loose cord is the edge from which you wish to pull the shade. Thread cords through all the tapes in this way, each time taking the cord across the top edge and down the side edge of the shade.

Making a Roman shade

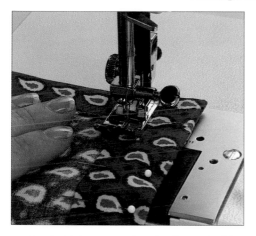

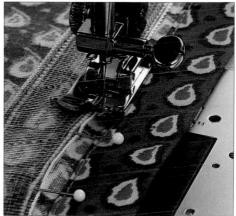

1 *Cut the fabric to the required size. Turn a double ½-inch hem to the wrong side along each side edge. Pin, baste and stitch. Turn a double 1-inch hem along the top edge of the shade. Pin, baste and stitch. Fold and press the fabric at 10 to 12 inch intervals across the width to provide guide lines for positioning the vertical tapes.*

2 *Cut strips of looped shade tape to the length of the shade plus ⅜ inch. Pin, baste and stitch the first strip close to the side hem, turning under ⅜ inch at the top. Stitch the tapes down the back of the shade following the fold lines, making sure that all the loops in the tapes line up horizontally right across the width of the shade.*

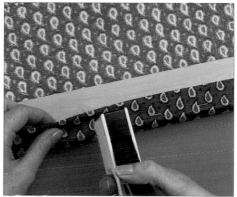

3 *Across the bottom of the shade, turn and press ⅜ inch, then fold up a 2-inch hem. Pin, baste and stitch to form a casing hem. Slot the wooden lath through the casing and slip-stitch the hem ends together. To help form neat, tailored folds when the finished shade is drawn up into pleats, baste and stitch ⅛ inch-deep horizontal tucks across the width of the shade to correspond to alternate rows of loops on the vertical tapes. Make the first tuck at the level of the second loop from the bottom of the shade (excluding the casing hem).*

4 *To make the tuck, fold and press the fabric wrong sides together and stitch ⅛ inch from the fold. Press the folds accurately, following the straight grain of the fabric, to ensure that they will make clean, evenly spaced horizontal lines across the shade when it is hung. Cut the wooden batten to the width of the shade. Spread out the shade right side down and place the batten across the top edge. Turn the top hem over onto the broad side of the batten and staple or baste across the width. This completes the shade and it is now ready to be fitted.*

Austrian shades

An Austrian shade creates remarkable impact with its loosely folded swags. The fullness comes from a gathered or pleated heading combined with the generous looping as the shade is drawn up. Light- and medium-weight cottons in bright colors or patterns have a sunny or vivid effect. A lightly textured or satinized surface provides an extra dimension, and sheers are also excellent, giving a beautifully softened look. Alternatively the shade can be made of a heavyweight fabric, which creates a more sculptured effect. The tapes should be about 12 inches apart when the shade is gathered, although the distance can be varied to suit the shape and size of the window.

Calculating fabric amounts

Length: Measure the window drop. Add 2⅜ inches for hem allowances.
Width: Measure the width of the window and multiply by 2 to 2½ to allow enough fabric width to form heading pleats. Add 1½ inches for side hem allowances.

Austrian shade
Bright yellow translucent fabric creates a sunny aspect, showing an Austrian shade to best effect. In contrast, the molded effect of a heavier fabric can be emphasized if the material has a surface sheen.

Making an Austrian shade

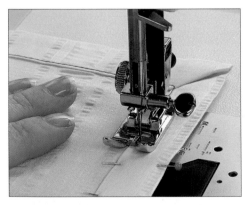

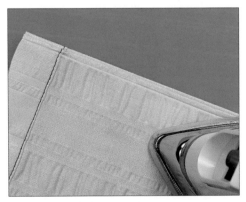

1 *Along the bottom and both sides of the fabric, turn a double ¾-inch hem to the wrong side. Miter the corners. Pin, baste and stitch the hems in place. Cut strips of looped shade tape to the length of the shade plus ⅜ inch. These strips of tape are to be positioned down the length of the shade at regularly spaced intervals of about 24 inches across the width.*

2 *Make sure that there is a loop ⅜ inch up from the bottom of each length of tape and that the strips are matched exactly so that when in position the loops will line up horizontally across the shade. Fold the fabric vertically accordian fashion at approximately 24-inch intervals across the width and press. The fold lines provide a guide for positioning the vertical tapes.*

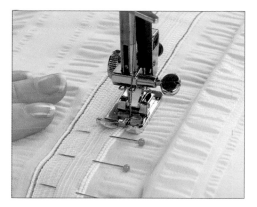

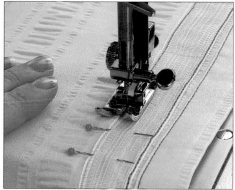

3 *If there are any seams in the fabric, arrange for them to be covered by the tape, but do not allow the spacing between the vertical strips to become irregular. Place the first length of tape down the length of the shade 1 inch from the side edge, close to the side hem. Turn the end of the tape under for ³/₈ inch at the hem edge, pin, baste and stitch down both edges of the tape, working both lines of stitching in the same direction so the tape does not pucker. Continue stitching the tapes at regular intervals across the shade.*

4 *As the tapes are positioned, check that the loops are matched down each length to line up horizontally and conceal any seams under the tapes. Turn ³/₄ inch of fabric to the wrong side across the top of the shade and press. Pin and baste the heading tape across the top of the shade to cover the raw edge of the turning. Stitch the heading tape in place. Then gather or pleat the heading tape until the shade is the width of the window. Thread the cords through the loops in the vertical tapes before mounting the shade in place.*

Adding a ruffle to shades

To make the shade more opulent, a ruffle of purchased eyelet or lace edging or a fabric ruffle can be added to the side and lower edges. There are many types of ready-made fancy edgings available which need only be hand- or machine-stitched to a seamline or hem. They can be bought in most fabric stores.

First decide the required finished ruffle depth and trim this amount plus 1 inch from the appropriate edges of the shade. For the ruffle length, allow 1½ times the length of the shade edges. For a double fabric ruffle, allow twice the required finished depth plus 1¼ inches for the depth of the ruffle.

Cut and join enough strips to make the ruffle the length you require. Then gather up the edge of the ruffle so that it fits the shade, arranging extra gathers at the corners of the shade. With right sides facing, stitch the ruffle to the edge, taking ⁵/₈-inch seams. Finally, trim the seam to ³/₈ inch and zigzag-stitch the raw edges together.

Making the shade more opulent
The decorative styling can be further elaborated by the addition of a ruffle across the bottom of the shade, even running the length of both sides as well for a really sumptuous finish. Ruffles can be bought in different widths and small, delicate patterns or loosely structured, chunky designs. These ready-made decorative trims have a firm binding along one edge, which you can stitch to the fabric by hand or machine.

Balloon shades

A balloon shade is similar to an Austrian shade, but although the swags are made by drawing up the fabric on a similar cording system, the balloon shade has additional ruching which keeps its effect even when the shade is fully let down. Narrow curtain heading tape is used for the vertical tapes on the shade and it is drawn up to make even gathers which remain permanently in place down the length. Small split curtain rings are inserted at regular intervals to accommodate the cording system.

The ruched finish works extremely well in light- and medium-weight fabrics – sheer, slightly textured or with a shiny surface. A translucent fabric creates romantic styling, and a lightweight shade can be teamed with heavily draped, floor-length curtains to create a luxurious effect. If the shade is used alone, a heavier fabric and rich, strong color emphasize warmth and privacy in the room when the shade is down.

Calculating fabric amounts

Length: Measure the window drop and multiply by 1½ for medium-weight or 3 for lightweight fabrics. Allow 2 inches for the top turning and the ruffle seam.
Width: Measure the width of the window area and multiply by 1¼ for medium-weight or 1½ for lightweight and sheer fabrics. Add 1½ inches for side hems and ⅜-inch seam allowances if you are seaming several widths of fabric together.

For the ruffle: You need enough 8 inch-deep strips of fabric to make up one long strip 1½ times the width of the shade fabric. You can make the ruffle out of the same material as the shade, or buy a ready-made trimming.

Balloon shade
Made from a filmy, translucent material, balloon shades can create a luxurious atmosphere. The fabric filters the light coolly, a boon on a hot summer day.

Double ruffle
The ruffle fitted to the balloon shade pictured left is a double ruffle. It is formed from a strip of fabric folded in half along its length. To finish the short ends neatly, fold the fabric in half lengthways with the right sides facing each other, baste and stitch across each end, then turn the material right side out once again, and press it carefully. Next, either hand-sew or machine-stitch two rows of stitches along the length of the fabric, and gather the material to the required length. Remember to allow some extra fullness at the corner, if necessary, so that the ruffle will not look skimpy as it turns the corner. The right side of the fabric shows on both sides of a double ruffle.

Making a balloon shade

1 *Turn a double ¾-inch hem down each side. To make the ruffle, fold the fabric lengthwise, right sides together, with the raw edges matched. Stitch a ⅜-inch seam across both short ends. Turn right side out and press. Work two rows of gathering stitches through both layers of fabric along the top edge of the ruffle. Pull until the ruffle equals the shade width. Knot the threads together.*

2 *Right sides together, align the raw edge of the ruffle with the bottom edge of the fabric. Stitch the ruffle in place. Press the ruffle seam upward on to the wrong side. Fold the fabric at intervals of 10 to 16 inches across the width and press. This provides guide lines for positioning the heading tape. The tape should be spaced evenly and positioned over the side hems and any seams joining fabric widths.*

3 *Cut the appropriate number of strips of tape to the length of the shade (excluding ruffle) plus ⅜ inch. Pin lengths of tape in position following the fold lines, turning under ⅜ inch to neaten the ends at the seamline of the ruffle. Beginning with the tape at the side hem, baste and then stitch each length of tape in place. Press the fabric from the wrong side, using a steam iron.*

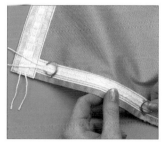

4 *Turn 1½ inches of fabric across the top of the shade. Position heading tape to cover the raw edge. Stitch in place, but keep the gathering cords clear of the horizontal stitching line on heading tape. Tuck the raw ends of tape under to neaten.*

5 *Slot small curtain rings into the vertical lengths of tape at intervals of about 8 inches. The top rings should be just below the heading and the bottom rings about 4 inches from the bottom of the shade. Space them so that the rings line up horizontally.*

6 *Pull the cords to gather up the shade evenly to the required drop. Tie off the cords. Hand-stitch neatly just below each ring to secure the cords to the fabric. Gather the heading tape at the top of the shade to the required width. Thread the cords through the rings.*

TAPES FOR BALLOON SHADES

Although balloon shades do not require much fullness in width, they may have a good deal of fullness lengthwise. The tapes for balloon shades should be about 12 inches apart when the shades are gathered, although this can be varied. On tapes with loops or rings attached make sure that one is positioned near the lower edge and that they line up horizontally on each tape.

Cottage shade

This pretty half-length shade effectively disguises an ugly window, or blocks out an undesirable view, but it is a permanent feature, suitable for a bathroom or small landing window, for example, where you do not need to vary the amount of light entering. It can be mounted on curtain wire or on narrow, rounded or flattened curtain rod, threaded through a casing on the fabric at top and bottom and attached to the window frame on either side. A valance at the top completes the effect.

Calculating fabric amounts

This shade is made from one piece of fabric and does not require a tuck to be made for the wire. It is therefore ideal if you wish to use a patterned fabric.

Length: Measure the window drop. Add 1¼ inches for the hem allowance and 2½ inches for making the top casing.

Width: Measure the width of the window area. Add on 1¼ to 1½ times width for fullness and ¾ inch for each side hem.

A traditional touch
The length of the valance can vary between a quarter to half of the shade's length.

Making a cottage shade

1 *Cut the shade fabric to the required size. Place fabric face down and turn a double ³⁄₈-inch hem along both of the side edges of the shade. Pin, baste and stitch in place. With the fabric still face down, turn a double ½-inch hem along the lower edge of the shade. Pin, baste and stitch in place.*

2 *Wrong sides together, turn under the top of the shade by ³⁄₈ inch then another 2 inches to make a double hem. Press in the fold. Pin, baste and sew in place ¼ inch from the inner edge. This will form the casing for the wire, which is inserted to make sure that the shade hangs evenly.*

3 *Measure 1¼ inches down from the fold at the top of the shade. Pin, baste and stitch across the width of the shade at this point. Make sure that this line of stitching is parallel to the first line of casing stitching.*

4 *Trim the curtain wire to the correct length. It will need to be slightly shorter than the distance between the hooks so that it is held taut. Screw eyes into the ends of wire and thread the wire through the casing.*

MAKING AN UNLINED VALANCE

Traditionally, a cottage shade over the lower half of the window is given a finished look by the addition of a short valance at the top. If you choose a print fabric with a clearly defined border section, this border used as the valance makes a pretty link between the top of the window and the bottom of the cottage shade. The valance is traditionally unlined. It is cut to the same width as the shade, and its length may vary between a quarter to half of the shade length, depending upon the size of the window. Add on the same top and bottom hem allowances as on the shade. The valance is made in the same way as the shade. Position the hooks, which will hold the curtain wire, about 1¼ inches down from the top of a recessed window. This will allow the fabric ruffle at the top of the curtain to stand up above the wire.

A cottagey print in glazed cotton is a highly suitable fabric choice; the treatment also lends itself to sheers or fancy fabrics such as Swiss muslin or eyelet.

ALTERNATIVES TO HAND-STITCHING

There may be occasions when you need to use a non-sew alternative to hand stitching. This may be for sheer speed, when you need to finish an item quickly and do not have time to hand stitch the hem, or as a temporary measure, which will later be replaced with stitching.

Fusible bonding is a web-like strip of adhesive, which is placed between the two fabric layers of a hem. The hem is then pressed to activate the adhesive which glues the hem in place. The bonding strip is about 1 inch wide; when used at that width it will fasten the hem securely, but may also stiffen the hem. To avoid the stiffening effect, cut the bonding into ¼ inch-wide strips and use these near the top of the hem allowance. This may not be quite as secure as the full width bonding when the item is laundered, but it will lessen the stiffening effect. Always try a test hem on spare fabric to check the finish which may vary on different fabrics.

Tacking tape is a very narrow sticky tape which has adhesive on both sides. This is purely a temporary measure, used to hold fabric in place before stitching. It can be very convenient if you wish to hang curtains to test the length before stitching the hem. The tape can be used to hold the trial hem in place, and can then be adjusted to correct the hem level while the curtains are hanging. Tacking tape can also be used as an alternative to basting where two wrong sides need holding together.

Trimmings for curtains and shades

Curtains and shades are often a major feature of the room, and it is wise to consider carefully the overall effect before applying any decorative details; if you overdo the trimming it may appear fussy or out of keeping with the rest of the décor once the curtains or shades are in place.

Traditional styles, such as dense, floor-length drapes in velvet or an elegantly satinized finish, benefit from furnishing-weight braid trims, fringes or tassels. These finishes look especially effective when applied to a matching valance.

A well-chosen border, ruffle or decorative edging can transform a plain shade into an interesting focal point, adding textural detail or contrast color which can dress up an inexpensive fabric and provide the perfect finishing touch.

The clean lines of a Roman shade require an unfussy trimming, such as a deep fabric border or flat braid stitched to the sides and hem, or across the pleats where it must be perfectly aligned. The softer styling of Austrian and balloon shades suggests ribbon trims, decorative tassels, bobbles or fringes to edge the bottom hem, or a softly ruched ruffle echoing the swagged effect of the shade. Cottage shades can be smart and simple or heavily ruffled and ornamented.

Trims and edgings for curtains
Tassels and fringes (right) make a luxurious finish for heavy, traditional-style drapes in fabrics such as velvet, chintz or damask. Many different styles are available in ready-made trims: silky textures or chunkier cotton trims; thick, short tassels or long and elegant fringes. These can be used on their own to make attractive tie-backs, or for edging on a wide, self-fabric tie-back. They also make a sculptured edging for valances or cornices. Stiff cornices can alternatively be decoratively finished with a matching or contrasting wallpaper border (above).

Trimmings for shades

The crisp lines of a roller or Roman shade are suited to decorative braid trims (far left), embossed and subtly colored, or sharply defined with bright motifs. Tasseled edgings (left) neatly finish the looped hem of an Austrian or balloon shade, complemented by silky pull cords hung with ornamental tassels, bobbles, or wooden acorns (below).

CHAPTER SEVEN

SEWING PROJECTS

Making your own sewing projects can add flair and originality to the overall décor of your home. Bedding, table linens and pillows can be given a lift with ruffles, gathers, trimmings and pleats. Modern patterned fabrics can make otherwise plain furnishings look bright and cheerful, or they can be combined for a subtly coordinated effect. Techniques such as quilting, embroidery and appliqué can produce unique and beautiful household items which will be treasured in years to come, while being practical articles for every day use.

Fabrics

The range of fabrics and trimmings is bewildering, and it is best to think through the overall effect you want to achieve before buying. For example, if you are making quilt covers, consider the furnishings in the rest of the room. Are there patterned materials elsewhere which would make a plain fabric a good choice? Or are you confident that you can mix patterns to the best advantage? If the décor is already plain and simple, would country-style ruffles or jazzy fabric be the better choice to give it more zest?

Basic bedlinen

The availability of extra-wide sheeting fabric has made it a very practical proposition to sew sheets, pillowcases and quilt covers in your own choice of color and pattern. Sheeting looks cheerful in bright colors, stunning in rich, deep hues, fresh and restful in pastels or subtly subdued designs. Polyester/cotton blends are the most practical form of sheeting.

Pillowcases use little fabric, and this is one occasion when you can get away with using printed dress fabrics to create an attractive toning or contrasting pillowcase – or just add a pretty print ruffle or deep lace border to a plain-colored sheeting pillowcase for a personal finishing touch.

Bedspreads

Bedspreads range from the easy, informal throw spread or lightweight, quilt-style comforter to a neat, fitted cover with a deep ruffle or boxed corner.

Cotton and cotton/synthetic blends are also a good choice for washable spreads. For a more traditional effect there is a wide range of chintzes, brocades or glistening velvets; hard-wearing, informal styles come from brightly colored canvases or various weights of corduroy. Linen and light wool fabrics are also a possibility, but check the cleaning instructions carefully. Practical, silk-look

Bedlinen
White bedlinen still has an inviting look despite the recent proliferation of fabric colors and patterns. Soft quilting and deep ruffling with a discreet color contrast creates luxurious styling by day or night.

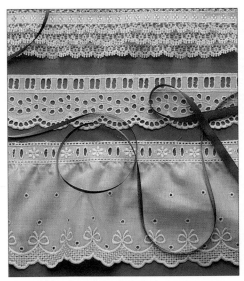

Trimmings
Lace, eyelet embroidery and shiny ribbons make beautiful decorations for traditional-style bedlinen in white or pastel colors, edging a pillowcase or a sheet turn-down.

synthetics can make a luxurious effect. Laces and sheers need simple styling – as a plain throw spread or fitted cover with a neat gathered ruffle.

Trimmings and fastenings for washable fabrics should also be washable, and colorfast. Check for possible shrinkage and deal with this before using. If you plan to add fabric trimmings, wash all the fabric first. Braids, ribbons, lace or fringe should be washed before they are attached, unless you are sure that they are colorfast and shrinkproof.

Tablecloths and fabric napkins

These are not necessities of modern living, but they set a mood and style – bright and fresh or elegant and luxurious – which can be enjoyed whether you are entertaining twenty people or dining alone. Alternatively, you may prefer to use table mats made from your own choice of fabric, or to combine mats with a tablecloth to create a fully coordinated effect. Table mats are simply constructed and can be made as plain or elaborate as you wish.

For practical tablecloths choose washable fabrics – many cotton/synthetic blends are also permanent press which is conveniently labor-saving. Solid colors lend themselves to smooth, easy styling and can be enlivened with decorative trimmings, appliqué and embroidery. A lawn, seersucker or plain-weave cotton is a suitable choice.

Pillows

Pillows are for comfort and are the best means of highlighting and adding contrast to a room scheme. You can let your imagination run wild with pillows because they can be of any shape, with an outer cover of almost any type of fabric, and as plain or elaborately decorative as you wish.

The great thing about pillows is that you can plan them to coordinate with a new scheme of room decoration, or just make them up as you have time and simply add to your collection whenever an appealing small piece of fabric comes your way. A jumble of pretty pillows gives your familiar furnishings a whole new and different look.

Table linen
A cheerful coordinating print will enliven plain dishes and flatware.

Pillow fabrics
Fabric remnants can be used for individual pillows, and careful choice of different, but complementary, fabric will give a lively effect.

DUST RUFFLES

A dust ruffle neatly and attractively covers the sides and foot end of the bed frame (page 202). It can be designed to go with the sheets and bedspread or to match the other furnishings in the room.

The dust ruffle can be made in one of three ways. A tailored style with inverted pleats at the corners uses the least fabric and gives the made-up bed a crisp, smart appearance. Pleated dust ruffles are well suited to traditional interiors and go well with quilts and down comforters. Ruffled dust ruffles can also be used with quilts or comforters and add a country ambience to the bedroom. Bedlinens and medium-weight cottons or synthetic fabrics are good for ruffling and fine pleats. Heavier chintzes and slubbed or textured-weave fabrics can be used, but these are best applied to the corner-pleated version, as they will not look well if gathered into a ruffle.

Types of fabric

Cotton is a natural fiber and is woven into a variety of fabrics. It can be blended with synthetic fibers. Cotton and cotton blends come with a variety of finishes, such as crêpe, chintz and seersucker, or with a pattern woven into the fabric – herringbone or gingham, for instance. Cotton takes printed patterns well, and is easy to work with and to launder, although it may shrink when washed and fade in harsh sunlight.

Pure silk is luxurious but extremely expensive. Silk blended with other fibers is more reasonable, and 100 percent synthetic silk substitutes cost a fraction of the price, while offering a comparable look. Moiré gives a wavy, watermark effect to silk, triacetate and acetate fabrics at the printing stage. It looks shiny and luxurious, although synthetic types tend to fray and are slippery to work with. Moiré must be dry-cleaned, or the pattern will

disappear. Any cloth with a pile shorter than 1/8 inch is known as velvet. It is available in cotton, silk, and synthetic fibers in a broad range of prices.

Unlike natural fibers, synthetics are all made entirely from chemicals. Different chemical combinations produce acetate, viscose, acrylic and polyester. They should not be confused with man-made fabrics, which may include natural, regenerated fibers as well as those made entirely from chemicals.

Quilted fabrics consist of light polyester padding sandwiched between a top layer and backing of fabric – usually cotton, silk and linen. Double-sided quilted fabrics are also available if you want to make a reversible item. Quilted fabrics are a good choice for upholstery, drapery and bedspreads.

Materials and trimmings
The silkiness of moiré, the richness of velvet, and simple cotton and synthetic prints cater to all tastes in decorating styles.

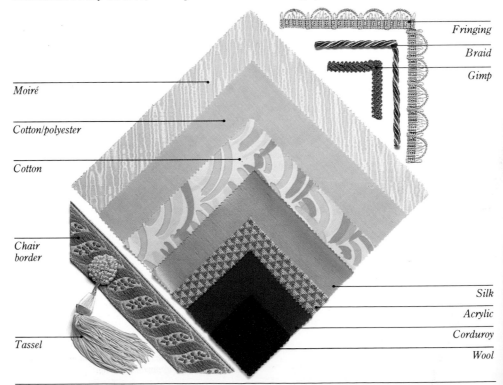

Moiré

Cotton/polyester

Cotton

Chair border

Tassel

Fringing

Braid

Gimp

Silk

Acrylic

Corduroy

Wool

Patterned fabrics

Patterned fabrics may be woven or printed on fabric, and you should see the effect of a drawn-out length from the roll. Remember, too, that the effect may vary under natural and artificial light. Check the pattern repeat and the wastage likely to be involved in matching the pattern if you are intending to make up a large item, such as slip covers.

Patterned fabrics are usually more practical than plain, since they do not show stains so readily, but remember to buy enough fabric to allow for matching of patterns. If you are unused to measuring, ask the sales person to go over your calculations and make sure that the pattern matches are easily made without too much wastage. Fabric pieces left over can be used to make pillow covers and other small items.

Miniprints come in abstract, floral or geometric designs, printed as a small, overall pattern. The majority are light- or medium-weight cottons or cotton/synthetic blends, although you may find that heavier upholstery weights are sometimes available.

Geometrics include circles, squares, diagonals and purely linear patterns. Remember that a close or fine-lined pattern may lose its identity at a distance and merge into a single shade, whereas bold, large-scale geometrics are likely to have a dramatic effect. These designs are commonly available in all fabric weights and may be printed or woven, in single-fiber or fiber-mix fabrics.

Traditional patterns are often developed from historical sources, chintz florals, oriental motifs and Art Nouveau patterns of serpentine foliage. Medium-weight glazed and unglazed cottons, heavier cottons or sturdy linen are available in such patterns, with designs on a large or small scale.

Contemporary style is a term which covers a multitude of design ideas – these may be completely abstract, splashy patterns or improvisations on traditional themes. Some of these will in time become classics in their own right, but when making your choice, remember that this year's fashion may look depressingly out of place in two years' time. You will find contemporary designs available in light and medium weights, in cotton, pure silk or synthetic materials.

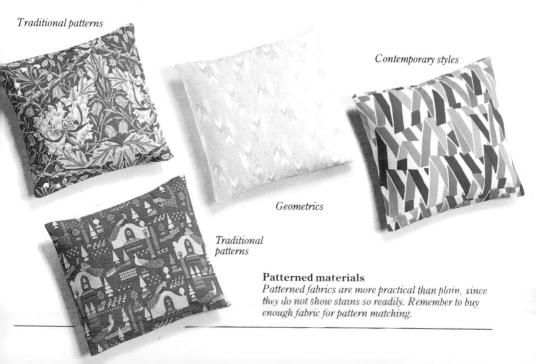

Traditional patterns

Contemporary styles

Geometrics

Traditional patterns

Patterned materials
Patterned fabrics are more practical than plain, since they do not show stains so readily. Remember to buy enough fabric for pattern matching.

Bedding

The bedroom is a personal retreat, the place where individual preference can be indulged without restraint. Fabric furnishings provide style and comfort, from the simplest pillowcase to a formal, fully fitted bedspread. But bedlinen should also be highly practical, to allow for frequent changing and washing. Fortunately, the great range of easy-care and washable fabrics offers plenty of scope for bright and sleek or soft and luxurious effects; but if you want to make a once-and-for-all, sumptuous choice of fabric for the outer bedspread, you can move into the dry-clean fabric range to find special effects of pattern and texture on more exotic fabrics – such as silk, velvet or brocade.

Flat sheets

A flat sheet is useful whether your bedspread is a throw or fitted spread. It is simple to sew, bringing the satisfaction of a practical result for little effort. When calculating fabric amounts add the mattress length to twice the mattress depth; add 20 inches for a 10-inch tuck-in allowance at each end. For the width, add the mattress width to twice the mattress depth, then add 20 inches.

Making a flat sheet

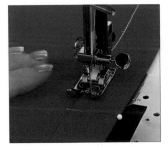 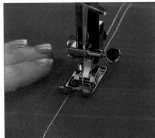 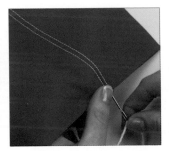

1 *Cut the fabric and turn a double ½-inch hem along both the long sides. Baste and stitch. Along one short edge turn a double 1-inch hem. Baste and stitch this hem. At the other short edge, turn under a double 3-inch hem. Stitch ⅜ inch from the fold.*

2 *Stitch again ½ inch from the fold to form a narrow channel. This deeply hemmed edge forms the turn-down on a top sheet. If you are making a bottom sheet to be tucked in at both ends of the mattress, stitch a double 1-inch hem at both the short edges of the fabric.*

3 *Using a long bodkin, carefully thread fine piping cord through the channel, across the full width of the sheet. Finally, secure the ends of the cord by stitching them firmly to the side hems, and neatly overcasting both the openings at either end of the channel. This completes the sheet.*

ALTERNATIVE FABRICS FOR SHEETS

If you have a taste for something a little different, look among the full range of suitable fabric weights for printed cottons, synthetics or even a washable cotton satin for a luxury effect. Handle the fabric before you buy it, to get a sense of its crease-resistance and durability.

Such fabrics will probably not be available in the width you need for full bed-size, so it will mean seaming sections together. Rather than joining two fabric widths, which will make a center seam that falls down the middle of the bed, cut one section in half lengthwise and seam on either side of a central panel, so that the seamlines can be placed toward the edges of the bed.

To avoid showing the wrong side of a printed fabric at the turn-down of the top sheet, stitch a same fabric or contrasting fabric facing to create a neat, attractive finish.

Fitted sheets

A fitted sheet covers the mattress neatly and makes bedmaking quick and simple. Easy-care, purpose-made sheeting fabric is the most practical choice. You can adapt the technique to make a top sheet with fitted corners at the foot end of the bed only – plan the most convenient style for the size of your bed and its accessibility when you have to change the bedlinen.

When calculating fabric amounts add the mattress length to twice the mattress depth; add 14 inches for a 7-inch tuck-in allowance at either end. For the width, add the mattress width to twice the mattress depth; then add 14 inches.

Making a fitted sheet

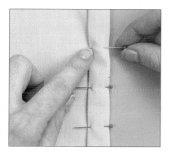

1 Cut the fabric to the required size. Then measure 14 inches along the edge from each corner on all sides and mark these lines with pins. From the position of each pin, chalk a line on the fabric at right angles to the edge and mark clearly where the lines meet. This gives you the position of the edges of the bed.

2 With the wrong sides facing, fold one corner between the point where the lines intersect and the corner, so that the 14-inch marker pins and chalked lines match. Pin together. Then stitch ³/₈ inch inside the pinned line. Trim the corner of the fabric to within ¹/₄ inch of the stitching line.

3 To complete the corner seam, press the seam open, then re-press, right sides facing and the seam at the edge. Pin, baste and stitch ³/₈ inch from the fold, to enclose the raw seam edges and form a French seam. Repeat step 1, step 2 and step 3 to complete seams at each of the other corners.

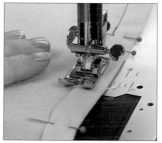
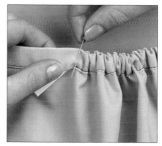

4 Turn under ¹/₂ inch all around the outer edge of the sheet. Then turn the fabric again to form a double ¹/₂-inch casing hem. Pin the hem securely. Next, miter the corners and slip-stitch the miters carefully so that there is a clean channel inside the hem to thread the elastic through.

5 Measure 13 inches along the pinned hem on either side of each corner seam; mark with pins. Stitch the casing hem along the straight edges and also around the corner section, leaving a gap of ¹/₂ inch at each mark to thread the elastic through. Cut four 9 inch lengths of elastic.

6 Thread elastic into the casing hem at each corner with a bodkin. Pin elastic through the casing hem at each opening. Tuck the ends of the elastic inside the casing hem. Repin the elastic ends parallel to the edge so that you can machine across the ends. Stitch the elastic ends and openings securely.

Plain pillowcase

The simplest type of pillowcase is made from a folded length of fabric with a fold-over flap on the inside which tucks over the inserted pillow. This pillowcase can be made in the same sheeting fabric as the sheets, or you may prefer a complete color contrast. Plain colors can be enlivened with ribbon trims, appliqué shapes or embroidery to form designs at each corner or a pretty border along the short edge of the pillowcase. These trimmings can be stitched on before making. When calculating fabric amounts, use a single piece of wide sheeting for each plain pillowcase. Measure the length of the pillow, double the measurement and add 8¼ inches for the flap and hems. Measure the width of the pillow and add 1¼ inches for the seams.

Making a plain pillowcase

1 *Cut the fabric to the required measurements. Along one short edge of the fabric piece, turn a double ¼-inch hem on to the wrong side. Pin, baste and stitch.*

2 *On the other short edge, turn 2 inches on to the wrong side and press. Turn in ⅜ inch at the raw edge; stitch in place. This edge will be at the front.*

3 *Fold the narrow-hemmed edge to make a 6-inch flap. Press and pin. Fold the fabric in half widthways, wrong sides together, aligning the wide-hemmed edge with the flap, and stitch the side edges.*

4 *Turn the pillowcase with right sides facing. Pin, baste and stitch the side edges ⅜ inch from the first seam to enclose the raw edges. Turn the pillowcase right side out and press.*

Pillow shams

Unlike a plain pillowcase, this is made with separate pieces for front and back, and the ruffle is another separate unit. The ruffle is made from a doubled-over fabric strip. You can use any printed cotton. Floral designs set off a pastel fabric, or use the same pattern with reversed colorways. When calculating fabric amounts, measure the length and width of the pillow. Add 1¼ inches to each measurement for ½-inch seam allowances all around. For the back, add 2½ inches to the length and 1¼ inches to the width. For the flap, allow the width of the front section, including seams, and a depth of 7 inches. Decide on the depth for the finished ruffle, double it and add 1¼ inches for seams. Allow a total length twice the total measurement around the pillow.

Making a pillow sham

1 *Turn a 2-inch hem on one short edge of the back piece. Turn under ⅜ inch at the raw edge. Turn a double ¼-inch hem on one long edge of the flap.*

2 *Seam strips of fabric to make a circular band for the ruffle. Divide it into four equal sections and mark with pins. Gather the ruffle separately in each section.*

3 *Mark the front piece of the pillowcase to match the sections on the ruffle. Stitch the ruffle in place. With right sides facing, align the hemmed edge of the back with the seamline on the front.*

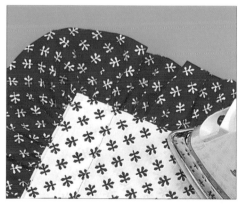

4 *Place the flap right side down, matching the long raw edge of the flap with the raw edge on the front. Pin and baste all around the pillow, turn it over and stitch from the front on the ruffle seamline. Press.*

Duvet covers

A duvet is designed to make life simpler, since it eliminates the more tedious aspects of bedmaking. Polyester/cotton sheeting is a suitable fabric. The basic duvet cover is very simply made and fastened with snap tape, velcro, or a zipper for quick removal. It consists of two rectangular fabric pieces, so you can make it all in one color or pattern, or choose different fabrics for the two sides to create a toned or contrasting effect. If you choose an unusual material for the upper side, you can seam panels of standard-width fabric and cut a single width of sheeting for the lower side. Make sure that the fabrics are compatible for washing; wash the top fabric before cutting out to eliminate any shrinkage. This method also lends itself to a patchwork or a strip-quilting for the upper side.

Calculating fabric amounts

Length: Measure the duvet length, usually 79 inches, and add 2¾ inches for the hem and the seam allowances.
Width: Measure the duvet width and add 1½ inches for the seam allowances.

Making a duvet cover

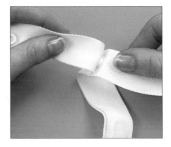

1 *Cut fabric to required size. Turn a double 1-inch hem along the bottom edge of both fabric pieces. Pin, baste and stitch the hems, then press them.*

2 *With right sides facing, baste 12 inches in towards the center from each side, leaving a central opening. Stitch the basted parts 1 inch from the outer edge.*

3 *Cut a length of snap tape 1¼ inches longer than the open section. Ensure there is a snap close to each end so that the closure will not gape.*

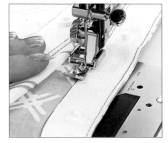

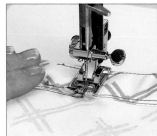

4 *Pin one length of tape along one side of the opening, with ½ inch of extra tape at each end. Baste and stitch using a zipper foot on the machine. Repeat on the other side, ensuring that the snaps match along the length.*

5 *Fold the cover with right sides facing. Make a double row of stitches vertically across the sides of the opening to enclose the tape edges. Finish the stitching securely, as it will undergo wear and tear when the cover is changed.*

6 *Turn the cover to wrong sides facing and make a French seam around the three open sides. Pin, baste and stitch ¼ inch from the raw edge. Trim seam to within ⅛ inch of the stitching. Turn to right sides facing and stitch.*

Fastenings

Fastenings are used mainly on items such as duvet and pillow covers, which must be removed for cleaning. There are many types of fastening and the choice is a matter of personal preference. For duvet covers there are two choices, a strip fastening or single fasteners.

Strip fasteners include snap tape, which comes with the snaps ready fastened to a tape; and touch-and-close tape, which is just pressed together to fasten. Single fasteners include sew-on rectangles and circles of touch-and-close fastening, and individual snaps, available in metal or plastic. For pillows where the opening needs to be firmly and neatly fastened a zipper is the best choice.

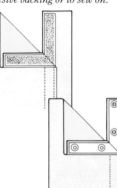 

Touch-and-close fastenings
These are available in the form of circular spots, rectangles and strips. One half of the fastening has fluffy loops and the other tiny hooks which adhere to the loops. The fastenings are available with an adhesive backing or to sew on.

Snaps and grippers
Metal snaps come in a range of sizes and in black, silver or colored enamel finishes. Small square white or clear plastic ones are also available; these are less sturdy than metal snaps but handy where a flat fastening is needed.

Grippers are non-sew press-studs. Each half of the gripper has a backing section which clips through the fabric to fasten the gripper in place. These types of fastenings are more suitable for loosely covered items, since they will come apart if subjected to strain.

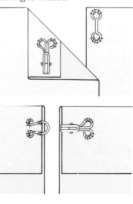 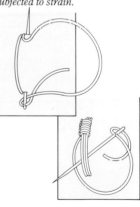

Fastening tapes
Touch-and-close tape and snap tape are ideal for fastening a duvet cover opening. Separate the two halves of the tape and stitch half to each edge of the opening along the long edges. Use a zipper foot on snap tape to pass by the snaps. The ends of the tape are usually finished into the end of the opening and hand or machine stitched across.

Hooks and eyes
For overlapping edges, sew the hook on the inside of the overlapping edge of the fabric and the bar on the outside underlapping edge. For abutting edges, sew both the hook and eye on the inside of the fabric. The eye should extend slightly over the edge. These are versatile fastenings, which can be used in clothing as well as soft furnishings.

Making a thread eye
A thread eye provides a decorative alternative to a metal eye, but is not as strong. Mark the two points where the eye should start and finish and sew a few long stitches from one point to the other, keeping them fairly loose. Secure the ends. Then sew closely spaced buttonhole stitches over the strands of thread to form the eye.

Dust ruffles

A dust ruffle creates an informal style while providing a neat cover-up for the bed base. The skirt of the dust ruffle is sewn to a flat section of fabric that spreads across the bed base underneath the mattress. This can be made from the same fabric as the skirt or a coordinated material. For economy, if the base section of the dust ruffle will not show, an old sheet can be used. Solid and patterned cottons are a practical choice for a ruffled dust ruffle, while a basic style can be enlivened with lace or ribbon stitched to the lower edge.

Calculating fabric amounts

Measure the mattress top and add 1⅜ inches to the length and 1¼ inches to the width. Measure the height from the floor to the top of the bed base and add 2½ inches. This gives the depth of the skirt. The total length of fabric needed for the skirt is four times the mattress length plus twice the width.

Making a ruffled dust ruffle

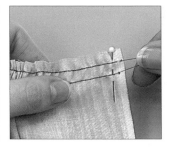

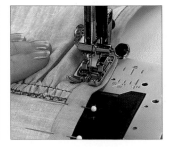

1 *Cut the main panel on the lengthwise grain. Curve the two base corners by drawing around the edge of a plate. Cut the curves. Cut strips of fabric to the depth of the skirt, adding ½-inch seam allowances.*

2 *Join the strips of fabric into one long strip using French seams. Turn under a double 1-inch hem on the wrong side of the fabric at the lower edge of the skirt. Then pin, baste and stitch the hem of the skirt in place.*

3 *Divide the total length of the skirt into six equal divisions and mark them with pins at the top. Work two rows of gathering stitches in each section. Pull up the threads to gather each section evenly and fasten them securely.*

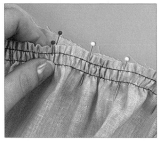

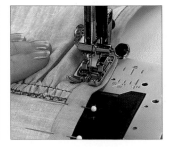

4 *Measure the sides and bottom edge of the main panel and divide by six. Mark the six equal divisions with pins. Match the marks on the skirt to those on the main panel. Pull the gathers in each section until the lengths are matched. Pin, with right sides facing.*

5 *Baste and stitch the skirt to panel ½ inch from the edge. Trim down the seam to ⅜ inch and stitch again close to the first line of stitching. Neaten the edges by working over them with machine zigzag stitch. Press the seam toward the main panel.*

6 *At the remaining raw edges of the main panel and valance (which will be placed at the top end of the bed), turn and press a double ⅜-inch hem on to the wrong side of the fabric. Pin, baste and stitch this hem firmly in place. This completes the dust ruffle.*

Ruffled bedspreads

A fitted bedspread with a deep ruffle needs a firmly woven fabric which handles easily and has good draping qualities. Cotton with a satinized finish gives a slightly luxurious feeling, or you might prefer a light wool for comfort with a plain or slightly textured weave.

Calculating fabric amounts

Main panel: Measure the length of the made-up bed top and add 8 inches to allow for the height of the pillows; measure the width and add 1¼ inches for the seam allowances.

Ruffle: Measure from the top of the bed to within ⅜ inch of the floor and add 2½ inches for the seam and hem allowances. This makes the depth of the ruffle. The full length of fabric needed is four times the length of the bed, plus twice the width, plus 1½ inches for side hems at the headboard end. Cut strips of fabric to the depth of the ruffle and seam them together to make up this length.

Making a ruffled bedspread

1 *Cut out the main panel on the lengthwise grain. Cut the lining to the same size. Curve the two base corners on both the fabric and lining by drawing around the edge of a plate. Trim the corners along the marked lines, making sure that the curves join into the straight edges in a smooth line.*

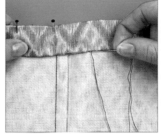

2 *Cut the strips for the ruffle and join them into one strip using French seams (page 223). Take ½-inch seam allowances and match the pattern details on the seams. Turn a double 1-inch hem onto the wrong side of the fabric at the lower edge of the ruffle. Pin, baste and slip-hem in place.*

3 *Divide by six the length of the two long sides and lower edge of the panel. Mark with pins. Divide the ruffle by six and mark with pins. Work two rows of gathering stitches along each section. Pull the gathers to match the divisions on the panel. Pin the ruffle to the panel, right sides together.*

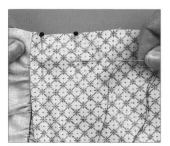

4 *Stitch ruffle to main panel ½ inch from the raw edges. Trim the seam to ⅜ inch and stitch. Position lining over panel, wrong sides facing. Turn under raw side edge at the ruffle seam. Baste.*

5 *Turn and press a double ⅜-inch hem on to the wrong side of the cover across the side edges of the ruffle and the basted top of the main panel. Pin the hem and machine-stitch it in place.*

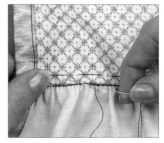

6 *Turn under the sides and lower edge of the lining and pin it to the wrong side of the ruffle, to cover the ruffle seam. Stitch the lining in place and secure the turned edges with hemming stitch.*

Throw bedspreads

A throw bedspread is simple to make and a clever choice of fabric can give a very rich effect. Medium-weight cottons are suitable, or, for a warm winter look, choose light wool, or textured fabric in glowing colors. When calculating fabric amounts, measure the bed with all the bedclothes in place, including pillows. Measure from the top of the mattress over the pillows to the end of the bed, then the depth to the floor. Add 4 inches for hems. Measure the width of the mattress and depth to the floor; double the depth. Add 4 inches for hems.

Making a throw bedspread

1 *Cut two widths of fabric and trim off the selvages from both sides of each length. Cut one piece in half lengthwise to make the side panels. Fold under a ¹/₂-inch seam along the edge of one side panel and place it over the seam on one side of the central panel, matching any pattern. Stitch together from the right side.*

2 *Repeat the previous step to attach the second side panel to the central panel, once again matching the pattern where possible. Machine-stitch the pieces together, making flat seams following the lines of ladder stitching. Neaten the raw edges of the seams and press open. Trim the side panels if necessary, allowing 2 inches for the hem on each side.*

3 *Turn and press a 2-inch single hem all around the edge of the cover, then fold in the raw edges ¹/₂ inch and press. Miter the corners by opening out the folded hem and cutting carefully across the corner diagonally just outside the fold line. Fold the hem back in place once more and press.*

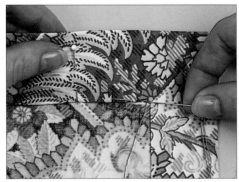

4 *Pin the hem in place and finish with hand stitching. Slip-stitch the edges of the mitered corner together and use hemming or blind hem stitch (page 167) to secure all four side hems. Finally, press the completed cover from the wrong side using a steam iron or a dry iron and a damp cloth.*

Comforters

A comforter is a lightweight quilt that can be used as a top cover over the other bedding, or if you combine it with a top sheet as a single covering for warm nights. Make the two sides from different fabrics. It looks particularly attractive when teamed with a dust ruffle.

When calculating fabric amounts, with bedding in place, measure from the head of the bed to just below the mattress at the foot. Measure across the bed and down to just below the mattress on either side. You need two panels of fabric and one panel of padding to these dimensions. Allow an extra ¾ inch on widths for joining sections of fabric or padding. Allow extra fabric to make bias strips (page 171).

] Making a comforter

1 *Cut the padding to length and stitch the sections together to make up the full width of the comforter. Overlap the edges of the padding pieces and join them with a broad herringbone stitch. Cut the fabric to the correct dimensions for the front and the back panels, joining the widths with flat seams (page 160) if necessary.*

2 *Spread out the back panel right side down and lay the padding on top of it, matching the edges carefully. Then spread the front panel over the padding right side up. Next, starting at the center, pin and baste all three layers together across the width. When basting, use large stitches and a contrasting colored thread.*

3 *Continue pinning and basting the layers, using rows of large stitching 10–12 inches apart, working from the center outward on both sides of the first row of stitching. Take the basting lines right to the edges of the fabric. When this is completed, baste all around the edges of the comforter ⅜ inch from the raw edges.*

4 *Run 1 inch-wide bias binding around all four sides of the comforter (you can also use matching fabric bias). Fold it over the raw edges of the joined fabric and padding. Pin and baste, overlap the ends of the binding and turn in the raw edge. Stitch in place.*

5 *Remove the basting threads and mark the positions for ties across the comforter with pins. To make a tie, thread a needle with embroidery cotton and make a short stitch through the layers of fabric, leaving a 2 inch end of thread. Make a second stitch in the same place.*

6 *To complete the tie, knot the ends of the thread and trim them to equal lengths. Work right across the length and width of the comforter, tying the layers of fabric firmly together at the pinned marks. This completes the comforter and it is ready for use.*

Boxed bedspreads

A smartly tailored bedcover is cleanly styled and practical, concealing the bedding completely. Inverted pleats at the corners make it easy to lift and relay the cover, but on the bed it settles neatly into a crisp, boxy finish. The handsome styling depends upon choice of a fairly firm, crease-resistant fabric that folds elegantly into the pleats.

Calculating fabric amounts

Main panel: Measure the top of the bed with the bedding in place. Add 8 inches to the length, for a tuck-in under the pillow, and 1¼ inches to the width for seam allowances. Skirt: The skirt is cut in three panels, one for each side and one for the foot of the bed. Measure from the top of the bed to within ⅜ inch of the floor and add 2½ inches for the seam and hems. This gives the depth of the skirt panels. For the side panels, measure the length of the bed and add 16 inches for the corner pleats and pillow tuck-in. For the foot panel, measure the width of the bed and add 16 inches for the corner pleats.

One-room living
This is a useful style for studio living; the bed is neat and unobtrusive when fully covered during the day, and if you remove the pillows the bed can effectively be turned into a sofa.

Making a boxed bedspread

 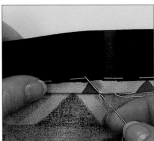 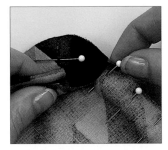

1 *Cut the panel on the lengthwise grain of the fabric. If the fabric pieces have to be joined to give sufficient width, use French seams to eliminate the raw edges on the wrong side. Draw a line at 45° from each of the base corners. Curve the corners slightly. With tailor's chalk, mark the position of the corner pleats on the line ½ inch from the raw edges.*

2 *Cut out the panels for the skirt and join them into one long strip. Be sure to join the side and foot panels in the correct sequence. Make French seams taking a ½-inch seam allowance. Turn a double 1-inch hem on to the wrong side of the fabric at the lower edge of the skirt. Pin, baste, then hem the skirt by hand. Then press the hem using a steam iron.*

3 *Mark the center of the top edge of the foot panel with a pin. Having done this, mark the center of the foot edge of the main panel in the same way. Next, with right sides facing, and matching the two pinned marks accurately, firmly pin the foot panel of the skirt to the edge of the main panel, right up to the pinned marks at the corners of the main panel.*

4 *Starting at the top end of the main panel, pin the skirt panels to the main panel, down to the pinned marks at the base corners. The surplus fabric in the skirt at each corner will be used to form the inverted pleats.*

5 *Fold the surplus fabric into a pleat at each corner, matching the center of the pleat to the mark at the corner of the main panel. Clip into the seam allowance of the pleat so that it will turn easily around the curve at the corners.*

6 *Baste and stitch the skirt in place. Neaten the raw edges of all the seams with machine zigzag stitch. Along the top edge of the cover, turn a double ⅜-inch hem. Pin, baste and stitch the hem in place. Press the finished cover.*

Pleats

Pleats give a tailored, slightly formal style furnishing, with a neat and tidy finish. Pleats can be formed either side-by-side or spaced further apart in groups. There are several types of pleats: the simplest and easiest to make are knife pleats, where the folds of fabric face in the same direction; there are also box pleats, where the folds are turned away from each other; finally, there are inverted pleats, where the folds are turned toward each other. These are the ones used in the boxed bedspread illustrated above.

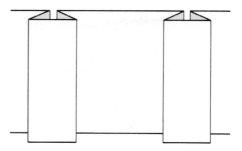

Box pleats
Each of the pleats has two folds which are turned away from each other. The back folds are facing and may meet on one line.

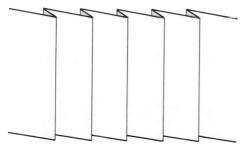

Knife pleats
Each pleat has one fold which is aligned with another line. All the pleats face in the same direction. Knife pleats are the simplest and easiest type of pleats, both to make and to maintain. An example of a knife pleated ruffle is shown on pages 224–5.

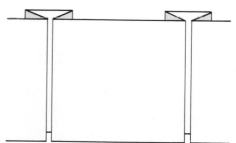

Inverted pleats
Each pleat has two folds which are turned toward each other and meet on one line. Back folds face away from each other. Inverted pleats, because they are hidden by the way the material falls, make a neat, unfussy finish.

Decorative finishes

Making your own decorative items is an opportunity to put your design skills to work, not only in the choice of fabric but also in terms of the details which make the project representative of your personal style and taste. In addition to the sewing methods involved in making the main item, there are many techniques of decorative stitching and applied decoration which can extend the range of your ideas for soft furnishings. Patchwork and appliqué are simple to learn and can produce original effects by allowing you to mix colors and patterns as freely as you wish on a small or large scale.

Patchwork quilts

Patchwork consists of a mosaic of small pieces of material joined together to form a pattern. To create an artifact of beauty and neatness, the choice of fabrics and shapes, and the accuracy of seams, must all be carefully considered. With patchwork thorough planning at the outset is a must.

For beginners, it is advisable to limit the number of fabrics you use, until you get a feel for mixing colors and patterns together. A checkerboard effect using only two different fabrics can have remarkable impact if you select the combination carefully. Colors can be highly contrasted or subtly moody; you can set off a discreet geometric pattern against a floral miniprint, with colors in common between the two. Use fabrics of the same basic weight to avoid puckering at the seams. As you gain more confidence with this technique, you can develop the patchwork patterning more freely.

Traditional, hand-stitched, "pieced" patchwork requires a methodical approach and is best used for relatively small items such as table mats, pillows and decorative panels. However, compared to machine patchwork, it is easier to work more complex designs, with diamonds, hexagons, stars and fan shapes. You can plan out the colors and patterns before you begin, or let the work grow piece by piece into the jeweled effect of mixed fabric patterns often seen in antique patchwork.

The fabric pieces are basted to templates of paper or thin cardboard with the edges turned under to the wrong side. With two pieces together, right sides facing, the edges are slip-stitched to create a firm, neat seam. The templates can be removed when individual shapes are completely surrounded by others and stitched on all sides.

Quilted table mats
Patchwork techniques can be adapted to regular shapes if the edges are accurately matched.

As with machine patchwork, fabrics should be of a similar weight, and if the finished item is to be washable, all must be shrink-resistant and colorfast. Printed cottons make beautiful patchwork and accommodate small shapes and intricate designs. Coordinated fabric ranges offer plenty of scope for patchwork designs, but there is great pleasure in selecting and combining fabrics from personal taste, and all sorts of scraps and remnants can be given useful life in this way.

Quilting
In items such as table mats and oven gloves, quilting provides the necessary thickness and an attractive finish for plain or patterned fabrics or patchwork pieces. Polyester batting is sandwiched between two layers of fabric and the quilted pattern is machine-stitched through all three layers. You can work the quilting and then bind the raw edges of fabric and batting. Alternatively, treat the front piece of fabric and the batting as one thickness, basting them together, and seam them to the back section on three sides; then turn out to the right side and neaten the remaining seam.

Diagonal quilting adds interest to a plain fabric or simple geometric. Patchwork quilted along the lines of the template shapes has a very decorative, neat effect. A similar technique is used in quilting the outlines of a fabric design, such as a large floral print; stitch around the edges of the main motifs to create a lightly raised relief surface.

Appliqué

Appliqué consists simply of applying one piece of fabric to another larger piece, and there are several ways in which an appliqué motif can be stitched to the base tabric.

The motif may be a single piece of fabric, or constructed from any number of pieces which are basted in place to form the design and then secured with finished stitching. The stitching is worked around all the edges of the appliqué, whether they are raw edges or neatened with a narrow turn-in. Closely worked machine zigzag stitch secures an appliqué motif in place, so that the fabric cannot fray or tear. If you use straight stitch, turn under the raw edges. Otherwise, the outlines can be overcast by hand.

As with patchwork, it is necessary to select the fabrics carefully, matching them for weight to avoid straining or puckering, and compatibility for washing or dry cleaning. Appliqué designs worked in small pieces of plain-colored fabrics have an attractive appearance particularly effective for borders and corners of sheets and pillowcases, but make sure that the colors are fast, or laundering will ruin your work. Avoid loose weaves which will eventually fray, however carefully they are stitched to begin with. You can also use embroidery stitches on appliqué to elaborate patterns.

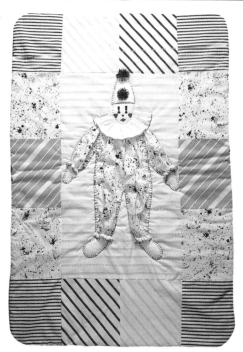

Combined techniques
Fresh, bright colors and textural detail make a decorative crib cover. A simple block patchwork provides the background with a jolly clown motif appliquéd at the center. Both the patchwork cover and the appliqué detail are padded; the clown's ruffled collar and pompon hat add three-dimensional interest.

Table linens

Table linens include tablecloths, mats and napkins. These are all easy and quick to make, and it is simple to add a personal touch to a complete set. It is more economical to make your own than to buy these items, and you also have a wider choice of materials and combinations of fabrics.

Table linens need to wear well and come up fresh when washed, but you may also wish to make beautifully decorative cloths for side tables or for the main table when it is not in use for dining. You can add a range of attractive and easy-to-sew trimmings, but ensure that they are compatible when washing.

Types of fabric

Printed cottons offer a wide range of different effects, from small, calico patterns in cool colors to rich, dark, swirling designs subtly glowing in a room lit for a leisurely evening at home. Gingham is a lively choice for the kitchen, the woven white-and-colored checks pretty but informal; you can choose a tiny houndstooth or bold checkerboard effect in fresh green or yellow, strong blue or red, brown or black. PVC-coated fabrics are a useful option for wipe-clean kitchen cloths, available in plain colors and a variety of attractive patterns.

The crisp and heavy textures of linens are pleasantly traditional, especially the natural creamy colors, lending themselves to discreet embroidered or cutwork borders and corner motifs. Pure linens need extra care, but linens/synthetic blends or linen-look fabrics are easier to care for.

Plain fabrics and woven-in patterns are suitable for matching napkins, and also for making table mats, which may be designed for use with other table linens or to be placed directly on the table-top. As table mats are made from a double layer of fabric, you can choose one-sided prints if preferred. Medium to heavy, hard-wearing materials are a good choice for mats in everyday use – fabrics such as denim, canvas or burlap, which are available in a range of colors and light or dark neutral tones. Brightly colored binding or a patterned braid edging lightens the purely practical emphasis. To make a thick mat you can insert a layer of batting, or you can use ready-quilted fabric instead.

Decorative effects
For decorative purposes, lace makes an ideal throw-over cloth, perhaps draped over a floor-length cloth of velvet or a rich silk or taffeta. Layered cottons look attractive as a daytime cover-up for a round table, in coordinated prints or contrasting colors, depending upon the effect you want to create. The top cloth should be considerably shorter than the lower layer and can also be a different shape. This treatment lends itself to decorative edgings such as scallops, braids, ribbons, cutwork embroidery or appliqué, to emphasize the layered effect. When adding trimmings match the weight of the trimming to the fabric weight, or you may get a distorted effect.

Coordinated table linens
Coordinating table linens will enhance any table. Matching quilted mats and napkins in bold, bright colors will complement modern tableware; or, for a more traditional setting, choose plain white with a little surface texture to form the perfect backdrop for elaborate tableware.

Design details

By making your own table linens, you can set the mood and atmosphere of your dining, whether for a leisurely summer breakfast or for an elegant dinner party. The choice of fabric should flatter your tableware and blend in stylishly with other furnishings. Small design details such as the trimmings and edging for tablecloths, place mats or napkins can make all the difference, lending a personalized touch that makes even the most basic table linens extra special.

Pick up cues on color and detail from the existing elements of your table. An attractively patterned dinner service may suggest an unusual color combination; gleaming silverware and delicate china look good against spotless white or subtly creamy table linens enhanced by the most discreet trimming such as a narrow satin binding, lace edging, or toning embroidery at borders and corners. Modern flatware and sturdy china benefit from bold colors and equally modern fabric designs. Dark hues and large-motif patterns can create a dramatic setting.

Borders and edgings
A neat, attractive way to create unusual styling for a tablecloth is to add a deep border in a coordinated or contrasting fabric. Wide strips of fabric stitched around the edges of the cloth can be doubled over with mitered corners. Plain color with a strong abstract or geometric border creates a good effect, while pretty flowered fabrics have an eye-catching finish when edged with an overall miniprint in coordinated colors.

Measuring

Unless you are copying the size of an existing cloth, the basic measurements you need are the size of the table-top and the required drop from the edge of the table downward. To judge a good length for everyday use, sit at the table on a chair in regular use and measure from the edge of the table to your lap. A little below lap-length – usually a drop of about 10–12 inches – is about right to avoid a skimpy appearance. The drop should hang gracefully even if it is short; too little fabric will stand out awkwardly from the table-top. For a full-length cloth, measure from the top of the table to within ⅜ inch of the floor.

When calculating the full amount of fabric needed, add twice the drop to the table length and width, or to the diameter of a round table, and add hem allowances. The hem is most easily kept to a narrow depth for convenience

in sewing, but you can make it deeper to add more weight, which helps the fabric to hang elegantly, especially on a floor-length cloth. Alternatively you can bind the edges of the cloth, so that no hem allowance is needed. This is effective on a round cloth, where a bias binding accommodates the curves neatly.

A tablecloth should be made from a single width of fabric, but if you need to seam widths together, make a central panel with equal side panels. This applies to rectangular and round cloths, never have a seam across the center of the table.

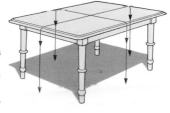

Calculating fabric amounts
Add twice the calculated drop to the width and length of the table.

Straight-sided tablecloths

Whether your table is square or oblong, a tablecloth gives a clean, finished effect, for daytime freshness or evening elegance. Basically, it is simply a hemmed rectangle of fabric, but the hem is neatened with mitered corners, a technique which gives a professional touch to many sewing projects.

Plain or printed cottons are a practical choice of fabric. If you are making up the cloth from seamed panels, you have the option to use one fabric for the central panel and a coordinated color or pattern for the outer panels, rather than the same fabric throughout. The traditional choice of white makes a crisp base for your table settings, and gives a sparkling effect for an evening dinner party, but you may prefer a darker color or busy pattern for daytime use.

Calculating fabric amounts

Measure the length and width of the table-top. To each measurement add twice the drop from the edge of the table. Add 2⅜ inches to the length and width for the hem. For a large table, you may need to join widths of fabric. If so, allow twice the length. Also allow extra fabric for positioning and matching any pattern.

Making a straight-sided tablecloth

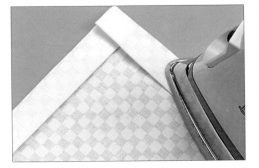

1 *Cut the fabric to size, or join widths (page 211). Along each edge of the fabric, turn ½ inch on to the wrong side and press. Fold over ½ inch again to make a double hem and press.*

2 *Open out one fold. Cut diagonally to within ¼ inch of the point at the inner fold. Refold the fabric and match the cut edges. Match the folded edges and pin them together to keep them level.*

3 *Pin and stitch a narrow seam along each diagonal cut. Stitch the seam ¼ inch from the raw edge, with the stitching line passing through the inner corner point. Press the seams. Turn the corners out.*

4 *Refold the double hem. The diagonal seam forms a neat miter. Stitch all around the edge of the tablecloth. At each end of the stitching line, pull the threads through to the wrong side and fasten.*

Round tablecloths

A round tablecloth is cut from a square of fabric: the fabric is folded in four and cut using a paper pattern of a quarter-circle. For everyday use a short cloth is neat and stylish, but a round cloth looks particularly elegant in a floor-length version, especially when made of a medium-weight fabric.

Fresh cottons are a good choice for informal styling, small-scale flower prints and random abstracts with small motifs minimize problems of pattern matching if you need to join widths of fabrics. For a more formal effect, choose a plain-weave linen or linen-look fabric.

Round cloths lend themselves particularly to a decorative layered style. Choose coordinated or contrasting colors and patterns and simply cut two paper patterns to make a floor length underlayer and a top cloth with a half-length drop.

Calculating fabric amounts

Measure the diameter of the table-top. Add twice the depth of the drop plus $1\frac{1}{4}$ inches for hem allowances. A round tablecloth creates the best effect if cut from a single width of fabric, but if you need to join widths, use the method described for the straight-sided tablecloth.

Making a round tablecloth

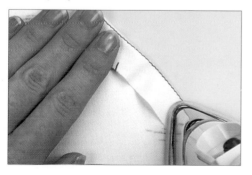

1 *Measure the radius of the table-top. Hold the measured point on the string at one corner of the paper. Move the pencil to draw a quarter-circle on the paper. Cut along the pencil line.*

2 *Fold the fabric in four. Pin on the paper pattern, aligning the straight edges of the paper with the folded edges of the fabric, then cut. Stitch around the outside edge of the cloth ½ inch in from the raw edge.*

3 *Press the edge on to the wrong side all around the cloth along the stitched line. The stitching will tend to roll over naturally just inside the fold, giving a good, smooth curve.*

4 *Turn under the raw edge to make a double hem. Pin and baste. Stitch all around the hem, keeping the stitching line close to the inner fold. Remove the basting and press.*

Table mats and napkins

Place mats and mats for serving dishes can be as plain and practical or as decorative as you wish, made as a basic rectangle or with neatly rounded corners. A quilted effect can be stitched by hand or machine, with a layer of polyester batting sandwiched between two pieces of fabric, or you have the option of a very handy short-cut, using ready-quilted fabric and simply binding two layers together. Fabric mats are not entirely heat-proof, so do not put down dishes straight from the oven without slipping a cork or plastic mat underneath the fabric one, but they provide sufficient insulation to protect the table-top from most warm plates.

If you are making a tablecloth, buy an additional length of fabric for a set of matching napkins; otherwise, this is an opportunity to use up remnants of fabric which are too small to be of use for any major projects. Make them coordinate or contrast with the tablecloth or place mats.

Napkins
Lacy edging in cool pink adds an attractively restrained touch of color for white linen napkins. The delicacy of the lacy edges gives a dainty finish to offset fine chinaware, or perhaps gleaming glassware and silver flatware.

Making a table mat

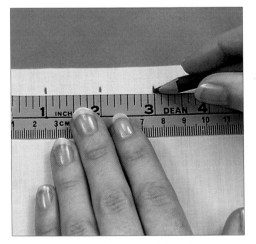

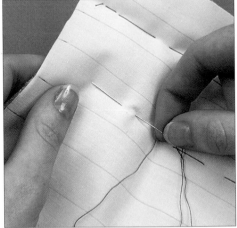

1 *Cut two pieces of the chosen fabric to the required size. With a hard pencil or tailor's chalk, mark evenly spaced lines about 1 inch apart along one of the shorter sides. Draw parallel lines from short side to short side. Then cut the batting to exactly the same size as the fabric.*

2 *Sandwich the batting between the wrong sides of the two pieces of fabric. Next, holding the three rectangles firmly between your finger and thumb, pin them together carefully. Then stitch rows of neat, even basting stitches between alternate drawn lines as shown in the picture above.*

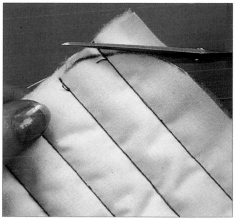

3 *Using the penciled or chalked lines as guide lines, sew several parallel rows of long machine stitches from one short side of the rectangle to the other. Do not sew them too close together, or the result will look cramped and fussy. You might also like to use a contrasting thread for working the quilting stitches, which can produce a very attractive effect.*

4 *Cups, saucers and plates can all be used as a guide to round the corners of the table mat. Decide how tight a curve you require and place the cup, saucer or plate on the first corner. Draw around it with tailor's chalk and repeat the same process for each corner. Then, cut along the curved lines and trim the corners neatly. Block lightly, if desired.*

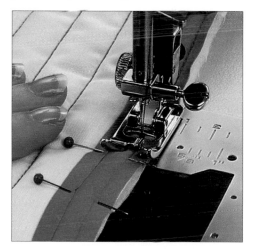

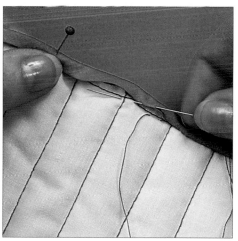

5 *To give a neat and stylish finish to the table mat, it is a good idea to edge it with binding. If you have used a contrasting color for the quilting stitches as suggested above, it is a good idea to use binding which is of the same contrasting color to give a unified look to the finished article. Open out one folded edge of the binding. Pin the binding around the mat with the right sides facing and the raw edges level. Stitch it in place along the crease on the binding as shown in the illustration above.*

6 *Fold over the edge to the wrong side. Press and stitch the binding in place. On the right side, machine-stitch on the inside edge of the binding to strengthen the mat around the edge. Napkins can be then easily made with any remnants. Cut out identical 18-inch squares. Fold and press a double 1/4-inch hem on all four edges of the napkin, taking care to fold in all the corners neatly. Pin, baste and stitch the hemmed edges close to the inner fold. Press each napkin carefully with a hot iron.*

Embroidered table linens

A craft long associated with home sewing, embroidery adds delicate detail to beautiful table linens. There are literally hundreds of different embroidery stitches that can be used singly or combined to build up pretty edgings, intricate corner motifs, deep borders and scattered color detail. Embroidering your own table linens is an opportunity to give elegance and originality to the atmosphere in which you dine.

Outline and filling stitches, cutwork embroidery, cross stitch and drawn thread work offer a range of decorative possibilities for application to a variety of fabrics. Successful embroidery requires patience and skill – a good effect depends upon neat, even stitching – but it is a rewarding craft, and embroidered items often become treasured family heirlooms.

To make a design for embroidery, you can use commercially available transfers which are ironed onto the fabric or traced over using dressmaker's transfer paper to leave a faint color outline on the fabric. Alternatively, draw up your own designs or trace attractive motifs from books or magazines, or even from the pattern of a favorite fabric. Flower patterns, small animal motifs and abstract symbols such as Greek keys or linked circles are traditionally popular embroidery motifs, but with a little invention you can adapt any type of form or symbol to a line drawing which forms the basis of a stitched motif.

Embroidery threads are available in glowing colors and subtly graded tones; stranded thread allows you to vary the thickness of the stitch and creates a smooth, silky finish, while the heavier cotton perlé yarn has a lightly textured sheen which is suitable for medium-weight fabrics.

Crewel work embroidery has a striking character all its own, although it is more usually used on heavier fabrics because the fabric weight must give firm support. Therefore, this technique is better suited to pillows or curtains rather than to the lighter fabrics used for table linens. Crewel-type stitches radiate from the center of the motif

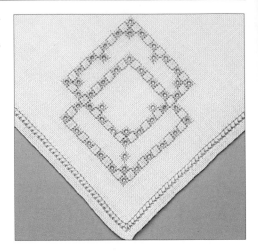

Drawn thread work
Drawn thread work is used to create borders or blocks of pattern. A good effect of subtle texturing is obtained by using an embroidery thread in a color close to that of the fabric. A more colorful appearance can be achieved by the use of a definite contrast between the thread and the fabric colors, and you can combine different threads in alternate or complex stitching. However, it is as well to limit the number of colors, or the overall shape of the design will become very confused.

A corner motif
An embroidered corner motif is attractively framed in a scalloped and pointed edging. Clear colors and the fresh contrast of pink and yellow against green on a natural linen background create an informal but eye-catching design. Variegated color thread secures the edges of the fabric. The design is traditional but not old-fashioned.

outward, filling the shape solidly. Long stitches tend to pucker and distort the fabric, so make sure that you judge the direction of the stitching carefully.

Satin stitch is one of the most common filling stitches in embroidery, for small blocks of color. The stitches should be even, closely spaced and not too long and the finished effect is a flat color area with an attractive surface sheen. The stitching is worked across the shape, to look rather like pencil or crayon shading in a drawing.

Outline stitches range from simple running stitch or back stitch to fancy linear effects such as chain stitch or feather stitch. Subtle coloring sometimes needs some outline detail to make the pattern more distinct.

Embroidered edgings give a well-finished look when interior detail is also embroidered. Bold outlines and strong colors match up to modern styles of furnishing; though there is a special charm to the traditional embroidery designs, it is an immensely adaptable craft which need never look old fashioned.

Cutwork embroidery

The intricacy and delicacy of cutwork embroidery makes it appear quite a complex technique, but it depends upon a basic type of stitching and careful organization of the design. This consists of outlines which are worked solidly with close buttonhole stitch. The inner sections are then cut away using an extremely sharp pair of scissors. The design must be carefully worked out so that no element becomes detached from its neighbors when the open areas are cut. The cut areas should be kept fairly small, or the fabric is weakened and does not retain a crisp finish. The main character of the design depends upon the balance between open and solid areas. Cutwork is especially suited to table linens. The fabric should be firmly woven and not too heavy, but not so lightweight that the stitching can cause distortion. Interwoven shapes and floral designs have always been particularly suitable types of design for cutwork.

Cross stitch

A remarkably simple but versatile technique, cross stitch provides a range of decorative effects, from single motifs and narrow edgings to deep, complex borders or even embroidered pictures. It is essential to use a base fabric in which threads can be counted to regulate the stitching, such as even-weave linens or heavy cotton. Special fabrics are also available with a grid-like weave of tiny holes, or you can follow the woven pattern of a finely checked fabric.

Pillows

Unlike the sofas and chairs on which they sit, pillows can simply be moved to another room if you get tired of them, or you can make up a different type of cover for little extra investment, so it is worth trying out ambitious design ideas on this small scale. At the least, you will end up with some unusual and individual focal points in your room which will give zest to the overall décor, and at best, it may give you confidence to start a larger project. Pillows of all shapes and sizes will add comfort and a warm welcoming atmosphere. Fabric remnants can be used for individual pillows, and careful choice of different, but complementary, fabric will give a lively effect. The pillows can be made plain or trimmed in a variety of ways – with piping, a ruffle, tassels and even appliquéd lace fabric.

Pillow fillings

The type of filling you choose depends mainly on how firm you want the pillow to be and how much you can afford to spend on it. Ready-made pillow forms can be bought in a variety of shapes and sizes. This is very useful as you then have a ready-made shape which only needs covering. But you can make a pillow form to any shape you please, just by seaming up a muslin or other plain-weave cotton inner cover and stuffing it with a suitable synthetic filling or with natural down.

Synthetic fillings are available in various types and qualities, usually of polyester or acrylic, both of which are fully washable. The best grades are siliconed for extra softness and there are special firm grades which may be a good choice for an unusual shape.

Down is light, soft and resilient, an expensive choice, but you will find that a little goes a long way. It is an appropriate filling for a pillow to be covered with a light and luxurious fabric such as silk. Feathers are less expensive than down but also less resilient.

They can be bought in ready-made pillow forms and are also available by the pound. Kapok and polyester fiber fill are cheap alternatives to feathers. Kapok, which is vegetable fiber, tends to become matted after a while. It is also not hand-washable. Fiber fill is a light filling which is washable and non-allergenic. One lb will be sufficient for an 18- to 20-inch pillow.

Latex and foam foundations are not as soft or as flexible as other fillings whether you use a block of foam or foam chips. They are, however, the best choice when you need firm cushions that will have to withstand some rough and tumble, in a child's playroom or bedroom, for example, or for use with garden or deck furniture.

Polystyrene beads are tiny, lightweight balls that are best used for irregular shapes such as "bean bag" floor pillows.

Pillow fillings
There are various types of pillow filling. Make sure that you suit the type of filling to the use of the pillow. Some fillings, such as down, are more luxurious and suited to expensive fabrics and tailored cushions.

Other types of filling, such as foam filling, provide a cheap, sturdy alternative for less formal cushions such as those for children's rooms. Shown here from left to right: down, foam filling, synthetic fiber fill, polystyrene beads.

Pillow trimmings

Trimmings range from neat piping inserted into outer seams to fringes, lace ruffles, braids, tassels or quilted appliqué motifs. Decorative ribbons may be plain or multi-colored, discreetly woven or heavily embossed. Hand stitched to the outer edges of the pillow cover, they define the outline of the shape while disguising the seamlines.

A very simple method of enlivening the basic rectangular pillow is to add a contrast edging stitched to the outer seams of the cover, or a heavy braid border sewn to the front of the pillow, aligned to the seam, or with an all-in-one border. An all-in-one border can also be created by making up the pillow cover a little larger than the form and stitching 1½ to 2 inches inside the seamlines all around. Lace makes an attractive appliqué design on the body of the pillow, and embroidery for borders and corners can also be appliquéd to the front section, particularly effective on a translucent fabric over a solid color background. Pretty handkerchiefs or scarves can be converted into pillow covers, stitched to a backing fabric in which the zipper is inserted.

Plain ribbons make pretty edging. Braided ribbons make an inner border for pillows or place mats, while woven into a block, they form a colorful panel which can be set into a pillow cover. Lengths of narrow satin ribbon can be stitched to sheer fabric to disguise the lines of seams and hems.

An important point to remember if you are machine-stitching ribbons to a flat piece of fabric, is to start at the same end when you machine down each side of the ribbon, otherwise there is a tension between the lines of stitching which pulls the ribbon out of shape and causes unsightly puckering.

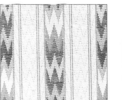
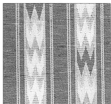

Pillow edgings
A small selection of braids, ribbons and furnishing trims suggests the range of possibilities for supplying additional color, texture and pattern to pillows with simple applied decoration.

Fabrics

Crisp cottons are a good choice if you are adding matching fabric ruffles to round or square pillows. For bolsters and boxed cushions you should use firm and hard-wearing fabrics, though bolsters are traditionally given a rich effect with satin or satinized fabric covers drawn up with silky tassels and cords. As you don't need a long length of fabric for pillows, it's a good opportunity to use luxury fibers, fancy weaves and unusual hand-printed patterns, which can give a real lift to the room, especially if your decorating scheme centers around solid color furnishings such as chairs, couch, carpeting and curtains.

Patterns and textures
Decorative pillows can be made from any fabric, but boxed cushions and bolsters should be covered in a firm, fairly heavy furnishing fabric. Lightly embossed and textured designs offer a number of different ideas for a coordinated look. Plain-colored piping creates a smart effect if the color is chosen to make a link between variations in the colorways of the fabric as shown above, or in the patterns.

Piping

Piping is made by covering a purchased piping cord with bias strips. This is then stitched into a flat seam to give pillows and other furnishings a smart, tailored and professional finish. The piping cord is available in different thicknesses for large and small items. Although it is most commonly used to outline the seaming around pillows and slip covers, it will also form an attractive edging on duvet covers and pillowcases, and also in the seaming of bedspreads. Piping can be made either from matching or from contrasting fabric, and, as the strips are cut diagonally on the fabric, you will find that striped and checked fabric can be used for special effect.

Covering piping cord

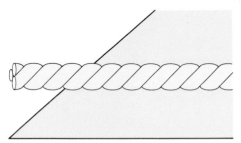

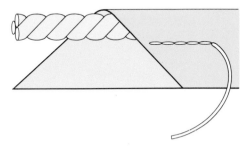

1 *Piping cord first has to be covered with bias binding. Press the bias binding strip flat, right side down, and place the piping cord in the middle.*

2 *Wrap the binding around the cord, wrong sides facing. Stitch the front and back together. Using a zipper foot, stitch close to the piping cord.*

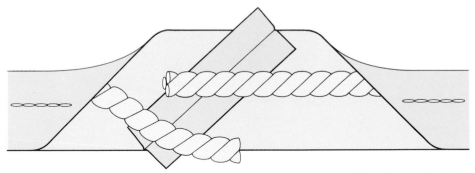

To join two pieces of cord
Join the bias binding strips with a flat seam along the grain (above). Trim the edges. Unravel the ends of

piping cord and trim to different lengths. Overlap the ends by 1 inch (below). Wrap the binding around the piping cord and complete stitching the cord.

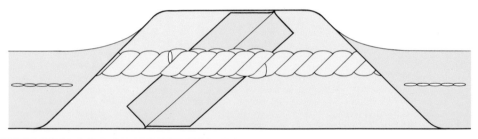

Inserting the piping

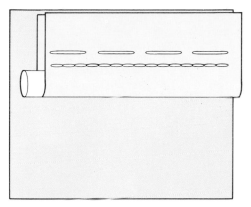

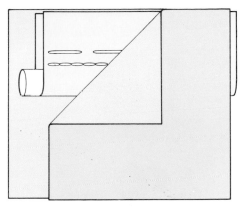

1 *The piping cord is sewn into the seam as you stitch the main seam. To begin with, place one piece of fabric with the wrong side facing downward. Then lay the piping cord on top of it so that the raw edges of the binding are facing outward. Make sure that the raw edges of the binding material properly match the raw edges of the piece of fabric. Then baste the piping carefully in place.*

2 *Place the other piece of fabric with the right side down on top of the first piece of fabric and the binding. Make sure that both the raw edges of both pieces match. Using a zipper foot on the machine, stitch the four layers together on the seamline. Remove the basting stitches. Then turn the material right side out. You will find that the piping cord makes a decorative edging along the seam.*

Shaping bolsters
Bolsters can benefit from being edged with piping, as it helps to retain the shape. Wash the piping cord before you cover it if it is not a pre-shrunk type. Allow it to dry thoroughly or it will shrink when you wash the cover itself. Note that 3 feet of narrow material makes approximately 73 feet of 1½-inch piping.

A neat finish
Piping is particularly effective on a round pillow to give it a neat, firm edging. If you are using covered piping (see opposite page), you will find it is far less time-consuming if you make a continuous length and cut it as you need it. Measure the length around the articles first to ensure that you make enough.

Square pillows

The simple symmetry of a square lends itself to a wide range of fabrics and treatments. If you have a plain sofa, select a lively range of well-coordinated, patterned fabrics; on patterned upholstery you can choose rich, plain colors and add luxurious fringing, silk cord edging or fancy braids. Piped edges are used for a tailored look, or to soften the shape, trim with a pleated or gathered ruffle.

The neatest and most secure way of fastening a square pillow cover is by a zipper placed across the back of the cushion. Alternatively you can insert a zipper in the side seam, or use snap tape or touch-and-close fastening in one side of the cover, but there is inevitably a slight distortion of the edge with these methods. Square pillow forms are available in a range of sizes, but it is a simple matter to seam and fill your own if you want a particular size of pad, perhaps to fit comfortably into an upholstered armchair.

Calculating fabric amounts

Front cover: Measure the length and width of the pillow form. Add a ½-inch seam allowance all around.

Back cover: You will need to cut two pieces of fabric for the back of the pillow so that you can add the zipper. Divide the area of the pillow form in half widthways and add a ½-inch seam to the center edges of both halves.

Themes and variations
The square pillow is one of the most varied and versatile furnishings in your scheme of decoration.

Pillows can either blend subtly with other fabrics, or provide bright splashes of color, and they are an opportunity to use edgings, piping or ruffles.

Making a square pillow

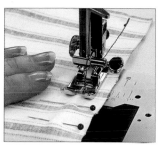

1 *Mark the square for the top of the cover and the two rectangles for the back on the straight grain. If the pattern needs matching, mark out one back piece and use this as a guide for the second back piece. Cut out the three sections.*

2 *Place the two back rectangles with the right sides facing. Sew a flat ½-inch seam along the center edges. Stitch for 2 inches in from each end, leaving the center of the seam open for the zipper. Press the seams open.*

3 *Insert the zipper into the opening with the wrong side of the fabric to the right side of the zipper. The open section of the seam should cover the zipper teeth. With the fabric placed right side up, baste and sew the zipper firmly in place.*

4 *Stitch the fabric and zipper as close to the teeth of the zipper as possible, and make sure that the stitching is evenly spaced. Carefully press the seams around the zipper. Then open the zipper, making sure that the fabric does not catch the teeth and that the ends of the zipper itself are stitched firmly.*

5 *For a piped edging, place the covered cord on the right side of the front fabric. Match the stitching to the seam ½ inch in, and align the raw edges of the piping with the raw edges of the cover. Pin. Unpick a few stitches at each end of the piping, join the fabric and cord ends and restitch. Sew in place.*

6 *Place the pillow back on the pillow front with the right sides facing and edges level. Stitch seam all around. If the edge is piped, use a zipper foot, keeping the stitching close to the cord. Press the seam open. If using heavyweight fabric, clip the corners to minimize bulk. Turn the cover right sides out.*

FRENCH SEAMS

This seam gives a very neat, strong finish with no stitching line or raw edges showing on the right side of the fabric. With the wrong sides of the fabric together, and raw edges matching, stitch a flat seam ¼ inch from the fabric edge.

Trim the edges to ⅛ inch and press. Turn the fabric back on itself so that the right sides are facing and the seam is on the fold, and baste the two layers together. Stitch another seam ⅜ inch down from the first seam, enclosing the raw edges. Remove the basting and press and turn the seam to the wrong side.

Round pillows

Ruffled, piped, fringed, braided, ribboned – like square pillows, the basic round pillow shape can be enlivened in any number of different ways, most simply by the choice of beautiful fabrics for the outer covers.

Round pillow forms are sold in various standard sizes. If you are using a smooth or shiny fabric, choose a firm foam and make sure that the cover fits closely, otherwise the edges will not stay crisp and any unevenness in the cover will be emphasized.

The circles for the front and back of the cover are cut from squares of fabric – you can make a paper pattern as a cutting guide or draw directly on the fabric with a tailor's chalk or pencil. The cover is fastened with a zipper. It is easier to sew a zipper across the back of a round pillow than to insert it in the edge.

Calculating fabric amounts

Measure the diameter of the pillow form; add a 1¼-inch seam allowance. You will need to cut a circular paper pattern of this diameter to be used directly for the front cover.
Ruffle: First decide the required finished depth

Variations on a theme
A group of plain, round pillows can be made up from a number of different fabrics with a unifying element, such as color or shape.

of ruffle. For a double ruffle cut the fabric strips to twice the required depth plus 1¼ inches. For a single ruffle, cut to the required depth plus 1 inch. For the ruffle length, measure around the pillow pattern ½ inch in from the edge. For a knife-pleated ruffle, as shown, allow twice the length around the pillow. Divide the length of the ruffle by the width of the fabric to find how many strips are needed. Multiply the number of strips by the depth of the ruffle to work out the extra fabric needed.

Making a round pillow

1 *Draw a circular paper pattern of the required diameter. Cut out the paper pattern and fabric circle for the front cover. Using the same circular pattern, rule a line across the pattern where the zipper is to be placed in the back of the cover.*

2 *The line should be 5 inches longer than the length of the zipper. Cut the paper pattern along the line. Pin the top section of the back cover pattern to the fabric. Allowing ½ inch for the zipper seam allowance on the straight edge, cut out the fabric.*

3 *Pin the bottom section of the paper pattern to the fabric, again allowing for the zipper seam, and cut out the fabric. Right sides together and raw edges matching, pin and baste the straight edges of the back cover together. Sew 2½ inches from either end along the seamline. Press the seam open. Remove basting.*

4 *With the fabric right side up, insert the zipper into the opening. The wrong side of the fabric should face the right side of the zipper, and the open section of the seam should cover the zipper teeth. Baste the zipper in place. Sew down both sides and across each end of the zipper, keeping close to the teeth. Open the zipper.*

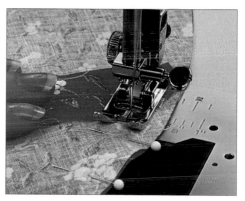

5 *Pin the front and back circles together with a ½-inch seam. To add a ruffle, align the raw edge with the raw edge of the front cover. Sew in place. Baste the right side of the back cover to the other right side of the ruffle, with a ½-inch seam.*

6 *Stitch the front and back covers together, sandwiching the ruffle in place if inserted. Notch the seam to minimize bulk inside the pillow. Turn the cover right side out through the zipper opening and insert the pillow form. Close the zipper.*

CIRCULAR RUFFLES

A ruffle can make an otherwise plain round pillow into an original and decorative article. It has the advantage of being easy to make. To make a circular ruffle, cut out a circle of fabric, and then cut out a smaller circle from its center. Clip the fabric around the inner edge of the circle; these small cuts will allow the fabric to be straightened out later on. Cut through from the outer edge of the fabric to the inner edge and flatten out the inner edge into a straight line, so that you produce fullness on the outer, longer edge. Stay-stitch (small machine stitch) the inner edge of the ruffle. With the right sides facing, pin and baste the inner clipped edge of the ruffle to the fabric. Machine-stitch carefully along the seamline and then turn back the ruffle so that the stitching is hidden. Press carefully with a hot iron.

Boxed cushions

Often made for a particular purpose – to fit a special chair or window seat – boxed cushions give a smart, crisp effect and are sturdy and practical in use.

You can use a suitable cushion foundation, or cut any shape you require from a thick foam block; this enables you to make regular geometric or irregularly shaped cushions, using the dimensions of the block to make a paper pattern before cutting out the fabric. The cover is opened and closed with a zipper in the side gusset, and you can pipe the seams to make a neat, strong finish.

Covers for boxed cushions need to be firm and close-fitting. Medium-weight cottons are highly practical, creating crisp lines and even seams. There is a wide choice of bold, plain colors, and patterns from traditionally pretty to powerfully abstract. The fabrics may have a matt or glazed surface, a textured weave or subtle figuring.

Calculating fabric amounts

Measure the length and width of the top of the pillow form; to each measurement add 1¼ inches for seam allowances. Allow for two pieces of fabric this size, for the top and bottom of the cover.

The gusset is made from four strips of fabric. Measure the depth of the form and the width on each side. For three sections of the gusset, add 1¼ inches to the length and width for ½-inch seam allowances all around. For the back section, add seam allowances all around and add 1¼ inches to the depth to allow for the zipper opening.

Round boxed cushions

When making a round cushion you will need to make a different type of gusset to accommodate the zipper. The gusset for a round cushion is made from two seamed strips, one shorter section enclosing the zipper. When attaching the gusset to the top and bottom cover pieces, ease the edge of the gusset onto the curve of the flat fabric, pin and baste to check the fit before machine-stitching all around the cover. To ensure that the seams do not pull when the cover is turned out to the right side, clip V-shaped notches in the seam allowances at regular intervals.

Making a boxed cushion

1 *Cut the back gusset piece in half lengthwise. Place the halves right sides together and baste a short seam on either side ½ inch from the long raw edges. Each seam should be 2 inches, leaving a central opening for the zipper. Press open the seam. Insert the zipper in the back gusset. Secure each end of the zipper with a short line of vertical stitching.*

2 *Seam the four gusset pieces firmly together at the short edges. Place them with their right sides together and stitch them carefully with a ½-inch seam. Make sure that you leave ½ inch unstitched at the top and bottom of each seam, but finish the stitching line securely. Then press the seams open on the wrong side of work.*

3 *Right sides facing, stitch the top edge of one section of the gusset along one edge of the top cover piece, taking a ½-inch seam. At the gusset seam, leave the needle in the fabric and raise the machine foot, turn the fabric and align the next section of the gusset on the cover piece. Lower the machine foot and continue stitching. Work all four sides in this way.*

4 *Clip the seam allowances diagonally across each corner close to the stitching. Open the zipper. Stitch the lower edges of the gusset to the bottom section of the cover. Clip the corner seams and press all the seams toward the gusset. Turn the cover out to the right side, through the open zipper. Ease and straighten out the seams and push out the corners.*

Zippers

Zippers are especially suitable as fastenings for cushions. They are neat and are more secure and less visible than snaps or hooks. They are available in a wide range of colors and are made of both plastic and metal. It is better to use a metal zipper if the pillow form is a tight fit in the cover, since a plastic zipper is more likely to pull apart under the strain.

INSERTING AN OFFSET ZIPPER

A zipper is inserted offset so that it is better concealed from view. Leave an opening as described previously. Position the zipper over the seam opening so that the teeth of the zipper arc in the center of the right seam allowance. Pin and baste one side of the tape in position ⅛ inch from the teeth of the zipper. Close the zipper and baste the other side of the tape through the other seam allowance near the opening. Turn the fabric right side up and, using the zipper foot attachment, top-stitch through all layers of the material, seam allowance and tape. Stitch as close as possible to the ends of the zipper. Remove the basting.

Inserting a zipper

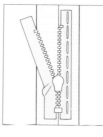

1 *Stitch a seam, leaving a gap. Center the zipper over it. Baste one side.*

2 *Close the zipper. Baste the other side as close to the teeth as possible.*

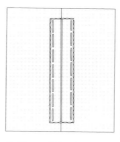

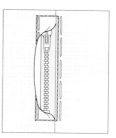

3 *Turn right side up and stitch the fabric, seam and tape.*

An offset zipper
This is placed to one side of the opening.

Bolsters

An elegant addition to a sofa, a window seat, or a chaise longue, bolsters can be a noticeable, comfortable and attractive feature of your room that can also be used as back supports on sofas and beds.

Your choice of fabric for bolster covers can make them roughly practical or luxuriously opulent, from matt-surfaced, textured weaves to shiny satin finishes with silky cords and floppy tassels.

There are three basic designs for bolster covers – fully fitted with flat ends; fitted with gathered ends; or a bag-like cover which pulls up with a drawstring at either end. The long, firm lines of a bolster lend themselves particularly well to directional designs such as stripes or trellises.

If you choose a heavily patterned fabric, it is best made up in the fitted style with a zipper closure, so that the pattern is evenly stretched around the bolster shape.

The gathered and drawstring versions can be informally styled in cottons and textured synthetic blends, more formally finished in

traditional chintzes or printed fabrics, or given a touch of glamour by a fabric with a definite surface sheen, which catches the light down the rounded length of the bolster and gives greater emphasis to the decorative effect of the gathers.

Although the simplest ones to make are those with no additional features, the steps opposite also show how to cover and attach the buttons for a bolster with a gathered end. Bolsters can also benefit from the use of piping (page 220), since it helps to retain the shape against wear and tear.

You can also use a bolster as an attractive part of a group of scatter pillows of various shapes and sizes.

Calculating fabric amounts

The steps below and opposite show a gathered bolster cover, which is made from a rectangle of fabric.

Length: Measure the length of the bolster form plus the diameter of the circular end. Add 1¼ inches for the seam allowances.

Width: Measure around the circumference of the bolster form; add another 1¼ inches for the seam allowances.

Making a bolster

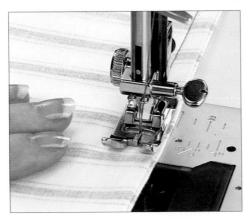

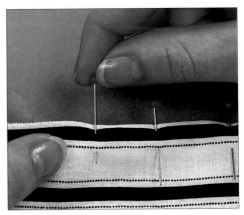

1 *Cut out a rectangle of fabric to the required size for the main body of the bolster. Fold it with right sides together and with the long edges accurately matched. Pin, baste and stitch the long edges together, making a French seam. Then turn the fabric tube right side out and press the seam on the right side with a warm iron.*

2 *Having done that, turn under a generous ½-inch hem at each end of the fabric, and pin it firmly in place. Then baste each hem in place securely, making sure that you use a contrasting color thread, as shown above. Finish the basting with a double stitch and then make sure that you remove all the pins.*

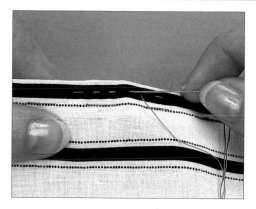

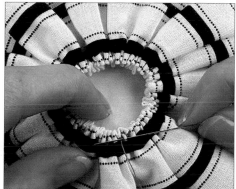

3 *At each end of the bolster, hand-sew a row of gathering stitches. Take care to position this stitching close to the fold and keep the stitches even. Insert the bolster form into the tube of fabric. Make sure that the cover fits snugly around the shape and is not loose along the body of the form.*

4 *Adjust it so that the projecting ends of fabric are equal. Pull up the gathering threads to bring the edges of the cover in to the center. Adjust the gathers to distribute them evenly from the center. Make sure that the hole left at the center will be covered by the button and fasten off the gathering threads with back stitch.*

Covering the buttons

Cut a circle of fabric generously larger than the button. Fold it over the top section of the button and push the edges of the fabric inside the button top. Use your finger to push the fabric onto the hooked spikes inside the button top; attach the fabric first at two opposite edges, then again at the other two opposite edges. Finally, work around the button, tucking in the remaining fabric smoothly.

Using double thread, pass the needle through the bobble of the tassel so that the thread end is hidden inside. Secure the thread with two small back stitches. Take a small stitch through the center of the button covering the fabric, then one through the top of tassel. Stitch securely and finish the thread end. Stitch buttons at each end of the bolster, concealing the gathered edges neatly.

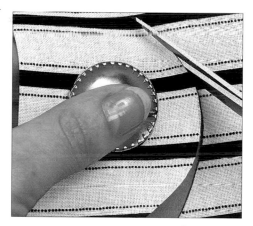

Bolster buttons
When making buttons for a bolster, you can simply buy the special buttons, as shown above. The fabric must be cut a good deal larger than the button. Push the fabric on to the spikes inside the button.

OVERLOCKING SEAMS

Overlocking is a way of enclosing the raw edges of a seam, thus hiding any fraying ends. It works best on lightweight fabrics. Pin the two pieces of fabric together, right sides facing and raw edges matching. Stitch a flat seam and press. Trim the top seam to ⅛ inch. Turn the edge of the other seam allowance under ⅛ inch and press. Turn it again, bringing the folded edge to the seamline, so that the trimmed edge of the top seam is enclosed. Press. Hand-stitch the seam to the fabric.

Shaped pillows

Once you have mastered the principle of pillow-making, you can consider decorative, unusual "fun" shapes based on flowers, fruits, animal motifs and so on.

The steps below and opposite show the construction of a triangular pillow form and cover. Draw up a paper pattern of the shape and make a second outline to allow for ½-inch seams all around each piece. Measure the pattern across the widest and longest sections.

If you are making the cover from fabric which just covers the width of the pillow, buy twice the length. If you can get two pattern pieces from the width, you need only the length of the pillow itself.

If the fabric has a pronounced directional pattern or large motif, allow extra if you want both sides of the pillow to include the same area from the repeats of the fabric design. Add an allowance for gusset strips if necessary.

Make your own shapes
Plain pillows do not have to be round or square – they can be triangles or diamonds, L-shaped or oval – or you can let your imagination wander into the range of slightly more complex shapes, such as hearts or fans. Any shape can be worked out as a paper pattern which can be used to make up your own pillow form and a suitable cover.

Making a shaped pillow form

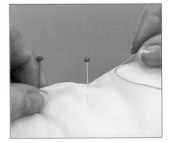

1 *Draw a paper pattern for the pillow form and add on a ½-inch seam allowance all around. If the shape is symmetrical, you can construct a pattern for half the shape and cut it out on a fold of the fabric, cutting through both layers away from the folded edge. The shape is then perfectly symmetrical when the fabric is opened out. Pin the paper pattern to the fabric and cut out the shape. Position the pattern separately for the front and back if the fabric has a definite printed or woven design.*

2 *Pin the two pieces of fabric right sides together and stitch around the edges taking a ½-inch seam allowance, and making sure that you leave an opening at least 6 inches long so that you can insert the filling. If the shape has a distinct point or a sharply curved section, you will find that it is best to place the opening along a relatively straight part of the seam opposite this point. Then you can push the filling firmly into the shape and it will not be distorted when it comes to closing the opening.*

3 *To give the seams extra strength, work a second row of stitching along the seamline on top of the first row. Then insert the filling through the opening in the seam. Make sure that you work it well into the contours of the shape and also make sure that it is distributed evenly so that the pillow form is firmly filled out but not lumpy. To close the opening in the seam, turn in the seam allowances neatly and pin the two sides of the gap together. Slip-stitch by hand making small invisible stitches.*

Making a shaped pillow cover

1 *Using the same pattern as for the form, cut pieces of fabric for the top and bottom of the pillow cover, but this time take a seam allowance of 3/8 inch beyond the edges of the paper pattern. The outer cover needs to be larger than the form to allow it to be inserted.*

2 *Put the pieces of fabric right sides together and pin. Stitch around the edge, taking a 1/2-inch seam allowance and leaving an opening in one side large enough for insertion of the form. It is a good idea to make a row of stitching to strengthen the seams.*

3 *Turn the pillow form out to the right side, pushing out the seams to achieve the correct shape. If necessary, cut diagonally across the corners to reduce the bulk of material. Then press the pillow cover, and try to ensure that the seams are even.*

4 *Insert the pillow form through the opening in the cover. Tuck in the raw edges neatly along the opening and slip-stitch them together as illustrated. This completes your shaped pillow. You can insert piping or ruffles as with any other pillow.*

SUITABLE FABRICS AND DECORATION

As with the more conventional pillow shapes, if the form is well constructed and evenly filled, you can choose any type of fabric for the outer cover to suit the style of the design. It can also be fun to try and match the fabric to the shape of the pillow – red for a heart shape, for example, or use a gray, textured fabric for an elephant shape. In addition, any decorative edging, such as piping or a ruffle, can be inserted in the seams, but stitched to one side of the cover only at the opening in the seam.

GLOSSARY

Alkyd paint A hard top coat paint, used for both exterior and interior wood and metal. It is solvent-based.

Anti-condensation paint Provides an insulating film between a cold surface and a humid atmosphere, and so reduces condensation.

Basting A long stitch used to hold fabric in place prior to the final stitching.

Batten A sawn strip of wood mounted on the wall or ceiling to support shelves or blinds.

Berber A type of carpet, made from undyed sheep wool, with a dense, looped pile.

Bias strips Lengths of fabric cut diagonally across the warp and weft threads of the fabric. They are used to bind edges and cover piping cord.

Binder bars Aluminum strips used to hold carpet taut and prevent it from fraying.

Buckram A strong, coarse cotton or linen cloth, impregnated with gum or other stiffening agents. It is used to stiffen fabric cornices and valances.

Butt joint Made by pushing one strip of wallpaper up against another to form a slight ridge. This disappears as the paper dries, and ensures there is no gap between the strips.

Colorways The color or combination of colors used in a fabric. Most fabrics have the same design produced in a number of different ways.

Cove A strip of material fitted to the angle between the ceiling and the wall. Used to hide cracks and provide a neater finish.

Cutting-in brush The slanting angle of the bristles means that the paint can be taken neatly right to an edge, such as a baseboard or the glass in a window frame without smudging.

Cutwork A decorative technique in which a motif or pattern is outlined in close blanket stitch and the fabric is then cut out in various sections of the design.

Dowel A small wooden peg which slots into holes in two pieces of wood, forming a joint.

Dress fabrics Those produced for the purpose of making clothing. Many are less durable than upholstery fabrics and are not fade-resistant in sunlight.

Edgings These are decorative trimmings that are used to finish the edge of an item. They may be made from fabric, such as a ruffle, or purchased, such as lace or eyelet. Edgings have one finished edge and one raw edge, by which they are attached to the hem.

Eggshell paint Has a flat finish, used for interiors and for some decorative finishes.

Embossed wallpaper A heavy wallpaper designed to be painted over. It has a texture pressed into it in a range of patterns.

Enamel A hard-wearing, high-gloss top coat paint.

Even weave Fabric that has warp and weft threads that are identical in thickness and provide the same number of threads over a given area, enabling stitches to be worked by counting the threads.

Expanded vinyl A lightweight material resembling a printed fabric. Pasted to the wall, it is warm to the touch, washable, and easy to strip.

Facings Used to finish edges in places where hems are unsuitable, such as a scalloped edge. The facing is made from a separate piece of fabric, cut to the same shape as the edge to be finished, and stitched to it.

Figurative designs Those which include life-like shapes within the pattern. The figures may represent birds, trees, flowers or scenery.

Figured weaves Those which have figurative designs woven into the fabric. The different areas of the design may be woven in different colors or with a contrasting texture.

Flat finish A finish for paint, tiles or fabric without any luster or reflective properties.

Flocked wallpaper A fine pile is added to selected areas of the paper or vinyl base to produce a flocked pattern.

Grout A powder, mixed with water, applied to the spaces between tiles to seal them. It is also called grouting.

Interlining A fabric which is placed between the main fabric and the lining to strengthen and stiffen the fabric, to give it extra body, or to provide more insulation. On fabric cornices and tie-backs the interlining is placed between the fabric and the buckram stiffening to mask the coarse weave of the buckram and give a softer, more pleasing feel to the finished side of the fabric.

Jigsaw A versatile power saw. It will make straight, curved, or scroll cuts in wood, wallboards, metals, plastics and other materials. The vertical blade cuts by moving rapidly up and down.

Joist A beam made of wood, steel or reinforced concrete. Used as a support for floors and roofs.

Knot Part of the pattern of the grain of wood. Knots should be covered with knot sealer before painting or varnishing.

Latex paint A water-based paint with a flat or semi-gloss finish, generally used for interior painting jobs on walls and ceilings. It is easy to apply and dries quickly.

Lathes Thin strips of wood which are inserted into the casings at the lower edges of Roman shades to keep the fabric stiff and straight.

Lining paper A plain paper applied to uneven walls or ceilings to provide a smoother surface for paint or paper.

Masonry paint A tough, weatherproof paint used for external decorations.

Mercerized fabric Fabric which has been treated under tension with caustic soda which causes the fibers to swell. It gives the fabric extra luster, and makes it softer to the touch.

Molding The trim around a door or window.

Mosaic tiles Small ceramic tiles attached to a mesh backing for easy installation.

Orbital sander A machine with a rectangular pressure pad which vibrates very rapidly. Sheets of sandpaper are attached to it.

Padding The layer of material, usually rubber or felt, laid down before the carpet is laid.

Parquet panels Polished pieces of wood fitted together to form a high-grade floor.

Pattern repeats The places where exactly the same motif is repeated again in the same position farther down the fabric or wallpaper. The length of a pattern repeat is the distance between these places.

Plumb and bob line A piece of cord with a weight attached. It is used to ensure straight lines.

Polyurethane seal A synthetic, transparent seal, used to protect wood or cork.

Primer Applied to wood to seal the pores and provide a stable base for undercoat.

Quadrant tiles Round-edged slivers of tiling used for borders on corners, such as window sills.

Returns The side edges of a cornice between the front edge of the cornice, or valance, and the window or wall.

Sander There are industrial sanders for rent, and also hand sanders, both are used for stripping wood floors and doors before staining or varnishing.

Sandpaper Sheets of paper in coarse to fine grades used for abrading.

Satin finish A paint finish midway between flat and gloss.

Scraper A metal implement used to remove paint.

Sculptured pile A woven or tufted carpet made up of a mixture of cut and looped pile.

Sealer A transparent liquid applied to wood to protect the surface.

Selvages The finished-off edges of fabric which run down both sides of the length of fabric.

Shag pile A luxurious carpet with a pile of 1 inch or more.

Shavehook For removing softened paint from wooden moldings around doors and windows. They are available with triangular, pear-shaped and combination edges.

Sizing A substance applied to fabric to improve its feel or appearance. When used to enhance fabric of an inferior quality, it may rub off or disappear when it is washed.

Stain For coloring wood. There are oil-based, solvent-based and

water-based varieties, used for different types of wood.

Straight grain This runs along the warp threads, parallel to the selvages in woven fabrics.

Strippable paper Wallpaper that can be peeled off the walls without using water.

Stripper There are peel-off, chemical and heat-based types of strippers. They are used for stripping paint from wood and metal surfaces.

Stud wall A hollow wall, made of two layers of plasterboard supported by wooden joists.

Sub-floor A floor laid under the surface flooring to provide a smooth, firm surface.

Tackless strips Plywood strips with spikes punched through them, fitted around the edges of the room with the spikes up, to grip carpet and hold it taut across the room or in place on stairs.

Textured paint Available both ready-to-use and in powdered form. Some leave a pattern automatically when applied, others are textured by hand after they have been applied.

Thixotropic paint Non-drip, alkyd paint.

Toggle bolts Enable fixtures to be secured to low-strength plasterboard and paneling.

Tongue-and-groove boards Wooden boards with a groove at one edge and a "tongue" or protrusion at the other. These enable the boards to be slotted into one another.

Warp threads Those which run lengthwise, parallel to the selvages in woven fabrics.

Weft threads Those which weave under and over the warp threads and run across the fabric between the selvages.

INDEX

Figures in italic refer to illustrations.

· Z ·

ACKNOWLEDGMENTS

Editor: Eileen Cadman
Editorial assistant: Joanna Swinnerton
Designer: Ron Samuels
Design assistant: Mark Davies
Illustrators: David Ashby, Kuo Kang Chen,
Kevin Maddison, Fraser Newman, Les Smith
Typesetting: Bournetype

Dorling Kindersley
Managing editor: Jemima Dunne
Managing art editor: Derek Coombes
Editorial assistant: Tom Fraser
Designer: Rachel Griffin
Production: Hilary Stephens
Contributor: Elaine Brumstead

Photography
(t=top, b=bottom, l=left, r=right)
Jon Bouchier: half title page, title page, 8t and bl, 9t and br, 10tl and bl,
11tr and br, 12t and bl, 13t and br, 17, 18, 19, 26, 27, 28, 30, 32, 33, 39,
41, 42, 43, 45, 51, 58, 59, 60, 61, 62, 63, 65, 66, 67, 68, 69, 70t, 78–9,
87, 88, 89, 90, 91, 92, 95, 96, 97, 103, 104, 105, 109, 111, 112, 113, 114,
124, 125, 126, 127, 128, 129, 131, 132, 133, 136, 137, 140, 141,
151, 168, 178, 179, 194.
Camera Press: 83tl, 83b, 110b, 118tl and r, 139tl.
"Coverplus" (Woolworth's): 23br.
Mark French: 195, 214t, 216, 217.
Stephen Oliver: 6–7, 14–5, 46–7, 74–5, 98–9, 134–5, 142–3, 190–1.
Steve Tanner: 8br, 9bl, 10tr, 11tl, 12br, 13bl, 145, 146–7, 148, 149, 150,
155, 156, 157, 160, 161, 162, 163, 164, 165, 166, 169, 170, 173, 174, 175,
176, 180, 181, 182, 183, 184, 185, 186, 187, 188, 189, 192, 193, 196, 197, 198,
199, 200, 202, 203, 204, 205, 206, 207, 208, 209, 210, 211, 212, 213, 214bl and br,
215, 218, 219, 222, 223, 224, 225, 226, 227, 228, 229, 230, 231.
Elizabeth Whiting Associates: 22, 23t and bl, 44br, 54, 55, 70bl and br,
82l, 83tr, 107, 110t, 118bl, 138, 139tr, 153.

For their generous assistance in supplying articles for the photographs on
pages 46–7, 74–5, 98–9, 134–5, 142–3 and 190–1, the authors and
publishers would like to thank the following:

Amtico: vinyl tiles.
William Armes Ltd: sisal, coconut, seagrass and woven plastic Danycord matting.
Laura Ashley: bedlinen, cushions, bolster, tablecloths, lace napkin,
wallpaper, wallpaper border, stencil, stencil brush, paints.
Astrohome Ltd: black and silver shelving.
Black and Decker: electric drill, Super Powerdriver, electric sander and heat gun.
C. Brewer & Son Ltd: white metal shelving, wallpapering tools and brushes, tiling tools.
Dixon Wallcoverings Ltd: textured wallcoverings.
Nairn Flooring: linoleum.
Nice Irma: rugs.
Wincanders (Great Britain) Ltd: woodblock flooring.
World's End Tiles: floor and wall tiles.